Repenser les relations entre sciences et philosophie

Repenser les relations entre sciences et philosophie

Sous la direction d'Anna C. Zielinska

Julien Blanc
Delphine Blitman
Florian Couturier
Pierre Fasula
Robin Lamarche-Perrin
Don Ross
Raphaël Sandoz
Sarah Troubé

RECHERCHES SUR LA PHILOSOPHIE ET LE LANGAGE
N°29 – 2013

Université Pierre Mendès France, Département de Philosophie
1251 Avenue Centrale, BP 47, 38040 Grenoble cedex 9

Imprimé en France

ISSN 0754-331X

ISBN 978-2-7116-8410-6

Les Auteurs

Julien BLANC	Université d'Aix-Marseille
Delphine BLITMAN	Institut J. Nicod
Pierre FASULA	Université de Paris I
Florian COUTURIER	Université de Grenoble II
Robin LAMARCHE-PERRIN	Université de Grenoble II
Don ROSS	University of Cape Town
Raphaël SANDOZ	Université de Genève
Sarah TROUBÉ	Université de Paris VII

Recherches sur la philosophie et le langage 29 (2013)
192 p., ISBN : 978-2-7116-8410-6, p. 7-10, Vrin.

Avant-propos

Au départ, ce volume a été une idée discutée au sein du groupe de recherche *Philosophie, Langages & Cognition* depuis un certain temps déjà : comment utiliser les données récentes de la psychologie, par exemple, pour éclairer les questions que la philosophie se pose depuis toujours ? Sont-elles d'un usage quelconque ? Depuis des siècles, et au XXe siècle en particulier, la philosophie a tenté de donner aux sciences des outils épistémologiques et méthodologiques qui ont permis à ces dernières de se forger des critères de plus en plus fins de leur légitimité. Ce sont les philosophes qui ont élaboré de différentes versions du critère de démarcation entre science et non-science. Et ces critères, comme on le voit notamment chez Karl Popper, ne permettent pas d'obtenir ce qu'on pourrait souhaiter, à savoir la méthode d'atteindre la vérité scientifique. Tout ce que l'on peut espérer, est de pourvoir à un moment dire, de façon définitive, qu'une théorie ne peut pas prétendre à la scientificité. Et pourtant, malgré son apparente modestie, la théorie de Popper a été critiquée pour son optimisme, et ceux qui lui ont succédé se sont de plus en plus éloigné de toute forme de réalisme (selon lequel les théories scientifiques refléteraient effectivement des lois de la nature)[1]. Certes, il y avait plusieurs tentatives pour faire revivre le réalisme, et

1. On peut penser ici évidemment à Thomas Kuhn, Paul Feyerabend et, plus récemment, à Bas van Fraassen.

le réalisme des entités[2] (et non plus des théories) en est l'une des plus réussies. Il semble toutefois que l'existence d'une difficulté dans l'interprétation du statut épistémologique des résultats scientifiques soit le seul consensus qui soit acquis en la matière, aussi bien chez les philosophes qui s'inscrivent dans la tradition critique du Cercle de Vienne que chez ceux qui sont plus proches de la tradition de l'épistémologie historique française, de Gaston Bachelard jusqu'à Michel Foucault et ses disciples.

Dans ce contexte d'incertitude, nous sommes confrontés à un phénomène à la fois séduisant et vertigineux. Après un siècle de philosophie des sciences florissantes qui enseigne surtout la prudence face aux résultats scientifiques, nous observons depuis une vingtaine d'années un retour de ces résultats au cœur des débats philosophiques, notamment en philosophie de l'esprit et en sciences cognitives. Un champ de recherche nouveau, la philosophie expérimentale, commence également à jouer un rôle important dans les relations entre les sciences et la philosophie, où ses résultats deviennent des arguments ou même des conclusions dans des débats. Peut-on se dire simplement que les sciences ont acquis elles-mêmes, peut-être grâce à la philosophie, une maturité suffisante, pour pouvoir enseigner la philosophie à leur tour ?

Le rôle de la philosophie est ici particulièrement délicat, ce que nous voyons notamment dans l'article de Don Ross publié dans le présent volume : dans un exercice critique de ses propres capacités, qui accompagnait la critique des sciences, la philosophie a de plus en plus de difficultés à trouver sa place. Ce qui est possible de sauver, selon Ross, n'appartient même plus à la théorie des sciences au sens de ce qui se faisait au XXe siècle, mais se réduit à la méthodologie des sciences, dépendante des perspectives adoptées par les sciences elles-mêmes. On se rapproche ici curieusement du point de vue de l'École de Lvov-Varsovie, qui, prenant ses distances avec le Cercle de Vienne, s'intéressait au perfectionnement des procédures très concrètes du raisonnement scientifique (notamment l'induction), en mettant en avant les aspects pragmatiques de celui-ci[3] et sans tenter

2. Présent notamment dans les travaux de Ian Hacking.

3. Le terme pragmatique doit être compris ici au sens non-technique, et les philosophes de l'École ne l'employaient pas non plus de façon univoque.

d'en proposer des théories philosophiques abstraites[4]. Ross va cependant plus loin. Il distingue la philosophie qui ne prétend pas fournir une description scientifique du monde et qui, de ce fait, n'entretient aucune relation avec la science, et celle qui au contraire propose une métaphysique qui correspondrait à la manière dont le monde est effectivement. Tant que les métaphysiciens contemporains de ce second type emploient le vocabulaire philosophique lourd d'un certain héritage, notamment en jouant avec la notion de nécessité, ils se fourvoient, selon Ross. Une métaphysique naturalisée ne peut qu'utiliser le langage scientifique, celui de la physique fondamentale en particulier, où la notion de nécessité a un sens différent de celui de la métaphysique classique. Elle devrait s'intéresser à la relation entre les mesures empiriques, les mathématiques et les statistiques, car ce champ constitue aux yeux de Ross un champ de travail privilégié pour la métaphysique naturalisée ou la méthodologie des sciences aujourd'hui. Le philosophe devrait alors tenter d'unifier les pratiques inférentielles à travers les sciences particulières, occupant un terrain entre « les mathématiques et l'informatique, se tenant informé des découvertes en physique fondamentale et étant motivé par les problèmes cibles des sciences spéciales »[5].

La position de Ross semble radicale, et invite à un renversement total de nos habitudes de travailler sur le terrain qui fait dialoguer la science et la philosophie. Cette position concerne toutefois principalement la métaphysique, avec ses ambitions fondatrices. Les textes réunis dans ce volume[6] s'intéressent à des questions plus concrètes concernant les rapports entre certaines branches de la philosophie et des sciences diverses, et ce qui les unit est leur capacité à démystifier ce rapport, à montrer qu'il ne peut pas constituer un problème facilement saisissable et aussi aisément critiquable.

4. *Cf.* Jan Wolenski, *L'École de Lvov-Varsovie. Philosophie et logique en Pologne (1895-1939)*, trad. fr. A. C. Zielinska, Paris, Vrin, 2012, chap. IX.

5. Ross, *infra*, p. 25.

6. Les articles qui composent ce cahier des *Recherches sur la philosophie et le langage* ont été présentés d'abord lors du colloque « Repenser les rapports entre science(s) et philosophie », qui a eu lieu à Grenoble, 6 et 7 juin 2011 (à l'exception du texte de Don Ross, écrit spécialement pour le volume). Le comité de rédaction a ensuite effectué un choix parmi les articles soumis selon les procédures habituelles (en « double aveugle »).

Après le texte fondamental de Ross, qui est l'invité spécial du présent numéro, nous verrons comment les problèmes dont il est question se présentent au sein des sciences cognitives (Delphine Blitman et Robin Lamarche-Perrin), de la psychologie (Sarah Troubé), de l'éthique dans sa théorie (Florian Couturier) et dans sa pratique (Julien Blanc) et enfin dans la philosophie des mathématiques (Raphaël Sandoz et Pierre Fasula). La diversité des approches permet de voir que l'utilisation des résultats scientifiques par les philosophes, si elle a lieu, peut être faite de façon suffisamment rigoureuse pour remplir les exigences d'une quelconque méthodologie des sciences. Cependant, il est nécessaire de rappeler que cela n'est possible que grâce à une formation historique et méthodologique minutieuse, et c'est souvent celle-ci qui manque quand on entre de façon trop enthousiaste sur le champ des sciences empiriques, comme le montrent des recherches récentes en « philosophie expérimentale ».

Mes remerciements vont avant tout aux membres du comité de rédaction crée spécialement pour ce volume, pour leur aide précieuse et leur travail sur les articles proposés. Grand merci aussi à Marion Renauld des Archives Poincaré pour son aide dans le travail sur le colloque qui s'est transformé en cette publication, et à Jérôme Dokic pour sa présence généreuse. Cette publication n'aurait pas pu se faire sans aide et sans soutien de Denis Vernant ainsi que sans l'assistance de Loredana Truong.

Anna C. ZIELINSKA *

* Anna C. Zielinska est docteure en philosophie. Sa thèse, consacrée à la praxéologie, la philosophie de l'action et la philosophie morale a été écrite et soutenue en 2009 sous la double direction de Denis Vernant et de Jan Wolenski. Depuis cette période, elle travaille sur la métaéthique, la philosophie du droit et l'analyse des usages de l'éthique dans la sphère publique. Elle enseigne actuellement à l'Université Paris I et est post-doctorante au laboratoire CERSES (CNRS / Université Paris V).

Recherches sur la philosophie et le langage 29 (2013)
192 p., ISBN : 978-2-7116-8410-6, p. 11-27, Vrin.

Will scientific philosophy still be philosophy?

Don ROSS*

ABSTRACT

The paper reflects on whether philosophy can pursue a genuinely naturalistic programme of inquiry, of the kind defended in Ladyman & Ross (2007), and yet avoid collapsing into the various empirical sciences. It is argued first that the relevant question more specifically concerns the autonomy of metaphysics from fundamental physics. Philosophers likely would remain institutionally alone in pursuing the metaphysical project of unifying the special sciences under constraints from fundamental physics, but for no deep reason of special expertise or on account of a special conceptual feature of the problem space; physicists will probably simply never be sufficiently interested in metaphysical questions to take them up. The paper then addresses the more complicated question of whether naturalized metaphysics à la Ladyman & Ross is not coextensive, both methodologically and with respect to its domain, with mathematics. The paper does not attempt to directly resolve this question. However, it identifies a plausible space for naturalized metaphysics in the matrix of the disciplines, which distinctively combines elements of computer science, mathematics and physics

* Don Ross is a professor at the School of Economics, University of Cape Town and in the Center for Economic Analysis of Risk, Georgia State University.

in addressing the unity of special sciences through pursuit of highly general principles of statistical inference.

RÉSUMÉ

Cet article s'interroge sur la capacité de la philosophie à poursuivre un programme d'enquête effectivement naturaliste, comme celui qui a été défendu dans Ladyman & Ross (2007), et cela en évitant de s'effacer au profit des sciences empiriques particulières. Il souligne que, premièrement, la question la plus pertinente concerne plus spécifiquement l'autonomie de la métaphysique de la physique fondamentale. Il est probable que les philosophes resteraient institutionnellement isolés dans leur poursuite du projet métaphysique d'unifier les sciences particulières conformément aux exigences de la physique fondamentale, mais cet isolement ne serait pas dû à une raison profonde quelconque, que ce soit son expertise unique ou la manière dont il rend compte d'une caractéristique conceptuelle particulière de l'espace-problème ; les physiciens ne seront probablement jamais suffisamment intéressés par des questions métaphysiques pour les reprendre à leur compte. L'article tente ensuite d'analyser une question plus compliquée, celle de savoir si la métaphysique naturalisée à la Ladyman & Ross n'est pas coextensive aux mathématiques, aussi bien du point de vue méthodologique que relativement à son domaine. L'article ne prétend pas répondre directement à cette question. Il identifie toutefois un espace plausible pour la métaphysique naturalisée dans la matrice des disciplines qui propose un arrangement original des éléments de la science informatique, des mathématiques et de la physique en s'intéressant à l'unité des sciences particulières à travers la poursuite des principes hautement généraux de l'inférence statistique.

1. SHOULD PHILOSOPHY BE OUTSOURCED TO SCIENTISTS?

Naively accepting, at least to begin with, a principle of excluded middle, let us begin with the proposition that either there are objective facts that are in principle beyond the reach of empirical science plus mathematics or there are not. If there are not, then it seems we should expect philosophy to continue to cede domains of authority to science and mathematics as the complexity of their collective resources deepens.[1] In this possible world, philosophy as an organized enterprise is most charitably regarded as the systematic comparison of such speculations as people offer while they wait for patches of ignorance to be cleared. Alternatively, if there are objective facts beyond the reach of empirical science and mathematics – facts, perhaps, about human moral obligations, or artistic value, or intuitions of meaningfulness – then philosophers have, and might be expected to go on having indefinitely, work to do that is independent of the development of science.

This syllogism bypasses the possibility that philosophers add value by thinking about something other than objective facts. On some important conceptions of the point of philosophy – shared by figures as diverse as Nietzsche, Heidegger, Wittgenstein and Rorty – philosophers elucidate implicit implications of sets of culturally constructed fictions that groups of people use to coordinate their affiliations and their joint projects. But are such implications not themselves facts about cultural practices, and is their elucidation different in any principled way from empirical anthropology? One possible response to this is that philosophical elucidation and regimentation of folk conceptual spaces is not merely descriptive but also *creative*; philosophical anthropology, it may be said, has affinities with both art and jurisprudence. Philosophy that lives up to this conception – as it surely does in the hands of Nietzsche, at least – is not engaged in the same sort of enterprise as science, and this why Ladyman and Ross (2007), in our criticism of non-scientific

1. Note that depth and range of modeling resources is a sense in which science has obviously steadily progressed, something we can maintain no matter how open we want to be to radical Kuhnian skeptics about progress with respect to truth.

metaphysics, ask "Heideggerians" to "go in peace" (p. 5). I add that it would be helpful if philosophers who do not view themselves as trying to discover objective facts would take greater pains than most do to make this explicit. This would help us to distinguish between philosophers who do not engage with science because it is tangential to their project from philosophers who are called to deep thought by their conviction that science is inadequate to the task of describing objective reality.

Nietzsche does not imagine that folk metaphysics and epistemology constitute proto-science – they are not, for him, in the truth-telling business to begin with. This sharply distinguishes his attitude from that of contemporary analytic metaphysicians, who take themselves to be engaged in discovering highly general truths about categories or modes or structures of being that are anticipated, however crudely, in everyday discourse and that are, they imagine, compatible with whatever detailed models will come to be favoured by fundamental physics (Merricks 2003).

Because analytic metaphysicians take themselves to be describing the same classes of events and structures as physicists, but at a higher level of abstraction, the argument against the value of their enterprise is straightforward. As Ladyman & Ross (2007, chapters 1 and 3) argue, almost all claims by analytic metaphysicians that are not anodyne are *refuted* by contemporary fundamental physics. Analytic metaphysics refines and regiments traditional metaphysical categories of object-hood and object interaction. But these traditional categories apply only to the parochial neighbourhoods of practical human intervention, and decisively fail to generalize. Sometimes, as Bas van Fraassen emphasizes, the problem with analytic metaphysics is that the propositions it considers are wholly disconnected from empirically testable implications; but more often the claims that its practitioners propound should be rejected because they are *false*. When we throw analytic metaphysics on the scrap-heap of misguided effort, most of analytic epistemology goes with it. Such epistemology typically analyzes a kind of state, knowledge, that can be attributed only by someone who is soundly confident about the conclusions of their underlying metaphysical analyses; but confidence in such conclusions cannot be sound.[2]

Nietzscheans and Heideggerians aside, this situation seems to confront philosophy with an existential crisis unless philosophers can identify a domain of objective discovery that science and mathematics cannot access without philosophical help. However, at this point we can start to put pressure on the naïve syllogism with which we opened. In order to find useful work for themselves, philosophers do *not* need to identify domains of discovery that scientists and mathematicians *can't* reach 'in principle'; there need only be domains that scientists, at least – I will now put mathematicians aside until later – are unlikely to *try* to reach, or reach only inefficiently and unreliably when they do try. Ladyman and Ross (2007) identify such a domain: an open set of structural facts about constraints on the flow of information that unify the scientific world view by explaining how mutually disconnected or only loosely connected special sciences non-redundantly characterize a single reality. We conceive of this reality as embedded on a structural toplogy provided by a body of fundamental physics from which the best models of the special sciences cannot be derived. (If they could be so derived, this would imply the prospect of both theoretical and ontological reduction, and metaphysics would be ultimately replaceable by fundamental physics.) We refer to the study of this domain as 'naturalized metaphysics', on grounds that it is continuous in motivation with the major metaphysical projects of (at least) Western intellectual history. We prefer not to quarrel over semantics with people who think the enterprise we describe should be called something else. The crucial point for present purposes is that, for reasons I will discuss, no one is likely to do it systematically except in institutional contexts (that is, journals, graduate student reading lists etc.) continuous with the traditions of philosophy.

This is not the place to attempt a précis of our positive programme for naturalized metaphysics. My aim instead is to expand on what Ladyman and I claim in our book is a stable – but

2. This of course does not apply to naturalized epistemology – which might less confusingly be called normative psychology – or to such epistemology as modestly examines relative rational acceptability conditions on different beliefs.

not 'principled' – difference in institutional objectives between naturalistic philosophers and scientists. Scientists tend to compartmentalize knowledge, even while continuing to award high prestige to general and elegant theories, leaving philosophers with the possible role – but only so long as enough of them will equip themselves with the mathematical tools for the job – of showing how the compartments jointly make up a single building.

2. THE PURSUIT OF UNITY

People have always liked to split up the world. The value of a second world, over and above the one which we all take to be characterized by physicists, is that it gives one a space in which to locate emotionally attractive objects – stable essences, sets, immortal souls, perfect creators, dead loved ones, things in themselves – that fit awkwardly at best into the generally intersubjectively accessible domain. One might naively imagine that philosophers, in their stern subservience to unsentimental reason, would all reliably see through this obvious cheap device for preserving hope and order in the face of ubiquitous entropy. But of course this isn't so and never has been; philosophers from Plato onwards have been at least as ready as anyone to divide reality into two or more compartments, though they have been more alert than most people to the need for a story about how awareness of esoteric spaces can be obtained from the mundane space. At the same time, no age of philosophy has been without dissenters against world-splitting: as Aristotle sought to reassemble the universe sundered by Plato, so Spinoza, Hume and the logical empiricists insisted on fundamental unity against the urgings of Descartes, Leibniz, and neo-Hegelian idealists.

Defenders of unity cannot claim to know on the basis of *observation* that everything that exists does so in dynamic interaction in a single multi-dimensional field, though that is what they effectively assume. If unificationists are not, then, motivated simply by sour resentment of the sweet dreams of others, their commitment to monism must be based ultimately on intellectual dissatisfaction with the *inelegance* of dualism, and with its associated failure of fortitude; to the monist, the dualist is like the mountain climber who turns back downward before the summit because it's getting cold. This attitude implicitly concedes a point: monism is worth defending because it's *difficult* and *challenging* to try to actually account for the full teeming variety of experience and thought in one coherent ontological model. When one seriously wonders, for example, how there can be something like an objective rate of monetary inflation that is constrained by fundamental physics but is at the same time not reducible to any kind of object described outside of macroeconomic theory, one confronts a cathedral-scale project. Ladyman and Ross (2007, chapters 4-6) merely sketch a preliminary outline of the general shapes of some big churches.

Monism has enjoyed much greater popularity since the scientific revolution than it ever did before. The reason for this is straightforward: science seemed for many decades to be making steady progress in weaving together the disparate strands of rigorous observation and experimentation into a single grand basket. However, during the past half-century or so this process of consolidation has gone into reverse. Traditionally, such specific aspects of ontological unification as have been achieved by science have usually been interpreted as progress toward realized monism by way of implicit physicalistic reductionism. But *that* thesis appears steadily less plausible as special sciences proliferate. The institutional processes of fundamental physics are as strongly attracted to the prize of a grand unified theory – or an altogether new theory that supplants one of the two recalcitrant pieces that so far won't fit together – as ever. But there is no serious prospect that the kinds of structures that feature in fundamental physics, however much they might *constrain* freedom of modeling in all other sciences, will *determine*, even stochastically, the characterizations even of all of the special applied domains of physics,[3] let alone the biological and social sciences. In the absence of good reason to expect such determination, there is no basis for confidence in unification of the sciences through global reduction, notwithstanding the occasional local success.[4]

3. See Batterman (2002).

4. Reductionism fails over and over again, at very specialized scales *within* sciences. For example, international trade economists used to favour a theory, refined from a model due to Ricardo, that reduced to the standard microeconomics of households. These economists abandoned this theory, and developed non-

Among philosophers, this conclusion has been embraced with both hands by radical disunity advocates such as Dupré (1993) and Cartwright (1999). Science, they argue, describes not a single reality but a patchwork of isolated islands of structure. Cartwright's explanation of this fact is especially illuminating because it does not appeal simply to institutional pressures for specialization. (These are certainly important, but they apply to philosophers of science just as to scientists; so it's not clear that we can lean on these pressures when searching for a reason to expect philosophers to preserve comparative advantage as unifiers.) Rather, Cartwright emphasizes that a main preoccupation of scientists, the isolation of causal networks, crucially relies in practice on artificially isolating locally stable clusters of regularities and shielding them from generally prevailing complexity. Science sheds powerful light on *hypothetically* abstracted machines by deliberately turning down the illumination on whatever has not been selected for isolation. Furthermore, clearly demarcating the boundaries of isolated systems is hard work – indeed, the *leading* source of difficulty in science. This explains why scientists are apt to become impatient – indeed exasperated – with philosophers and others who seek to over-generalize scientific results or try to unify them too hastily.

As both Cartwright and the philosopher of economics Uskali Mäki have emphasized, this logic is nicely exemplified in the science I know most intimately, microeconomics. Where that discipline is concerned, the currently fashionable behavioural economists (e.g. Loewenstein 2008, Ariely 2008) relentlessly nag modelers towards shotgun unification with psychology, calling on us to liberally scatter exogenous psychological influences among the independent

reducing 'gravity models' (Feenstra et al 2003), when empirical evidence was found that refuted the Ricardian story as a general account. A comprehensive book on failures of reductionism since the 1980s would be very long. The temporal reference here has an explanation: the run of success for reductionistic models was due mainly to the fact that limited computational capacities encouraged closed-form high-level models that tended to bury non-reducing processes in black boxes. With the recent explosion in number-crunching capacity, the black boxes open one after another. (See Humphreys 2004.)

variables in our models.[5] Most microeconomists resist this campaign, for good reason. Every new exogenous variable appears in a structural model with a little flotilla of parameters, like remoras around a shark.[6] The consequence, if these variables are received with any attitude other than extreme deliberation and suspicion, will be the wholescale surrender of the ambition to achieve what the microeconomist most wants: a *general* theory of the responses of goal-driven general information-processing systems to changes in relative opportunity costs of choices.

Thus it is explicable why economists are at best reluctant unificationists. However, it would be rash, to put it mildly, to conclude from this that there is on the one hand 'an economic world' and, on the other, a disconnected 'psychological world'. Minds as described by psychologists participate – non-tangentially – in computing relationships described by economists; and to refuse in principle to ever try to integrate these descriptions is to decide to forego access to some information that is bound to be relevant to both prediction and explanation.[7]

Let us consider an example. Glimcher (2010) musters a sustained case for the integration of processing models inspired by empirical neuroscience with the axiomatic framework of standard microeconomics. He stresses that this integration, like any well managed marriage, requires responsible modification of both parts of the proposed whole. Whether the details of Glimcher's

5. One sometimes gathers that we're to do this whenever an experimental subject responds in any surprising way in the lab. This is advice implicitly pitched at the extravagantly lazy: why resort to hard modeling when you can always just add a new parameter or two?

6. One way of trying to avoid this problem, recently urged by some influential econometricians, is to minimize the use of structural models (Angrist & Pischke 2009). I think this proposed cure is worse than the disease, both because the instrumental variables on which we are then forced to rely are much rarer than these 'new empiricists' suggest, and because we so far lack the kind of fully generalized statistical theory of unbiased model estimators we would need to obtain broad-scope causal generalizations in the absence of structural models. The anti-structuralist programme in econometrics makes a fetish out of local causal modeling; so it will appeal to philosophers of disunity.

7. Some rash economists do urge that we avert our gaze from such complications; see Gul & Pesendorfer (2008).

programme will ultimately carry the day must be decided by a pending experimental history, not a priori assessment. But it would clearly be simplistic to suppose that Glimcher has been motivated to develop his integrated 'neuroeconomics' simply by serendipitous observations; unification has had to be actively pursued The relevant measurements on which Glimcher's project finds its empirical legs are mainly of neurons in the brains of monkeys, who were placed in ecologically bizarre task settings by Glimcher and his colleagues because they recognized that economic and psychological processes must constrain one another and wanted to isolate – a la Cartwright – the mechanisms that transmit the constraints in question. The design details of the research programme would be incomprehensible without recognition that Glimcher and his associates believed that economists and neuroscientists model a single shared world but that, furthermore, the abstractions of neither theoretical framework reduce to those of the other.[8]

When integrative projects such as Glimcher's succeed, they constitute evidence against the philosophers of disunity – because, as I have just urged, such projects actively and by design test disunity as a null hypothesis. But of course they test it piecemeal. We can only test the *generalized* disunity hypothesis by showing that the special sciences are constrained by fundamental physics. The reason for this, as argued by Ladyman & Ross (2007, chapter 1), is that among the empirical sciences only fundamental physics is in the business of offering generalizations that are implicitly tested by every measurement of every magnitude in the universe. If philosophical metaphysics were in fact to be outsourced to an empirical science, the science in question would have to be fundamental physics,[9] for exactly this reason.

But – and this brings us to the main conclusion at which I have been aiming – physicists are not going to take up this job. They will decline it not because it is beyond their capacity, but because its opportunity cost is too high in light of their institutionalized

8. Glimcher is explicit and insistent about the second point.

9. Ladyman & Ross demarcate 'fundamental' physics by reference to this principle of universal measurement applicability, thereby legislating that thermodynamics, for example, is non-fundamental. We do not deny that this is circular; it is intended as a recursive definition, not an empirical claim.

mission. This point could readily be misunderstood. There are physicists who study complexity in general and who find useful test phenomena for modeling in the biological and social sciences (see Zurek 1990), and in financial markets (Challet et al 2005). However, this work all depends on refinements and extensions of thermodynamics that takes the Second Law for granted. This isn't *fundamental* physics, because both quantum theory and spacetime theory have physically possible models in which the Second Law doesn't apply; and we have no reason to believe that these models might not characterize regions of the universe we haven't yet accessed.

This demarcating stipulation about fundamentality isn't special pleading. Metaphysicians often try to distinguish their project from scientific ones by claiming an interest in necessity. This tips straight into anti-scientific metaphysical analysis if necessity is understood in terms of the semantics of possible worlds. However, necessity can be understood in a less tendentious way as involving reference to *universal* – but physical – constraints on transmission of information across the universe, and which thus restrict the acceptable classes of models in all sciences. Interest in fundamentality in this sense is thus motivated by interest in unification.

The last point signals that we have identified a job that will be done only by philosophers.[10] Physicists are of course interested in the scopes of the generalizations they discover, but not because they entertain hypotheses about possible biologies or possible economies. In doubting that (many) physicists will be motivated by this sort of concern, even if they come to clearly recognize it, I claim no novel insight into the sociology of science; nor do I deny that social circumstances could conceivably arise that might rivet everyone's

10. Physicists often speculate about what we are calling metaphysical unification in popular books of varying quality. Among recent ones, Deutsch (2011) is among the most entertaining and, thanks to its author's imagination and self-confidence, frequently enlightening. But Deutsch is clearly engaged mainly with the philosophical rather than the physical tradition of debate, as evidenced by his recurrent discussions of Popper, Socrates, Kant and so forth. This is notwithstanding his determination to argue that his favorite (Everettian) interpretation of the quantum measurement problem is the winner logically *and* physically.

attention, including that of mainstream physical theorists, on, say, 'econophysics'. I claim only that there are no evident trends in this direction. Thus metaphysicians who are institutionally embedded in philosophy departments can retain an intellectually sound project in the same sense that immigrants from poor regions can reliably find work in labour-intensive agriculture in rich countries: nobody else, at least for the moment, wants the job. Of course, intellectual soundness is no guarantee that naturalistic metaphysicians will succeed in overcoming the grip of the analysts *within* philosophy departments, nor that institutional philosophy won't be overwhelmed by political-economic stresses that currently threaten it, regardless of what philosophers do.

3. IS NATURALIZED METAPHYSICS COEXTENSIVE WITH MATHEMATICS?

A thread remains dangling. I opened the present essay by comparing the scope of philosophy, as a contributor to objective knowledge,[11] with the conjoined scope of empirical science and mathematics; but then I set mathematics aside. It cannot be left unconsidered, however. Mathematics has claim to universal scope in a stronger sense than fundamental physics does. Furthermore, the kind of naturalized metaphysics briefly described here, and in detail in Ladyman & Ross (2007), should not be expected to be expressible in natural language, which builds a pre-scientific ontology of discrete actions and events into its very syntax.[12] Naturalized metaphysics requires formal representation. Finally, the ontology of abstract structures 'all the way down' that Ladyman & Ross argue to be the only ontology consistent with quantum theory, deliberately obscures the distinction between physically interpreted and

[11]. The reader should infer from earlier remarks that I here use 'knowledge' only its everyday sense of 'well established collective belief'.

[12]. Of course, as Deutsch (2011) argues, natural language could change in this respect. Our claim about its inadequacy for naturalized metaphysics is contingent, as are indeed all claims in our book.

uninterpreted mathematics.[13] It seems to follow from all of this that if there is a naturalized metaphysics to be had – that is, a formal model of universal structures that embed all empirically adequate scientific models without generally reducing them to one another – then it is an as-yet unidentified part of mathematics.

I will raise a problem based on two premises. First, suppose that mathematics as a whole is unifiable.[14] This need not be interpreted as requiring that all of mathematics be shown to rest on a finite set of axioms; mathematics is unified in a weaker and more plausible sense merely if there is no part of it that is structurally isolated from the rest. Next: if the development of naturalized metaphysics is mathematical activity, it in no way follows that we should expect it to correspond to a distinctive sub-branch of mathematics; contributions might be expected from *any* part of mathematics. From these two assumptions it seems to follow that people have been doing naturalized metaphysics, in the sense of Ladyman and Ross, all along; for naturalized metaphysics in that sense is just co-extensive with mathematics!

Many philosophers are likely to think that unless there is a decisive way of blocking this implication, naturalization of metaphysics by way of Ladyman & Ross's 'ontic structural realism' (OSR) is a shipwrecked project. Several points of reflection, however, suggest that this would be a hasty conclusion.

Ladyman & Ross's overall view, Rainforest Realism (RR), is historically located as a motivational relative of two salient projects in recent philosophy: Peircean pragmatism and logical positivism. The latter, in turn, is understood, following Friedman's (1999) excavations, as a species of neo-Kantianism. We might say, a bit

13. Dorr (2010) is one of several critics of Ladyman & Ross (2007) who regards this as an objection to our 'ontic structural realism'. We don't know why it should be presumed that mathematics and physics have a sharp or clear boundary, except with respect to an institutional feature: physicists, but not mathematicians, will turn their attention away from modeling approaches that go too long without identifying relevant and performable measurement tests, as exemplified by the current plight of string theory. If string theory is thus mathematics but not physics, this needn't reflect any intrinsic property of the theory that should be expected to have a deep or general philosophical explanation.

14. It might not be.

anachronistically, that the themes uniting these views as a family are scientism and verificationism. The logical positivists sought formal foundations for philosophy and denied, like Ladyman & Ross, that interesting philosophical truths can be well expressed in natural language. The unachievable ambition on which their project foundered was to reduce science and mathematics to logic; and this went hand-in-glove with a mistaken commitment to deduction from axioms as the core model of scientific reasoning. But the positivists had no stronger basis for distinguishing philosophy from mathematics than Ladyman & Ross do. It is seldom if ever suggested that *that* is a decisive objection to positivism. It would be a forceful concern if the metaphysical project were presumed to be co-extensive with the aims of Lewis and Kripke; but such a presumption would egregiously beg every question of interest here.

The Peircean connection is still more important. We follow Hacking (1990) in interpreting Peirce as seeing the world, in its widest angle, as a kind of directed graph in which the edges are statistical relationships. As Hacking (p. 181) notes, Peirce would likely have found terrific inspiration for refining this vague insight had he lived after instead of before the rise of quantum-theoretical fundamental physics. Ladyman & Ross (2007) might reasonably be read as an effort to say some of what a post-Copenhagen Peirce might have articulated, no doubt more perspicuously. We are, indeed, attracted by the following gloss on RR that mimics Wittgenstein: the world is the totality of non-redundant statistics. Now, the three-cornered relationship among empirical measurement, mathematics, and statistical inference is famously complex and unresolved, is indeed the current hothouse of activity in scientific methodology that occupies theorists in various corners of the academy. It has particularly flourished since the coming of massive new computational capacities has turned a range of formerly abstract, speculative questions into practical ones.

Consider just one example of a pressing question in the foundations of statistical inference: is there a generally consistent estimator of time-series count data on distributions of independent variables that are neither normal, binomial nor Poisson?[15] The urgency of the question derives directly from applications in the social and biological sciences. The work involved in seeking to answer it requires division of labour between computer scientists – who are effectively doing the relevant epistemology – and mathematicians, who might reasonably be interpreted as responsible for the metaphysical aspect of the problem. (I call it 'metaphysical' with the Ladyman-Ross understanding of that word in mind: the aim is to unify inferential practices across special sciences by means of a fundamental constraint on information transmission that might objectively exist and be discoverable.) The semantic field in which researchers must operate is not a refined version of everyday folk categories, and formal conceptual representation is indispensible.

Continuity of this work with some of the most venerable of philosophical questions has been prominently noted. In a practical vein, Pearl (2000) interprets the unfolding theory of statistical inference as the project of understanding causality in general; with a more explicitly philosophical agenda, Woodward (2005) concurs, and exploits Pearl's practical insights. Whether one agrees with the details or not, this is naturalized metaphysics. At its core is mathematics. No one can know in advance how much or how little of mathematics will turn out to be useful for later stages of the inquiry or for new research programs to which it gives rise.

These reflections of course do not directly answer the question of the section title, which would require at least book-length treatment. Deep issues within mathematics are also relevant to it. Mathematicians and philosophers of mathematics have wondered for many decades about whether certain parts of mathematics – for example, the theory of transfinite numbers – are importantly set apart from other provinces of the discipline precisely in having, in principle, no physical applications. In this context, the naturalist must doubt that anyone can know which mathematics don't have physical applications in advance of the future history of physics.

Thus if many philosophers, remaining in a distinctive institutional niche, were to take up naturalized metaphysics as we

15. The common current practical hack is to pretend that such distributions are Poisson and then correct in a case-specific way for the obviously false assumption.

Ladyman & Ross characterize it, they may end up doing a mix of mathematics and computer science, closely informed by discoveries from fundamental physics and motivated by target problems in the special sciences. The boundary between this alluring – at least to me – discipline and its associated neighbours would be murky, like most disciplinary boundaries. As Humphreys (2004) concludes his book by saying, the wider home for such philosophy would be in the sciences, not the humanities; and it isn't evident that these scientific philosophers would have much to say, professionally, to the Heideggerians in the Humanities schools from whom they had peacefully separated. Philosophy in the other sense, as part of the pursuit of the best model of objective reality, would go on as philosophy; and it would be science.

REFERENCES

Angrist, J., & Pischke, J-S. (2009). *Mostly Harmless Econometrics.* Princeton: Princeton University Press.

Ariely, D. (2008). *Predictably Irrational.* New York: Harper Collins.

Batterman, R. (2002). *The Devil in the Details.* Oxford: Oxford University Press.

Cartwright, N. (1999). *The Dappled World.* Cambridge: Cambridge University Press.

Challet, D., Marsilli, M., & Zhang, Y-C (2005). *Minority Games: Interacting Agents in Financial Markets.* Oxford: Oxford University Press.

Deutsch, D. (2011). *The Beginning of Infinity.* London: Allen Lane.

Dorr, C. (2010). Review of *Every Thing Must Go: Metaphysics Naturalized. Notre Dame Philosophical Reviews.* Accessed at http://ndpr.nd.edu/news/24377-every-thing-must-go-metaphysics-naturalized

Dupré, J. (1993). *The Disorder of Things.* Cambridge, MA: Harvard University Press.

Feenstra, R., Markusen, J., & Rose, A. (2001). Using the gravity equation to differentiate among alternative theories of trade. *Canadian Journal of Economics* 34: 430-447.

Friedman, M. (1999). *Reconsidering Logical Positivism.* Cambridge: Cambridge University Press.

Glimcher, P. (2010). *Foundations of Neuroeconomic Analysis.* Oxford: Oxford University Press.

Gul, F., and Pesendorfer, W. (2008). The case for mindless economics. In: A. Caplin & A. Schotter, eds., *The Foundations of Positive and Normative Economics: a Handbook* (pp. 3-39). Oxford: Oxford University Press.

Hacking, I. (1990) *The Taming of Chance*. Cambridge: Cambridge University Press.

Humphreys, P. (2004). *Extending Ourselves*. Oxford: Oxford University Press.

Ladyman, J., & Ross, D. (2007). *Every Thing Must Go*. Oxford: Oxford University Press.

Loewenstein, G. (2008). *Exotic Preferences*. Oxford: Oxford University Press.

Mäki, U. (1992). On the method of isolation in economics. In C. Dilworth, ed., *Idealization IV: Intelligibility in Science*. Special issue of *Poznan Studies in the Philosophy of the Sciences and the Humanities* 26: 319-354.

Merricks, T. (2003). Replies. *Philosophy and Phenomenological Research* 67: 700-703.

Pearl, J. (2000). *Causality*. Cambridge: Cambridge University Press.

Woodward, J. (2005). *Making Things Happen*. Oxford: Oxford University Press.

Zurek, W, ed. (1990). *Complexity, Entropy and the Physics of Information*. Boulder: Westview.

Recherches sur la philosophie et le langage 29 (2013)
192 p., ISBN : 978-2-7116-8410-6, p. 29-46, Vrin.

L'esprit n'est plus un objet philosophique ou comment les sciences cognitives nous aident à penser les rapports entre science et philosophie

Delphine BLITMAN*

RÉSUMÉ

Les sciences cognitives contemporaines ont en partie pris le relais de la philosophie dans l'étude de l'esprit humain. Quelles leçons la philosophie doit-elle tirer des découvertes empiriques qui sont faites en neurosciences ou en psychologie, par exemple : doit-elle se contenter d'enregistrer les résultats scientifiques et voir son territoire de plus en plus empiété, ou conserve-t-elle un rôle spécifique à jouer dans la compréhension de l'esprit humain ? Dans ce domaine, on peut reformuler la question des rapports entre science(s) et philosophie en demandant si l'esprit est (encore) un objet philosophique. La position que je défends se présente comme une réponse négative nuancée à cette question. Je prendrai l'exemple, paradigmatique en sciences cognitives, de la théorie de Chomsky sur le langage. Je montrerai d'abord que les débats philosophiques classiques sur la nature du langage ont été complètement reformulés par les sciences cognitives contemporaines et la

* Delphine Blitman est titulaire d'un doctorat de philosophie des sciences de l'EHESS. Elle a enseigné la philosophie notamment à l'Université de Paris 1 et à l'EHESS. Ses recherches ont porté jusqu'à présent sur la théorie de Chomsky sur le langage et la question de l'inné et de l'acquis.

philosophie doit prendre acte de la manière scientifique de reformuler ces problèmes. Cependant, j'argumenterai aussi pour soutenir que la philosophie n'est pas passive face à ces résultats ; avec ses méthodes propres, notamment celle de l'analyse conceptuelle, elle contribue d'une manière décisive à déterminer leur portée et leur signification.

ABSTRACT

Mind is no more a philosophical object, or how cognitive science helps us to rethink relationships between science and philosophy

Contemporary cognitive science has replaced philosophy in the study of the human mind. What lessons should philosophy draw from, for instance, empirical results in neuroscience or psychology? Should the philosopher just note these scientific results and see her competence more and more contested, or does she maintain a specific role to play as regards the understanding of the human mind? In this domain, the question of the relationships between science(s) and philosophy may be rephrased as the question of knowing whether the mind is (still) a philosophical object. The position I take is a nuanced negative answer to this last question. I will rely on the case, paradigmatic for cognitive science, of Chomsky's theory of language. I will argue first that the classical debates in philosophy about the nature of the language faculty were completely reformulated by contemporary cognitive science and that philosophy must take into account the scientific way of approaching these issues. However, I will also defend the idea that philosophy does not maintain a passive attitude in confrontation with scientific results. With its own method, notably conceptual analysis, it contributes in a decisive way to determining their scope and meaning.

INTRODUCTION

Depuis la naissance de la science moderne, engendrée par la révolution scientifique des XVIe, XVIIe et XVIIIe siècles, la philosophie a besoin de se justifier. Au mieux, elle n'est plus la forme nécessaire et unique du savoir ; au pire, sa capacité même à connaître le monde est remise en cause au profit de la science, ou, vaudrait-il mieux dire, des sciences. Les rapports entre la science en générale et la philosophie en sont devenus problématiques : où et comment situer les frontières de la philosophie par rapport aux sciences ? La philosophie a-t-elle un domaine d'objets propre auquel la démarche scientifique n'a pas accès ? Comment définir la connaissance philosophique en la distinguant de la connaissance scientifique ?

Il me semble que les réponses à ces questions peuvent emprunter trois chemins principaux, qu'il y a trois façons très générales de concevoir, en première approche, les rapports entre science et philosophie. La première consiste à affirmer que la philosophie a ses domaines réservés, ses objets propres, auxquels la science n'a pas accès et qu'elle seule peut connaître. Pour la deuxième, la science concurrence et évince progressivement la philosophie dans son entreprise de connaissance du monde, de sorte que la philosophie devient inutile à toute entreprise de connaissance. La troisième, tout en reconnaissant qu'il n'y a pas, à proprement parler, de connaissance philosophique, considère néanmoins que la philosophie, comme épistémologie, comme philosophie des sciences, a un rôle propre à jouer face à la science, qu'il faut définir. C'est cette troisième position que je voudrais défendre en m'appuyant sur une analyse des relations entre sciences cognitives et philosophie.

Le travail du philosophe des sciences consiste traditionnellement en deux tâches principales. Il s'agit de comprendre et d'expliciter la démarche scientifique pour dégager un modèle général du raisonnement scientifique d'une part, et d'autre part d'analyser et d'interpréter les résultats scientifiques dans les différentes disciplines. Dans le cas des sciences cognitives cependant, qui cherchent à comprendre les phénomènes mentaux et neurobiologiques, le fait que la connaissance scientifique de l'esprit/cerveau en soit encore à ses débuts laisse certainement une part plus grande à la philosophie. De fait, la philosophie est considérée aujourd'hui comme l'une des disciplines qui constituent les sciences cognitives, aux côtés de la psychologie cognitive, de la neurobiologie ou encore de l'intelligence artificielle, et qui contribuent à la connaissance et à la compréhension de l'esprit/cerveau humain. L'analyse philosophique joue dans les sciences cognitives un rôle heuristique qu'elle n'a manifestement plus dans les autres sciences. Les philosophes développent des intuitions, élaborent des modèles, des distinctions conceptuelles qui peuvent fournir des outils aux scientifiques. En même temps, l'interprétation des résultats scientifiques y est plus délicate que dans d'autres domaines, au sens où la signification d'une découverte neurobiologique pour le fonctionnement mental d'un individu est souvent loin d'être évidente, ce qui laisse, là aussi, davantage de place à l'analyse philosophique[1].

Ainsi, s'appuyer sur l'exemple des sciences cognitives pour chercher des réponses aux questions qui concernent les relations entre la science et la philosophie me paraît particulièrement intéressant parce que les sciences cognitives rendent précisément ce problème des rapports entre science(s) et philosophie plus aigu. La philosophie a, dans les sciences cognitives, une place et des prétentions plus importantes que dans d'autres domaines ; elle fait valoir dans l'étude de l'esprit la valeur de ses intuitions ou de ses expériences de pensée, là où elle n'oserait pas le faire en physique par exemple. On pourrait donc reformuler notre question initiale en demandant si l'esprit est (encore) un objet philosophique. La position que je voudrais défendre se présente comme une réponse négative nuancée à cette question.

Dans cet article, je m'appuierai sur l'analyse d'un cas paradigmatique en sciences cognitives, celui du langage. Le linguiste américain Noam Chomsky, en proposant d'étudier le langage comme un objet naturel dans l'esprit/cerveau du locuteur, a contribué à la fondation des sciences cognitives au milieu des années

1. On peut songer, par exemple, à la discussion suscitée depuis plus de 15 ans par la découverte des « neurones miroirs » (voir pour la découverte de ces neurones G. Rizzolatti, L. Fadiga, V. Gallese & L. Fogassi, « Premotor cortex and the recognition of motor actions », *Cognitive Brain Research*, 3, 1995, p. 131-141, et, pour un aperçu de la discussion, le colloque en ligne « What Do Mirror Neurons Mean? », archivé à l'adresse http://www.interdisiplines.org/archives.php, consulté le 30 août 2011).

1950. Il s'agit donc, à partir du cas du langage, de réfléchir à ce que peut être le rôle de la philosophie face aux hypothèses scientifiques et aux découvertes empiriques des sciences cognitives. Dans une première partie, je montrerai comment Chomsky reformule de manière scientifique un problème philosophique ancien, et, dans une seconde partie, je dégagerai les implications que l'on peut tirer de cet exemple concernant les rapports entre science et philosophie.

I.

Chomsky a pour ambition de faire de la linguistique une science, sur le modèle des sciences naturelles.

C'est d'abord par la définition de son objet que la linguistique chomskyenne se caractérise. Chomsky propose de définir le langage comme un objet naturel. Pour lui, étudier le langage comme un objet naturel, c'est avant tout lui appliquer la méthode de la science, ce qu'il appelle le « naturalisme méthodologique »[2] :

> Je voudrais examiner une façon d'aborder l'esprit qui considère le langage et d'autres phénomènes similaires comme des éléments du monde naturel devant être étudiés avec les méthodes ordinaires de la recherche empirique[3].

Comme on le voit, Chomsky récuse la distinction entre sciences de l'esprit et sciences de la nature. Il faut étudier les phénomènes mentaux comme on étudie n'importe quels phénomènes physiques. Cela implique notamment que les lois qui gouvernent les phénomènes mentaux sont aussi éloignées du sens commun que le sont les lois physiques.

Que le langage soit un « objet naturel » signifie aussi que le langage est un objet réel, une partie de la nature. Et s'il existe quelque part, ce doit être dans l'esprit/cerveau des locuteurs. De cette façon, la linguistique est considérée par Chomsky comme une

2. N. Chomsky, *New Horizons in the Study of Language and Mind*, Cambridge, Cambridge University Press, 2000 ; trad. fr. *Nouveaux horizons dans l'étude du langage et de l'esprit*, Paris, Stock, 2005.

3. *Ibid.*, p. 235.

partie de la psychologie[4], qui est elle-même une partie de la biologie[5]. Le langage est défini comme une « capacité cognitive »[6] : la maîtrise de sa langue maternelle par un locuteur est représentée dans son esprit/cerveau, autrement dit, la grammaire a une réalité psychologique[7]. L'adoption d'une perspective mentaliste sur le langage est ainsi une autre conséquence du naturalisme méthodologique. La théorie linguistique se présente alors comme une théorie de ce qu'est la faculté de langage dans l'esprit/cerveau d'un individu humain.

A l'appui de son ambition scientifique, Chomsky introduit ensuite l'idée que les lois du langage doivent être formulées dans un langage formel. Son approche est fondée sur la conviction qu'on peut rendre compte de la grammaire maîtrisée par le locuteur dans les termes formels d'un calcul dont la description emprunte ses outils aux mathématiques. La théorie linguistique proposée est donc liée à une conception particulière de l'esprit humain, comme système computationnel de traitement de l'information. Souscrire au computationnalisme, c'est admettre que les processus mentaux sont des processus de traitement de l'information ; ces processus sont des calculs sur des symboles en fonction de leurs caractéristiques formelles ou syntaxiques. Le computationnalisme est le modèle classique des processus mentaux en sciences cognitives (ce qu'on appelle le paradigme cognitiviste). Chomsky applique au langage le modèle des systèmes computationnels de règles qui forment et modifient des représentations. L'expression de « grammaire générative », qui définit la théorie chomskyenne du langage, désigne ainsi l'élaboration de modèles computationnels explicites des mécanismes grammaticaux grâce auxquels une phrase est dérivée de structures syntaxiques sous-jacentes.

4. Voir par exemple N. Chomsky, *Reflections on Language*, New-York, Pantheon Books, 1975; trad. fr. *Réflexions sur le langage*, Paris, Flammarion, 1981 : « La théorie du langage est simplement la partie de la psychologie humaine qui traite d'un « organe mental » particulier, le langage humain » (p. 49).

5. *Ibid.*, p. 52.

6. *Ibid.*

7. Ce point a fait l'objet d'une intense polémique, notamment avec les philosophes contemporains du langage et de l'esprit. Voir, par exemple, M. Devitt, *Ignorance of Language*, Oxford, Oxford University Press, 2006.

Chomsky oppose donc aux grammaires traditionnelles descriptives la notion de grammaire générative[8]. Il emprunte aux travaux mathématiques et logiques de Turing et Church et à la théorie des fonctions récursives, issue, à l'origine, de la théorie de la calculabilité, les concepts et les outils nécessaires à la grammaire générative. Il introduit la notion centrale de récursivité dans la définition des grammaires génératives. La récursivité désigne la propriété d'une règle de pouvoir se ré-appliquer indéfiniment à son propre résultat. Selon Chomsky, une grammaire d'une langue naturelle ou formelle est un système de règles récursives, c'est-à-dire de procédures récursives d'engendrement des phrases. Pour le dire autrement, on peut définir la grammaire d'une langue naturelle par une fonction générative dotée de propriétés récursives. On rend ainsi compte de la langue non pas en énumérant exhaustivement les structures qu'elle autorise, mais de manière générative, parce qu'on peut engendrer à partir des règles de la grammaire toutes les phrases bien formées dans cette langue et seulement elles.

Cette formalisation et cette mathématisation contribuent, pour Chomsky, à rendre le traitement du langage qu'il propose scientifique. Si la volonté de faire de la linguistique une science n'est pas nouvelle, pas plus que ne l'est la tentative de formalisation des grammaires naturelles qui accompagne cette ambition, Chomsky propose une étude mathématique des propriétés formelles des grammaires qui va plus loin que tout ce qui a été fait précédemment.

Au mentalisme, défini comme l'adoption d'une perspective mentaliste ou cognitive sur le langage, et au computationnalisme, il faut ajouter un troisième élément pour terminer de caractériser l'approche chomskyenne du langage. Cet élément est l'innéisme. Selon Chomsky, admettre le naturalisme méthodologique dans l'étude de l'esprit humain implique aussi d'admettre que les structures mentales ont, comme toutes les structures biologiques, un fondement inné[9]. L'hypothèse principale sur laquelle repose la

8. Voir N. Chomsky, « Current Issues in Linguistic Theory », *in* J. Fodor & J. Katz (eds.), *The Structure of Language: Readings in the Philosophy of Language*, Englewood Cliffs, New-Jersey, Prentice-Hall, 1964, p. 50-118.

9. Pour une analyse plus détaillée du lien établi par Chomsky entre naturalisme et innéisme, et de la critique de l'empirisme qui l'accompagne, on peut consulter D. Blitman, « Chomsky et l'empirisme : de la critique de l'empirisme au sens de

théorie chomskyenne du langage concerne précisément la nature du fondement inné de la faculté de langage : il s'agit pour Chomsky de soutenir non pas seulement qu'il existe des principes ou des mécanismes innés sur lesquels repose le fonctionnement du langage, mais que ces principes ou ces mécanismes de fonctionnement sont propres au langage, spécifiques, qu'ils sont déjà de nature linguistique. Chomsky parle pour cette raison du langage comme d'un « module de l'esprit »[10] ou d'un « organe mental »[11], ces expressions reprenant à la fois l'idée d'un fondement biologique inné et l'idée d'une spécificité des principes de fonctionnement du langage[12]. La faculté de langage est constituée par un contenu inné qui lui est propre, elle consiste dans un corps de connaissances linguistiques innées.

Cette hypothèse de l'innéité de la faculté de langage est avancée par Chomsky en réponse au problème de l'acquisition du langage. Un bébé humain est capable d'acquérir la connaissance de la grammaire de la langue parlée par les membres de sa communauté, quelle qu'elle soit, à partir des données linguistiques primaires disponibles (c'est-à-dire à partir des stimuli linguistiques qui lui sont fournis par son environnement). Comment y parvient-il ? Contribuer à résoudre le problème de l'acquisition du langage, c'est explorer les mécanismes innés dont disposent les bébés humains pour analyser les données linguistiques primaires. Chomsky défend l'idée qu'il existe une faculté humaine de langage, universelle et innée, qui guide l'apprentissage du langage par le jeune enfant et qu'il appelle la Grammaire Universelle. La grammaire universelle est non seulement l'ensemble des principes universels auxquels sont soumises toutes les langues humaines, mais aussi la base innée à partir de laquelle se développe l'acquisition du langage chez l'enfant. C'est pourquoi

l'innéisme et du rationalisme chomskyens », *Histoire, Epistémologie, Langage*, 32/1, 2010, p. 139-168.

10. N. Chomsky, *Knowledge of Language: Its Nature, Origin, and Use*, New York, Praeger Publishers, 1986, p. 13.

11. N. Chomsky, *Rules and Representations*, New-York, Columbia University Press, 1980 ; trad. fr. *Règles et représentations*, Paris, Flammarion, 1985, p. 61 et 226.

12. La notion de modularité se définit bien, pour Chomsky, par la *spécificité* des principes de fonctionnement d'un module (en anglais, on emploie le terme *domain-specificity*).

Chomsky caractérise la grammaire universelle comme un « mécanisme d'apprentissage du langage », « Language Acquisition Device » ou « LAD » en anglais [13]. La théorie linguistique a donc une double tâche : découvrir la grammaire des langues particulières et découvrir les principes dont est constituée la Grammaire universelle.

L'hypothèse de l'innéité de la faculté de langage se veut, conformément à la démarche générale de Chomsky, une hypothèse scientifique et non un *a priori* philosophique. Avec cette hypothèse centrale, Chomsky place pourtant au cœur de sa théorie du langage une question philosophique : la question de l'inné et de l'acquis, de la part de la nature et de la culture dans le développement de la cognition humaine. C'est là une question ancienne, élaborée en particulier par la philosophie classique, et Chomsky s'inscrit délibérément dans cette tradition [14]. Il se revendique de l'innéisme classique de Descartes et plus généralement du rationalisme. Cependant, la question philosophique qui était au cœur de la controverse classique entre Descartes et ses successeurs d'une part et Locke et ses successeurs d'autre part [15], laisse place, chez Chomsky, à un problème scientifique. Chomsky reformule le problème classique en lui donnant un contenu scientifique, et c'est toute la portée de ce changement qu'il conviendra d'évaluer.

Ce changement intervient, selon moi, sur deux points essentiels : sur la méthode de recherche et sur le contenu des hypothèses innéistes, qui devient un contenu empirique, testable empiriquement et donc falsifiable.

Le premier point sur lequel intervient un changement par rapport à la question classique du rationalisme et de l'empirisme concerne donc la méthode utilisée pour aborder les problèmes posés. Il s'agit de délaisser l'introspection au profit de théories explicatives des phénomènes mentaux, autrement dit d'authentiques

13. Par exemple, N. Chomsky, *Knowledge of Language: Its Nature, Origin, and Use*, *op. cit.*, p. 3.

14. Voir N. Chomsky, *Cartesian Linguistics: A chapter in the History of Rationalist Thought*, New-York, Harper and Row, 1966 ; trad. fr. *La linguistique cartesienne : un chapitre de l'histoire de la pensée rationaliste*, Paris, Le Seuil, 1969.

15. Voir R. Descartes, *Méditations métaphysiques*, Paris, Garnier-Flammarion, 1641/1992, et J. Locke, *Essai sur l'entendement humain*, Paris, Vrin, 1690/ 2001 et 2006, notamment le Livre II, chap. 1, § 2.

théories scientifiques. Selon Chomsky, « [l]a plus grande lacune de la philosophie classique de l'esprit, rationaliste ou empiriste, [...] semble être sa supposition incontestée que les propriétés et le contenu de l'esprit sont accessibles à l'introspection »[16]. Ce n'est plus l'accès privilégié en première personne qui compte, mais la construction d'une théorie objective du langage. Instaurer une distance avec le sens commun est la condition pour parvenir à une explication scientifique réelle des phénomènes mentaux comme des phénomènes physiques. Les phénomènes mentaux aussi, comme les phénomènes physiques, requièrent d'être expliqués par des théories qui postulent des systèmes de règles et de principes gouvernant ces phénomènes. Dans le cas du langage en particulier, bien qu'« [e]n tant que locuteurs nous [ayons] à notre disposition un vaste ensemble de faits », il ne faut pas croire « qu'il n'y a rien à expliquer, que les principes organisationnels et les mécanismes sous-jacents, quels qu'ils soient, doivent être « donnés » avec les faits »[17]. Au contraire, « [l]a recherche de théories explicatives doit commencer par une tentative de déterminer ces systèmes de règles et de mettre au clair les principes qui les gouvernent »[18].

Concernant le second point, le contenu des hypothèses innéistes, rappelons que la question philosophique classique concerne la part respective, dans la constitution de la connaissance, de l'expérience (sensorielle) et de ce qu'on appelle la raison, qui renvoie à l'esprit humain avec ses principes et ses contenus naturels, *a priori*. Elle porte sur l'origine de la connaissance : les connaissances humaines viennent-elles de l'expérience ou sont-elles innées ? Le problème que pose Chomsky est bien plus précis : quelle est la nature de la faculté humaine de langage et comment le langage est-il acquis par l'enfant ? Cet abandon de la généralité de la question pour favoriser une étude empirique d'un domaine précis est le second élément qui signe le passage à la science.

Ainsi, Chomsky ne défend pas une « hypothèse de l'innéité » en général, mais des « hypothèses explicatives particulières concernant

16. N. Chomsky, *Language and Mind*, New-York, Harcourt, Brace & World, Inc., 1968; trad. fr. *Le langage et la pensée*, Paris, Payot, 1969, p. 65.

17. *Ibid.*, p. 67.

18. *Ibid.*, p. 67-68.

l'état initial génétiquement déterminé pour l'apprentissage du langage dans la mesure où elles paraissent crédibles et empiriquement confirmées »[19]. Si Chomsky tient à ce point, c'est qu'il met en jeu le caractère scientifique de la théorie qu'il avance. Le linguiste propose des hypothèses concernant, d'une part, la nature de la compétence grammaticale du locuteur-auditeur natif, c'est-à-dire de la maîtrise ou de la connaissance de la grammaire de la langue maternelle qu'un locuteur a acquise et qui est représentée dans son esprit/cerveau[20], et d'autre part les principes de la grammaire universelle censés expliquer l'acquisition de cette compétence. Dans le débat soulevé par la théorie de Chomsky, les hypothèses en présence ne sont pas l'innéisme et l'empirisme en général, mais des hypothèses particulières sur les mécanismes d'apprentissage du langage : ce qu'on appelle souvent « l'intelligence générale » suffit-elle à rendre compte de l'apprentissage du langage ou faut-il supposer qu'il existe des mécanismes d'acquisition du langage spécifiques à ce domaine ? Reformulé avec des notions propres aux sciences cognitives, le problème scientifique que pose Chomsky concerne la généralité ou la spécificité des mécanismes d'acquisition du langage[21]. Comme il le souligne :

> Toute « théorie de l'apprentissage » qui vaut seulement la peine d'être prise en considération contient une hypothèse d'innéisme. [...] La question n'est pas de savoir si l'apprentissage présuppose une structure innée – cela est évident ; et personne n'en a jamais douté –, mais plutôt de savoir quelles sont ces structures innées dans chaque domaine[22].

Ou encore :

19. N. Chomsky, « Discussion des commentaires de Putnam », in M. Piattelli-Palmarini (éd.), *Théories du langage, théories de l'apprentissage : le débat entre Jean Piaget et Noam Chomsky*, Paris, Le Seuil, 1979, p. 444-461, p. 445.

20. Sur la notion de compétence linguistique, voir N. Chomsky, *Aspects of the Theory of Syntax, Cambridge*, MIT Press, 1965 ; trad. fr. *Aspects de la théorie syntaxique*, Paris, Le Seuil, 1971.

21. On parle en anglais de « *domain-specificity* » pour désigner ce qui est propre à un domaine cognitif donné.

22. N. Chomsky, *Réflexions sur le langage*, *op. cit.*, p. 23.

> L'existence d'une structure mentale innée ne prête évidemment pas à controverse. On peut s'interroger, en revanche, sur sa nature et sur la mesure dans laquelle elle est spécifique pour le langage[23].

Pour découvrir les mécanismes spécifiques qui sous-tendent l'acquisition du langage et formuler des hypothèses innéistes précises, Chomsky s'est appuyé sur un type d'argument fondamental, l'argument dit « par la pauvreté du stimulus ». Cet argument consiste à montrer que certains principes syntaxiques sur lesquels repose la grammaire d'une langue ne peuvent pas être dérivés des données linguistiques auxquelles l'enfant a accès. Il en conclut alors par une inférence à la meilleure explication que les principes syntaxiques en question sont innés, qu'ils font partie de la Grammaire universelle dont est dotée tout cerveau humain à la naissance.

Pour illustrer cet argument, Chomsky prend souvent l'exemple, devenu fameux, de la dépendance à la structure[24]. On peut envisager deux façons possibles de former des interrogatives polaires à partir de déclaratives du type : « *The man who is here is tall* ». La première hypothèse consiste à proposer, pour former des interrogatives, d'inverser et de mettre en début de phrase le premier auxiliaire rencontré. On aurait alors l'interrogative suivante : « *Is the man who here is tall?* ». La seconde hypothèse maintient que c'est l'auxiliaire de la proposition principale qu'il faut inverser, de sorte qu'elle fait appel à une analyse de la structure de la phrase en constituants. Avec cette seconde hypothèse, on obtient la phrase : « *Is the man who is here tall?* ». La première hypothèse peut sembler plus simple, puisqu'elle ne présuppose pas une connaissance de la structure de la phrase. On pourrait donc s'attendre à ce que ce soit cette hypothèse que l'enfant utilise en apprenant à former des questions. Or ce n'est pas ce que l'on constate. La deuxième hypothèse, dépendante de la structure, est toujours préférée au sens où, quand l'enfant apprend la langue, il

23. N. Chomsky, « The Formal Nature of Language », *in* E. Lenneberg, *Biological Foundations of Language*, New-York, Wiley and Sons, 1967 ; trad. fr. *La nature formelle du langage*, Paris, Le Seuil, 1969, note 5, p. 131.

24. C'est l'exemple constamment utilisé par Chomsky pour illustrer l'argument par la pauvreté du stimulus. Je suivrai ici l'argumentation développée par Chomsky dans N. Chomsky, « L'approche linguistique », *in* M. Piattelli-Palmarini (éd.), *Théories du langage, théories de l'apprentissage : Le débat entre Jean Piaget et Noam Chomsky*, *op. cit.*, p. 169-193, p. 173 et suiv.

ne commet pas d'erreurs du type de celles qui seraient induites par la première hypothèse.

Comme le souligne Chomsky[25], la deuxième hypothèse requiert d'analyser la phrase en syntagmes abstraits. Or cette analyse n'est pas quelque chose que l'on peut inférer ou induire des données. La dépendance à la structure n'est pas une propriété observable des énoncés. Ce n'est donc pas l'expérience ou les données qui apprennent à l'enfant à choisir entre les deux hypothèses[26]. Parce que les données ne permettent pas de trancher, l'apprentissage de la règle gouvernant la formation des questions ne peut s'expliquer que par le fait qu'il est guidé par une connaissance innée, en l'occurrence une contrainte sur la dépendance à la structure des règles du langage. C'est là en tout cas la meilleure explication que l'on puisse avancer.

Cet exemple montre que, si l'argument par la pauvreté du stimulus prend souvent chez Chomsky une forme générale, qui peut conduire à y voir – à tort – un argument *a priori* ou logique, il s'agit en réalité d'un argument empirique : il faut faire un argument particulier pour les différents éléments de la grammaire que l'enfant vient à maîtriser, chaque argument visant à établir l'innéité d'un principe linguistique précis. L'argument par la pauvreté du stimulus doit ainsi être établi pour chaque principe syntaxique que l'on a des raisons indépendantes d'accepter comme vrai. Et pour l'établir, il faut en préciser empiriquement les trois aspects fondamentaux : la nature de la connaissance acquise (c'est-à-dire le principe linguistique dont l'analyse linguistique a montré qu'il faisait partie de la grammaire de la langue acquise par l'enfant), la nature des données linguistiques primaires et la nature des mécanismes d'apprentissage impliqués (pour savoir si des mécanismes généraux, et non spécifiques au langage, peuvent suffire à expliquer l'acquisition du principe linguistique en question). Savoir s'il y a une pauvreté du stimulus qui permet de faire l'inférence à la meilleure explication en faveur de l'existence de principes innés spécifiques de la faculté de langage est bien une question empirique, et les hypothèses innéistes

25. N. Chomsky, « Discussion des commentaires de Putnam », art. cit., p. 444-461.

26. L'enfant sait qu'il faut faire des inversions pour former des questions, parce qu'il en a entendues, mais selon Chomsky, il n'a pas de données concernant la formation de questions à partir de déclaratives contenant des propositions relatives.

que la théorie générative formule en s'appuyant sur l'argument par la pauvreté du stimulus ont un contenu testable et falsifiable.

Ainsi, comme j'ai voulu le montrer, la question de l'inné et de l'acquis dans le cas du langage est devenue un authentique problème scientifique, de sorte que ce sont des données empiriques qui permettent d'argumenter en faveur d'une hypothèse innéiste ou d'une hypothèse empiriste. Aujourd'hui, sans être définitivement tranché, le débat s'est nourri des données neurobiologiques, génétiques, évolutionnistes, et surtout psycho-linguistiques accumulées par les sciences cognitives[27].

De manière plus générale, comme l'illustre le cas paradigmatique de la faculté de langage, il semble bien que le débat sur l'inné et l'acquis tel qu'il a existé dans l'histoire de la philosophie soit aujourd'hui caduc et qu'il laisse la place à des débats scientifiques, spécifiques aux différents domaines de la cognition, concernant les structures innées éventuellement propres à ces domaines dans l'esprit/cerveau des êtres humains. En effet, à l'instar de la théorie chomskyenne du langage, les sciences cognitives ont développé l'étude naturaliste d'autres facultés mentales, transformant ainsi les thèses philosophiques rationaliste et empiriste en hypothèses scientifiques.

II

Je voudrais dans la deuxième partie de cet article développer les implications que l'on peut tirer concernant les rapports entre science et philosophie de cette transformation par les sciences cognitives d'un problème philosophique en un problème scientifique, transformation que j'ai analysée dans le cas de la faculté de langage. Je dégagerai trois implications générales qui, selon moi, découlent de l'exemple du langage. La première prend acte de cette transformation et de ce qu'elle signifie ; les deux suivantes précisent les relations qui s'établissent alors entre science et philosophie dans le

27. Pour une revue de ce riche débat empirique, voir D. Blitman, *Innéité et sciences cognitives : la faculté de langage*, thèse de doctorat, 2010.

cadre des sciences cognitives et développent le rôle que la philosophie peut être amenée à jouer vis-à-vis de l'entreprise scientifique.

Premièrement, dans le domaine de la connaissance, les questions philosophiques sont reformulées pour devenir des problèmes scientifiques, de sorte que la réponse qu'on peut y apporter s'appuie sur un raisonnement scientifique et des preuves empiriques. L'étude de la faculté de langage par Chomsky, dans la mesure où l'on admet qu'elle est paradigmatique, par sa méthode, de ce que font les sciences cognitives pour les différentes facultés mentales, montre que l'esprit lui-même n'est plus un objet de connaissance philosophique. Comme nous l'avons expliqué précédemment, Chomsky s'est efforcé de poser les bases d'une étude scientifique de la faculté de langage, en lui appliquant une méthode naturaliste. Il a par là même profondément transformé l'ancienne question philosophique de l'inné et de l'acquis, en lui donnant un contenu empirique précis et testable. La philosophie se trouve ainsi dessaisie d'un objet qui a été le sien. Chomsky a montré que l'on pouvait produire une théorie scientifique de la faculté de langage reposant sur des hypothèses innéistes, qui prend ainsi la place des anciennes questions philosophiques sur la nature de la faculté de langage. De ce point de vue, on peut dire que la science évince bien la philosophie.

Deuxièmement, précisément parce que l'esprit a longtemps été l'un des objets par excellence de la philosophie, parce que nombre de problèmes scientifiques dans le champ des sciences cognitives ont d'abord été des questions philosophiques, tout un travail d'analyse conceptuelle, en amont et en aval de l'étude scientifique, n'en est pas moins nécessaire. Dans le cas que j'ai étudié, les notions d'inné et d'acquis sont chargées du poids de la tradition philosophique ; elles sont connotées philosophiquement, voire idéologiquement, reliées aux contextes philosophiques dans lesquels elles sont apparues. La notion d'innéité par exemple est liée, depuis son origine platonicienne jusqu'à sa réactualisation chez Descartes et ses successeurs, à l'idéalisme : les idées innées sont d'abord des idées qui ne viennent pas de l'expérience, qui sont accessibles à la raison et non aux sens, et qui sont la source d'une connaissance bien plus certaine que celle que procure l'expérience sensible. Quand Chomsky formule son hypothèse innéiste, l'hypothèse de l'existence d'une Grammaire Universelle fondée dans la biologie humaine, il faut ainsi entreprendre à nouveaux frais de donner un sens à la notion d'innéité, différent de celui qu'elle avait dans la tradition philosophique. Le contexte scientifique dans lequel Chomsky utilise la notion en modifie profondément le sens. Tout le problème est de comprendre que Chomsky ne réactualise pas la thèse innéiste de Descartes, bien qu'il s'y réfère constamment. Il inscrit le concept d'innéité au sein d'une théorie scientifique du langage qui lui confère une signification nouvelle.

Comme philosophie des sciences cognitives, comme épistémologie, la philosophie a ainsi un rôle important à jouer de clarification et d'analyse conceptuelles. Même si la nature de ce travail sur les concepts est essentiellement philosophique, il n'est pas exclu que ce soient les scientifiques eux-mêmes qui l'accomplissent. Cela est assez significatif qu'en lieu et place des philosophes engagés dans un travail scientifique existent aujourd'hui des scientifiques épistémologues, capables de prendre un recul philosophique sur les concepts mis en jeu par leur discipline. Tous les scientifiques ne se posent évidemment pas nécessairement le problème de la nécessité ou non d'un tel travail philosophique, mais quelle que soit la division du travail entre philosophes des sciences et scientifiques, les sciences cognitives actuelles supposent cette part de réflexion conceptuelle.

Troisièmement, il s'agit aussi pour la philosophie des sciences cognitives d'isoler dans les débats scientifiques eux-mêmes le noyau scientifique de la part philosophique qui peut y être mêlée. De fait, dans notre cas d'étude, les références au débat philosophique classique brouillent d'une certaine façon le débat scientifique. Nous avons évoqué la référence permanente chez Chomsky au rationalisme cartésien et sa critique de l'empirisme sous toutes ses formes[28]. Cette référence n'est certainement pas étrangère aux polémiques et parfois au violent rejet que la théorie de Chomsky a suscités. Au lieu de montrer en quoi l'hypothèse de l'innéité de la faculté de langage qu'il avance rompt, par son contenu scientifique, avec la tradition philosophique innéiste, Chomsky a mis l'accent sur la continuité entre sa manière de poser la question de la nature de la faculté de langage et de son acquisition et celle qu'avaient les rationalistes depuis Platon de poser la question de l'acquisition de la

28. Voir par exemple N. Chomsky, *Cartesian Linguistics: A chapter in the History of Rationalist Thought*, New-York, Harper and Row, 1966.

connaissance[29]. Le contenu scientifique de son hypothèse se retrouve ainsi dilué dans un contexte philosophique qui, en réalité, ne change rien à la validité de cette hypothèse : ni les rationalistes ni les empiristes classiques ne peuvent fournir d'arguments concernant la validité ou la fausseté de l'hypothèse chomskyenne, puisque leurs arguments ne sont précisément pas scientifiques, riches d'un contenu empirique qui les rendrait testables. La référence aux débats classiques marque plus les préférences ou les préjugés philosophiques de Chomsky, sans que ce dernier terme ait ici une connotation péjorative, qu'elle n'apporte des éléments au débat scientifique qu'il soulève. Et, en un sens, chercher à répondre sans *a priori* à la question de savoir s'il existe une grammaire universelle innée qui guide l'apprentissage du langage suppose de se défaire de ses propres préjugés philosophiques pour examiner le problème scientifique nouveau qu'a formulé Chomsky.

Si l'on généralise ces remarques concernant le débat sur le caractère inné ou acquis de la faculté de langage, il semble qu'il y ait un travail de séparation à faire entre ce qui relève de la science et ce qui relève de la philosophie, y compris contre ce que disent parfois les scientifiques eux-mêmes. Les scientifiques ont inévitablement leurs propres préférences, préjugés ou *a priori* philosophiques, encore une fois sans attacher à ces termes une dimension négative. En d'autres termes, les scientifiques ont leur philosophie, consciente ou inconsciente. Le rôle de la philosophie est alors aussi de défendre la science contre les préjugés des scientifiques eux-mêmes, de démasquer la philosophie sous-jacente qui peut interférer avec les débats proprement scientifiques. C'est peut-être particulièrement le cas dans le domaine des sciences cognitives en raison de leur objet. Isoler les débats scientifiques des interprétations philosophiques auxquels ils sont parfois mêlés est ainsi également l'un des rôles de la philosophie des sciences cognitives.

29. Voir la formulation par Chomsky de ce qu'il appelle le « problème de Platon » dans N. Chomsky, *Knowledge of Language: Its Nature, Origin, and Use*, *op. cit.*, 1986.

Ainsi, j'ai montré qu'au sein des sciences cognitives, si l'on s'appuie sur l'exemple de la théorie chomskyenne du langage comme sur un cas paradigmatique, l'esprit comme objet philosophique disparaît au profit de problèmes scientifiques dont la formulation suppose de rompre avec la formulation philosophique antérieure. Cependant, j'ai insisté, dans la seconde partie de mon article, sur le fait que l'examen de la question de l'inné et de l'acquis dans le cas du langage permet aussi de mettre en évidence le rôle que la philosophie, comme épistémologie ou philosophie des sciences cognitives, conserve face à la science, un rôle de clarification et d'analyse conceptuelles, mais également, en un sens, de démystification des débats scientifiques.

Recherches sur la philosophie et le langage 29 (2013)
192 p., ISBN : 978-2-7116-8410-6, p. 47-65, Vrin.

Des collaborations possibles entre Intelligence Artificielle et philosophie de l'esprit[1]

Robin LAMARCHE-PERRIN*

RÉSUMÉ

Dans cet article, les relations logiques entre deux problèmes paradigmatiques concernant l'intelligence des machines (IA faible et IA forte) servent à exemplifier les rapports possibles entre Intelligence Artificielle et philosophie de l'esprit. Après avoir écarté la méthode béhavioriste de Turing (IA faible ⇒ IA forte) et l'hypothèse computationnaliste de Newell & Simon (IA faible ⇔ IA forte), l'article s'intéresse à la démarche critique adoptée par Dreyfus. Son analyse du computationnalisme, appuyée sur l'examen de ses origines philosophiques, constitue une stratégie logique féconde pour penser les rapports entre Intelligence Artificielle et philosophie de l'esprit (IA forte ⇒ IA faible). Cette stratégie peut également être exploitée pour résoudre des difficultés conceptuelles relatives à la simulation informatique des phénomènes émergents. Le concept

* Robin Lamarche-Perrin est en train d'écrire une thèse d'Intelligence Artificielle au Laboratoire d'Informatique de Grenoble, il est titulaire du master de philosophie à l'Université Pierre-Mendès-France et du diplôme d'ingénieur à l'Ensimag de l'Institut Polytechnique de Grenoble (Grenoble INP).

1. Les thèses présentées dans cette article ont été défendues dans un mémoire de recherche en philosophie. Nous invitons le lecteur à s'y référer pour plus de details : R. Lamarche-Perrin, *Des collaborations possibles entre philosophie et Intelligence Artificielle*, dir. Denis Perrin, Université Pierre-Mendès-France, Grenoble, 2012.

d'« émergence épistémique », emprunté aux controverses de la philosophie britannique, induit notamment des résultats méthodologiques intéressants pour l'Intelligence Artificielle. Ce rapprochement particulier (IA forte ⇒ IA faible) débouche sur un second mode de collaboration (non IA faible ⇒ non IA forte) au sein duquel l'Intelligence Artificielle devient à son tour une philosophie expérimentale, *i. e.* une science au service de la philosophie.

ABSTRACT

In this paper, the logical relationships between two paradigmatic problems regarding the intelligence of machines (strong AI and weak AI) are used to exemplify the possible relationships between Artificial Intelligence and philosophy of mind. Having rejected the behaviourist method of Turing (weak AI ⇒ strong AI) and the computationalist hypothesis of Newell and Simon (weak AI ⇔ strong AI), this paper focuses on the critical approach adopted by Dreyfus. His analysis of computationalism, based on the examination of its philosophical origins, constitutes a fruitful logical strategy to think up the relationship between Artificial Intelligence and philosophy of mind (strong AI ⇒ weak AI). This strategy can also be exploited to resolve conceptual difficulties regarding the simulation of emergent phenomena. In particular, the concept of "epistemic emergence", borrowed from the controversies of British philosophy, induces interesting methodological results in Artificial Intelligence. This particular relationship (strong AI ⇒ weak AI) leads to a second kind of collaboration (not weak AI ⇒ not strong AI) in which Artificial Intelligence becomes an experimental philosophy, *i.e.* a science which serves philosophy.

INTRODUCTION

Cet article s'intéresse aux collaborations possibles entre Intelligence Artificielle (IA) et philosophie. Une première approche évidente consiste à définir une *philosophie de l'IA*, au sens usuel de *philosophie des sciences*. Une épistémologie, donc, qui s'intéresse de manière extra-théorique aux fondements, aux objets et aux méthodes de l'IA. Nous soutenons cependant qu'il existe un endroit où IA et philosophie collaborent *à un même niveau*, c'est-à-dire au sein d'une même théorie et à propos des mêmes objets. Nous examinons pour cela le rôle particulier de la *philosophie de l'esprit* dans l'élaboration de l'IA moderne. Nous souhaitons également rendre compte du baptême administré par Daniel Andler dans l'avant-propos à l'édition française de l'ouvrage d'Hubert L. Dreyfus *What Computers Can't Do*. Andler y désigne l'IA comme « science de la philosophie », comme « *science philosophique* » par excellence[2]. Cet article vise également à comprendre les termes d'un tel baptême.

La distinction entre IA faible et IA forte, introduite à plusieurs reprises par John R. Searle[3], offre de bons jalons pour discuter des rapports possibles entre IA et philosophie de l'esprit. L'*IA faible* pose un problème pratique : peut-on réaliser des machines qui *simulent* les comportements intelligents et qui résolvent ainsi des problèmes techniques ou conceptuels habituellement appréhendés par l'homme ? L'*IA forte* répond à un problème de nature plus philosophique. Elle s'intéresse à l'ontologie même des machines : sont-elles *réellement* intelligentes ou ne font-elles que *simuler* l'intelligence ? Plusieurs critères peuvent être introduits pour distinguer ce qui est

2. H. L. Dreyfus, *Intelligence Artificielle : mythes et limites* (*What Computers Can't Do: The Limits of Artificial Intelligence*, 2nd ed., 1979), trad. fr. R.-M. Vassallo-Villaneau, avant-propos de D. Andler et J. Perriault, Paris, Flammarion, 1984, p. XIV.

3. Cette distinction apparaît pour la première fois dans J. R. Searle, « Minds, Brains, and Programs » (1980), *in* M. A. Boden (ed.), *The Philosophy of Artificial Intelligence*, Oxford/New York, Oxford University Press, 1990, p. 66. Elle est souvent réitérée par Searle et utilisée par des chercheurs en philosophie et en IA. Les acceptions retenues dans cet article sont celles de S. Russell et P. Norvig, *Artificial Intelligence: A Modern Approach*, 3rd ed., Upper Saddle River, New Jersey, Prentice Hall/Pearson Education, 2010, p. 1020.

de l'ordre de la véritable intelligence et ce qui est de l'ordre de la simulation. Les discussions les plus classiques font intervenir les notions d'états mentaux, d'intentionnalité (est-ce qu'une machine est capable d'états intentionnels ?) ou de conscience (est-ce qu'une machine peut avoir une vie phénoménale, une conscience de soi, *etc.* ?)

À première vue, les chercheurs qui travaillent sur ces deux problèmes appartiennent à des communautés distinctes. Il y a d'une part les spécialistes de l'IA, dont l'objectif premier est la production de comportements intelligents, et pour lesquels la question d'une « véritable intelligence » a peu de sens[4]. Tout comme un ingénieur en aéronautique se demande rarement si un avion « simule le vol » ou s'il « vole réellement »[5], la plupart des chercheurs en IA considèrent qu'une machine est intelligente lorsqu'elle peut résoudre des problèmes difficiles, peu importe la similarité de fonctionnement avec l'intelligence naturelle. Ainsi, les travaux des spécialistes font très marginalement référence aux notions de conscience et d'états mentaux[6]. Les philosophes, d'autre part, lorsqu'ils s'intéressent au problème de la conscience des machines (un sous-problème de l'IA forte), n'ont pas d'avis sur les possibilités et les difficultés de l'IA faible. La plupart n'émettent simplement aucune objection de principe[7].

Aucune collaboration n'est possible, dès l'abord, entre spécialistes de l'IA et philosophes de l'esprit. Les chercheurs

4. « Most AI researchers take the weak AI hypothesis for granted, and don't care about the strong AI hypothesis – as long as their program works, they don't care whether you call it a simulation of intelligence or real intelligence. » S. Russell et P. Norvig, *op. cit.*, p. 1020.

5. Cette analogie est empruntée à *ibid.*, p. 3 et 1021.

6. Par exemple, dans l'appel à la célèbre conférence de Dartmouth, où le terme même d'« Intelligence Artificielle » a été décidé, et dans l'ensemble des travaux de « simulation cognitive » qui lui ont succédé, les conjectures concernaient seulement la *simulation* de l'intelligence : « every aspect of learning or any other feature of intelligence can in principle be so precisely described that a machine can be made to simulate it. » J. McCarthy, M. L. Minsky, N. Rochester et C. E. Shannon, « A Proposal for the Dartmouth Summer Research Project on Artificial Intelligence » (1955), *AI Magazine*, vol. 27, n°4, 2006, p. 12.

7. *Cf.* par exemple la position de Searle : « I have no objection to the claims of weak AI, at least as far as this article is concerned. » J. R. Searle, *op. cit.*, p. 67.

n'aspirent simplement pas à résoudre les mêmes problèmes. Cependant, l'indépendance de ces problèmes est à mettre en question. Dans cet article, nous envisageons les cas où une dépendance logique ou empirique apparaît entre les hypothèses de l'IA faible et de l'IA forte. De telles dépendances témoignent d'interconnections entre le problème pratique et le problème philosophique. Elles nous servent ainsi à exemplifier les rapports possibles entre IA et philosophie de l'esprit, comme un cas particulier des rapports entre science et philosophie. Dans la première section, les dépendances « IA faible $\Rightarrow$ IA forte » et « IA faible $\Leftrightarrow$ IA forte »[8] sont abordées à partir de deux paradigmes classiques de l'IA : le behaviorisme d'Alan M. Turing, en 1950, et le computationnalisme, à l'origine de l'« IA classique » dans les années 1960. La deuxième section examine deux approches critiques de l'IA, argumentées par Searle et par Dreyfus. Le travail de Dreyfus est exploité pour établir une collaboration constructive entre les deux disciplines, sur la base de la dépendance « IA faible $\Leftarrow$ IA forte ». Les termes de cette collaboration sont développés et généralisés dans les deux dernières sections. Elles montrent comment les modèles philosophiques peuvent offrir une base saine au travail empirique et comment celui-ci peut en retour aider la philosophie à évaluer ses théories.

1. LES DÉBUTS DE L'INTELLIGENCE ARTIFICIELLE

Le behaviorisme. Dans son article de 1950, Alan M. Turing donne à l'intelligence une définition strictement comportementale : une machine est intelligente lorsqu'elle *se comporte comme un homme*[9]. Le désormais célèbre « Test de Turing » constitue une méthode empirique pour détecter une faculté psychologique à partir de ses propriétés observables, *i. e.* les comportements qu'elle engendre. Il hérite ainsi du behaviorisme méthodologique apparu en psychologie au début du siècle. Le test répond au problème de l'IA faible

8. Les symboles $\Rightarrow$ et $\Leftrightarrow$ désignent respectivement l'implication et l'équivalence logiques. Les expressions « IA faible $\Rightarrow$ IA forte », « IA forte $\Rightarrow$ IA faible » et « IA faible $\Leftrightarrow$ IA forte » sont explicitées ci-après.

9. A. M. Turing, « Computing Machinery and Intelligence » (1950), *in* M. A. Boden (ed.), *The Philosophy of Artificial Intelligence*, *op. cit.*, p. 40-66.

(simulation de l'intelligence). Mais, en évitant de s'adosser aux qualités internes de la faculté, il reste muet quant au problème de l'IA forte (intelligence réelle).

Il est intéressant de noter que Turing se positionne également vis-à-vis du problème de l'IA forte et notamment vis-à-vis du problème difficile de la conscience appliqué aux machines. Pour Turing, il est impossible de déterminer si une machine a *e.g.* une vie phénoménale, à moins bien sûr d'« *être* la machine et de se sentir penser soi-même »[10]. Face au *problème des autres esprits*, réputé parmi les philosophes, Turing recommande d'avoir « la convention polie (*the polite convention*) que tout le monde pense »[11]. C'est effectivement la solution que l'on adopte quotidiennement pour échapper au solipsisme. Cependant, en déployant toutes les conséquences de sa proposition, Turing aurait pu postuler en faveur d'un behaviorisme logique, plus radical que son homologue méthodologique. Ici en effet, le concept de conscience n'a aucune signification en dehors de ses propriétés observables. Il s'agit une propriété analytique que l'on réduit à une simple convention entièrement déterminée par l'implication « IA faible ⇒ IA forte » : le constat empirique de comportements intelligents définit *à lui seul* la notion de conscience. Les concepts de la philosophie de l'esprit sont dès lors inadéquats pour résoudre le problème de l'IA forte. Ils sont éliminés et remplacés par la « convention polie » de Turing qui récuse alors toute collaboration possible entre IA et philosophie de l'esprit[12].

Le computationnalisme. Les sciences cognitives se sont organisées autour d'une critique véhémente du behaviorisme. Dans les années 1960, parmi les hypothèses fondatrices du cognitivisme, le computationnalisme est directement influencé par les avancées de l'IA. Une acception technique en est donnée par Allen Newell et Herbert A. Simon sous le nom de « Physical-Symbol System Hypothesis: A

10. *Ibid.*, p. 52.

11. *Ibid.*

12. Turing n'ira pas jusque-là. Pour lui, plus simplement, le problème de l'IA faible peut être résolu sans qu'on ait résolu celui de l'IA forte. Cf. *ibid.*, p. 53. À l'indépendance des deux problèmes, postulée par Turing, nous appliquons ici la position plus stricte du béhaviorisme logique visant à la réduction et à l'élimination de l'un des deux problèmes.

physical symbol system[13] has the necessary and sufficient means for general intelligent action »[14]. Il s'agit d'une hypothèse double. Par « suffisant », on entend que les ordinateurs, en tant que systèmes symboliques physiques, peuvent en principe agir intelligemment. En ce sens, l'hypothèse de Newell & Simon est ni plus ni moins une généralisation de l'hypothèse de l'IA faible. Par « nécessaire », on entend que le cerveau humain, puisqu'il est capable d'engendrer des comportements intelligents, doit lui aussi être une sorte de système symbolique physique. En un sens, le cerveau est donc similaire à l'ordinateur et l'esprit aux programmes qu'il exécute. La théorie computo-représentationnelle de l'esprit, dont Jerry A. Fodor est sans doute le plus grand défenseur du côté de la philosophie[15], affirme que (1) l'esprit est un système symbolique implémenté par un cerveau et que (2) la cognition consiste en un calcul sur ces symboles, *i. e.* une *computation.* Par ailleurs, cette analogie apporte une solution au problème de l'IA forte : à l'instar de leurs analogues biologiques, les ordinateurs sont en principe capables d'engendrer la conscience.

L'hypothèse computationnaliste a participé à l'essor des sciences cognitives, notamment parce qu'elle amenait de nombreuses disciplines (psychologie, neurobiologie, linguistique, philosophie, Intelligence Artificielle, *etc.*) à étudier de concert une seule catégorie d'objets : les systèmes symboliques et leurs implémentations physiques. L'hypothèse double de Newell & Simon affirme en effet l'équivalence des objets et des problèmes : « IA faible ⇔ IA forte ». Elle donne une possibilité de collaboration intra-théorique maximale entre IA et philosophie de l'esprit.

Pourtant, le computationnalisme – et plus généralement le cognitivisme – ont été très largement mis en cause à partir des années

13. Un *système symbolique* est constitué d'un ensemble de symboles (le vocabulaire) et d'opérations (la syntaxe). Un *système symbolique physique* est la réalisation matérielle d'un tel système. Les ordinateurs sont des exemples canoniques de *systèmes symboliques physiques.*

14. A. Newell et H. A. Simon, « Computer Science as Empirical Inquiry: Symbols and Search » (1976), *in* M. A. Boden (ed.), *The Philosophy of Artificial Intelligence*, *op. cit.*, p. 111.

15. J. A. Fodor, *The Language of Thought*, Cambridge, Massachusetts, Harvard University Press, 1975.

1980. Nous arrêtons donc ici l'analyse de cette collaboration particulière pour nous concentrer sur les critiques qui lui ont été opposées.

2. LES CRITIQUES DE L'INTELLIGENCE ARTIFICIELLE

La critique searlienne. La critique du computationnalisme par John R. Searle, dont l'argument le plus célèbre est celui de la « Chambre Chinoise »[16], souffre de plusieurs défauts. Avant toute chose, elle est souvent mal renseignée sur les recherches en IA qui lui sont contemporaines. L'argumentation ne couvre qu'une catégorie limitée de programmes et n'atteint pas l'universalité qu'elle prétend avoir. Par exemple, dans le cas de la « Chambre Chinoise », seuls le behaviorisme de Turing et une forme « linéaire »[17] du computationnalisme sont réellement mis en cause. De plus, lorsqu'on l'examine avec précaution, l'objection majeure de Searle apparaît comme étant avant tout une objection *de principe.* Il est optimiste en ce qui concerne le rôle des neurosciences dans la résolution du problème difficile de la conscience *humaine.* Par contre, si les cerveaux ont la base biologique nécessaire à l'intentionnalité et à l'émergence d'une conscience, Searle soutient que les transistors de

16. J. R. Searle, « Minds, Brains, and Programs » (1980), *in* M. A. Boden (ed.), *The Philosophy of Artificial Intelligence*, *op. cit.*, p. 67-88.

17. Nous qualifions de « computationnaliste linéaire » tout programme qui associe de manière linéaire ses entrées (*inputs*) et ses une sorties (*outputs*) sans tenir compte d'éventuelles variables internes. Il semble que le premier programme pris en exemple dans l'expérience de Searle est bien de ce type : un simple dictionnaire d'associations linéaires. Daniel C. Dennett dénonce la simplicité de l'argument fondé sur « the (unwarranted) supposition that the giant program would work by somehow simply "matching up" the input Chinese characters with some output Chinese characters ». Les autres exemples présentés dans l'article de Searle, dont la complexité reflète mieux celle des programmes développés à l'époque, limitent cependant la clarté de son argument. Pour Dennett justement, « complexity does matter » (D. C. Dennett, *Consciousness Explained*, New York, Hachette Book, 1991, p. 431-455).

silicium ne disposent pas d'un tel pouvoir causal[18]. Irrémédiablement, il nie ainsi la possibilité d'une IA forte.

En ce qui concerne les rapports entre IA et philosophie, le défaut majeur de la critique searlienne est qu'elle s'intéresse uniquement au problème de l'IA forte (intentionnalité et conscience des machines). Searle ne fournit aucune analyse des possibilités de l'IA faible et son travail ne peut donc être exploité par les spécialistes de la seconde communauté.

La critique dreyfusienne. La critique d'Hubert L. Dreyfus ne présente pas les mêmes défauts. Premièrement, à l'inverse de Searle, Dreyfus est bien informé des avancées et des résultats de l'IA. En témoigne la première partie de *What Computers Can't Do*[19] dans laquelle il établit un bilan critique de vingt années de recherches, entre 1957 et 1977.

1. Parmi les projets que Dreyfus analyse, le *General Problem Solver*[20] (GPS) de Newell & Simon constitue une application canonique du computationnalisme. Le programme consiste en un ensemble d'algorithmes génériques et de fonctions heuristiques travaillant à la résolution de problèmes formalisés. Par exemple, à partir de l'ensemble des règles du jeu d'échecs (*base de règles*), de la position des pièces sur l'échiquier (*base de faits*) et d'un *objectif* à atteindre, le GPS peut en théorie proposer un coup régulier et viable sur le plan stratégique. Newell & Simon supposent de plus que tout problème peut être modélisé par un système symbolique (faits et règles) et que sa résolution peut être engendrée par un calcul sur ces symboles (exécution d'algorithmes génériques). Outre les difficultés spécifiques aux problèmes abordés par le GPS, notamment liées à l'explosion combinatoire des faits et des opérations possibles, cette

18. « Whatever else intentionality is, it is a biological phenomenon, and it is as likely to be as causally dependent on the specific biochemistry of its origins as lactation, photosynthesis, or any other biological phenomena », J. R. Searle, « Minds, Brains, and Programs » (1980), *in* M. A. Boden (ed.), *The Philosophy of Artificial Intelligence*, *op. cit.*, p. 86-87. Dennett s'oppose à cette pétition de principe : D. C. Dennett, *op. cit.* et D. J. Chalmers, *The Conscious Mind*, New York, Oxford University Press, 1996, section IV.9.1.

19. H. L. Dreyfus, *op. cit.*

20. A. Newell et H. A. Simon, « GPS, A Program that Simulates Human Thought », *in* E. A. Feigenbaum et J. Feldman (eds.), *Computers and Thought*, New York, McGraw-Hill, 1963.

approche computationnaliste rencontre deux difficultés de taille. Premièrement, il est très difficile d'agréger les problèmes modélisés pour augmenter la portée du GPS. Les « micromondes »[21] ne s'imbriquent pas aisément et le programme, perdu dans la multitude des problèmes possibles, n'atteint pas la généricité escomptée. Deuxièmement, certains problèmes sont très difficiles à formaliser en termes de faits et de règles, notamment ceux dont l'espace des états possibles n'est pas autant contrôlé que celui du jeu d'échecs. Exemple parmi d'autre, la motricité dans un environnement complexe, dynamique et incertain résiste à une description symbolique intégrale. Dreyfus montre comment, face à ces difficultés, l'idée d'un programme générique, capable de résoudre « tout type de problème », s'est soldée par un échec et a été finalement abandonnée.

2. La deuxième partie de l'ouvrage s'efforce d'expliciter les soubassements philosophiques des approches computationnalistes. Pour Dreyfus, trois postulats non-avoués sont à l'origine de l'échec du GPS et de toute autre tentative d'application du computationnalisme. Le *postulat psychologique* est l'hypothèse computo-représentationnelle elle-même, associant cognition et computation. Le *postulat épistémologique* affirme que « tout savoir peut être explicitement formulé »[22]. Le *postulat ontologique* affirme que « tout ce qui existe est un ensemble de faits, dont chacun est logiquement indépendant de tous les autres »[23]. Dreyfus montre comment ces présupposés héritent d'une longue tradition philosophique. On peut citer par exemple Thomas Hobbes et son « "reason" […] is nothing but "reckoning" »[24], Descartes et l'idée que l'esprit est un « miroir de la nature », Leibniz et l'espoir de construire un langage algorithmique capable de venir à bout des problèmes philosophiques, l'idée kan-

21. Les « micromondes » sont des modèles simplistes de problèmes réels. Il s'agit d'univers clos, certains, discrets, dont la complexité des variables d'état est largement atténuée. Le jeu d'échecs peut être considéré comme un micromonde dans la mesure où un état du plateau et ses coups réguliers peuvent être décrits intégralement et avec certitude.

22. H. L. Dreyfus, *op. cit.*, p. 192.

23. *Ibid.*, p. 193.

24. T. Hobbes, *Of Man, Being the First Part of Leviathan* (1651), The Harvard Classics, vol. XXXIV, partie 5, New York, P. F. Collier & Son, 2001.

tienne que tout comportement humain est régi par des règles transcendantales qu'il faut s'efforcer d'expliciter, le premier Wittgenstein et l'atomisme logique, *etc.* Dreyfus montre également comment le poids de ces traditions a amené l'IA à se forger un paradigme dominant, lequel a méticuleusement étouffé les approches hétérodoxes qui faisaient pourtant l'économie de certains de ces présupposés[25].

3. Dreyfus propose de dépasser la tradition philosophique et ouvre ainsi la voie à une « nouvelle IA ». Sa stratégie consiste à emprunter aux critiques de la tradition cartésienne – notamment du côté de la phénoménologie – des arguments qu'il oppose aux démarches computationnalistes. Par exemple, la distinction entre *knowing-how* et *knowing-that* révèle les limites du modèle computationnel[26]. Le *knowing-that* (ou « *savoir-que* ») désigne notre aptitude à résoudre des problèmes rationnels de manière logique. Il nécessite une halte de l'esprit et une séquence d'attitudes propositionnelles (croyances, désirs, *etc.*). Le GPS de Newell & Simon implémente avec précision cette faculté épistémique de « haut-niveau ». Cependant, la phénoménologie rappelle qu'une seconde aptitude cognitive, le *knowing-how* (ou « *savoir-comment* »), distinct et irréductible au *knowing-that*, est responsable d'une grande part de notre activité quotidienne. Elle consiste en des processus continus, souvent inconscients, qui gèrent les facultés de « bas-niveau » telles que la perception, la motricité, les émotions, *etc.* Le *knowing-how*, contrai-

25. C'est par exemple le cas du connexionnisme, véritablement écrasé par la recherche computationnaliste, alors qu'il répondait notamment aux critiques de Searle concernant l'impossibilité d'une sémantique non-arbitraire dans les systèmes symboliques. L. Dreyfus et S. E. Dreyfus, « Making a Mind Versus Modeling the Brain: Artificial Intelligence Back at a Branchpoint » (1988), *in* M. A. Boden (ed.), *The Philosophy of Artificial Intelligence*, *op. cit.*, p. 309-333.

26. La discussion de Dreyfus se trouve principalement dans H. L. Dreyfus et S. E. Dreyfus, *Mind over Machine: The Power of Human Intuition and Expertise in the Era of the Computer*, Oxford, Blackwell, 1986. Les termes « *knowing-how* » et « *knowing-that* » sont introduits pour la première fois par Gilbert Ryle pour argumenter contre le mythe cartésien du dualisme. G. Ryle, *La Notion d'esprit* (*The Concept of mind*, 1949), trad. fr. S. Stern-Gillet, Paris, Éditions Payot & Rivages, 2005, p. 93-140. Cependant, la critique de Dreyfus est moins fondée sur les concepts de Ryle que sur la distinction heideggérienne entre « *Vorhandenheit* » et « *Zuhandenheit* » (resp. « être-sous-la-main » et « être-à-portée-de-la-main »).

rement à son analogue rationnel, n'utilise ni symbole, ni logique. De plus, il est sensible aux contextes : corporel, environnemental, social, *etc.* De fait, il est difficile (voire impossible) de modéliser chacun de ces contextes par un système symbolique approprié. Il est donc difficile (voire impossible) d'implémenter le *knowing-how* à l'aide d'un programme tel que le GPS. Cette faculté épistémique non-rationnelle échappe au computationnalisme.

Cependant, la critique dreyfusienne ne doit pas être entendue comme un rejet intégral du computationnalisme. Si on tire toutes les conséquences de son argumentation, il existe encore des domaines de l'intelligence pour lesquels les systèmes symboliques sont efficaces. Lorsqu'on cherche par exemple à résoudre un problème hautement rationnel, facilement formalisable, tel que celui du jeu d'échecs, les approches classiques peuvent encore faire leurs preuves – en témoigne la victoire de Deep Blue sur Garry K. Kasparov en mai 1997[27]. Cependant, la phénoménologie insiste sur le fait que la plus grande part de l'activité humaine, contrairement à ce qui y paraît, est de l'ordre du *knowing-how* : l'usage du langage, la motricité quotidienne, la reconnaissance et la classification de formes sont autant d'activités aux soubassements non-symboliques et non-rationnels. Si elles constituent les objectifs des spécialistes de l'IA, alors il faut trouver *une nouvelle voie*. Pour résumer :

- Le travail de Dreyfus est bien informé des recherches et des résultats de l'IA ;
- Il ne constitue pas une opposition de principe à l'IA, mais cible son paradigme dominant (le computationnalisme) et son utilisation inadéquate pour résoudre une large quantité de problèmes ;
- Il s'intéresse enfin à l'IA faible. L'enjeu de la critique ne porte pas sur l'ontologie des machines, mais sur leurs capacités concrètes de résolution.

Ce dernier point distingue fondamentalement les travaux de Searle et de Dreyfus. *What Computers Can't Do*, à partir de la position

27. Cela-dit, même pour les grands joueurs d'échecs, une bonne part de la stratégie n'est ni explicite, ni rationnelle. La psychologie, le bluff, l'utilisation du temps forment un contexte global qui s'ajoute à la simple connaissance des positions des pièces et des règles de déplacement.

philosophique de l'auteur, opère une critique constructive des méthodes *pratiques* de l'IA. Les deux sections suivantes généralisent cette démarche pour définir les termes d'une collaboration véritable entre IA et philosophie.

3. LA PHILOSOPHIE AU SERVICE DE L'IA[28]

Avec le temps, le travail de Dreyfus est passé des mains des critiques à celles des praticiens. Les modèles phénoménologiques de la cognition, en réaction aux modèles de la tradition cartésienne, offrent l'opportunité d'un nouveau paradigme pour l'IA faible. Nous formulons ainsi la démarche de Dreyfus : « IA forte ⇒ IA faible ». Autrement dit, une théorie de l'esprit adéquate, si elle est correctement appliquée, donne de bons résultats en pratique. Ainsi, à partir des années 1980, suite aux nombreuses critiques du computationnalisme et aux sollicitations de la phénoménologie, l'IA connait une véritable crise fondationnelle. Des chercheurs en philosophie et en informatique œuvrent pour l'édification de nouveaux paradigmes. Le connexionnisme refait son apparition avec les débuts de l'Intelligence Artificielle Distribuée et de la Vie Artificielle. De nouveaux modèles voient le jour en robotique : tels le modèle énactif de la cognition, la robotique incarnée, la robotique évolutionniste. Apparaissent également des modèles antireprésentationnalistes (systèmes réactifs, intelligence sans représentation, systèmes dynamiques, *etc.*). On parle aussi du « tournant pragmatique » de l'IA[29].

28. Le travail présenté dans cette section a fait l'objet d'une communication pour la plateforme *AFIA 2011* (Association Française pour l'Intelligence Artificielle). R. Lamarche-Perrin, « Conceptualisation de l'émergence : dynamiques microscopiques et analyse macroscopique des SMA », *in Plateforme AFIA 2011, atelier FUTURAMA*, 2011.

29. Sur la nouvelle robotique et l'anti-représentationnalisme : R. A. Brooks, « Intelligence without representation », *Artificial Intelligence* 47 (1991), p. 139-159. Sur le connexionnisme et le modèle énactif de la cognition : F. J. Varela, E. Thompson et E. Rosch, *The Embodied Mind: Cognitive Science and Human Experience*, Cambridge, Massachusetts, MIT Press, 1991. Sur les systèmes dynamiques : T. van Gelder, « Dynamics and cognition », *in* J. Haugeland (ed.), *Mind Design II*, Bradford/MITP, 1996. Sur la notion de « tournant pragmatique » : A. K. Engel, « Directive Minds:

Afin de généraliser la démarche « IA forte ⇒ IA faible » inaugurée par Dreyfus, un autre exemple de collaboration est présenté dans cette section. L'objectif n'est plus ici la simulation de comportements intelligents, mais la simulation de « phénomènes émergents », c'est-à-dire de propriétés et processus globaux d'un système induits par les propriétés et processus locaux de ses parties. L'émergence distingue ainsi au moins deux niveaux de description. La difficulté réside dans la modélisation et simulation simultanées de ces deux niveaux au sein d'un même programme. Par exemple, comment simuler les dynamiques globales d'une ville ou d'un pays ? Comment rendre compte des relations entre la dynamique locale des individus et la taille de la ville, sa politique générale, son marché immobilier ? De quelle manière ces variables macroscopiques dépendent-elles des comportements microscopiques ? Ce type de problème est très répandu en IA[30]. Nous soutenons que la philosophie peut aider à clarifier la notion d'émergence et à résoudre certaines difficultés théoriques liées à la simulation des phénomènes macroscopiques. Dans ce qui suit, nous faisons l'analyse de la notion d'émergence telle qu'elle fut historiquement développée par la philosophie britannique au tournant du XIXe siècle[31]. Les concepts et les enjeux du débat philosophique nous permettent d'élaborer une définition adéquate dans le cas des simulations informatiques. Ainsi, à partir de problématiques et de contraintes *philosophiques*, nous exprimons des problématiques et des contraintes d'ordre *méthodologique*.

How Dynamics Shapes Cognition », in *Enaction : Toward a New Paradigm for Cognitive Science*, MIT Press, 2010, p. 219-243. Pour un retour de Dreyfus sur ces nouvelles approches, une vingtaine d'années plus tard : H. L. Dreyfus, « Why Heideggerian AI Failed and How Fixing It Would Require Making It More Heideggerian », *Philosophical Psychology*, vol. 20, n°2, 2007, p. 247-268.

30. Pour une analyse non-exhaustive des différentes conceptualisations de l'émergence en IA : R. Lamarche-Perrin, *op. cit.* et J. Deguet, Y. Demazeau et L. Magnin, « Element about the Emergence Issue : A Survey of Emergence Definitions », *ComPlexUs*, vol. 3, 2006, p. 24-31.

31. Pour une analyse historique détaillée de cette controverse, à laquelle participent notamment J. S. Mill, C. D. Broad et S. Alexander, voir : T. O'Connor et H. Y. Wong, « Emergent Properties », *Stanford Encyclopedia of Philosophy*, 2006, (http://plato.stanford.edu/entries/properties-emergent/, mis en ligne le 24 sept. 2002, révisé le 23 oct. 2006, consulté le 1 mai 2011).

Dualisme et monisme. Prenons un problème auquel sont confrontés scientifiques et philosophes : comment rendre compte des phénomènes du vivant ? Comment expliquer leurs spécificités ? Comment expliquer les différences essentielles qui existent entre un être inanimé et un être vivant ? Sommairement, au XIXe siècle, deux positions s'affrontent : le *vitalisme* et le *mécanisme*. Le *vitalisme* est un « dualisme non-réductionniste » : il postule l'existence de deux substances (la matière inanimée et un principe de force vitale) pour rendre compte des deux catégories d'objets, la seconde substance ne pouvant être entièrement déterminée par la première. Autrement dit, le non-réductionnisme affirme que les lois de la biologie ne peuvent être « déduites de » ou « réduites aux » lois physico-chimiques. Le dualisme, parce qu'il multiplie les postulats d'existence, est *ontologiquement coûteux*. Le *mécanisme* au contraire fait une économie ontologique en affirmant que les phénomènes du vivant sont entièrement explicables par les lois de la physique et de la chimie. Cependant, en effectuant cette réduction, le monisme participe à l'élimination des sciences spéciales. Puisque le vocabulaire de la biologie peut être exprimé à partir de celui de la physique, son usage est rendu caduc. Dès lors, un seul mode de connaissance est privilégié : celui de la physique fondamentale. Il devient difficile de rendre compte et d'expliquer la distinction entre êtres inanimés et être vivants. Celle-ci est amenuisée, voire radicalement éliminée. On dira donc que ce « monisme éliminatif » est *épistémiquement faible.*

Émergence épistémique. La position émergentiste consiste à trouver une voie moyenne entre vitalisme et mécanisme, entre « dualisme non-réductionniste » et « monisme éliminatif ». Comment défendre une position à la fois économe sur le plan ontologique et forte sur le plan épistémique ? Comment concevoir un « monisme non-éliminatif » ? La notion d'*émergence épistémique*[32] répond justement à ces attentes. Elle soutient que le principe de force vitale, même s'il est en principe réductible à la matière inanimée, constitue une abstraction utile au scientifique. La distinction entre êtres inanimés et êtres vivants n'est pas d'ordre ontologique : elle est « dans l'œil du

32. On parle d'« émergence épistémique » par opposition à l'« émergence ontologique », notion que l'on associe parfois au dualisme. Pour une analyse conceptuelle plus détaillée : T. O'Connor et H. Y. Wong, *op. cit.*

scientifique », elle est *épistémique.* Cette position est compatible avec le monisme puisque les lois de la biologie peuvent *en principe* être réduites à celles de la physique. Elle est de plus non-éliminative, puisque la biologie présente *en pratique* des lois et des modèles utiles et nécessaires à la compréhension des phénomènes complexes.

Pour appliquer la notion d'émergence épistémique aux simulations informatiques, nous exploitons l'analogie suivante : ce qui est *ontologique* pour un système, c'est ce qui est relatif à sa conception, *i.e.* en amont de son exécution (le modèle du programme, son code source, son implémentation matérielle, *etc.*) ; ce qui est *épistémique*, c'est ce qui est relatif à l'analyse *a posteriori* de l'exécution du programme (les outils d'observation, de description et d'analyse). L'ontologie relève du système *per se* ; l'épistémologie se rapporte au système relativement à *un point de vue donné.* Dans ce qui suit, le concept d'émergence épistémique est traduit sur la base de cette analogie. Deux contraintes méthodologiques sont engendrées : le *monisme microscopique* et le *non-éliminativisme.*

Monisme microscopique. Par analogie, qu'est-ce qu'une simulation « dualiste » en informatique ? Il s'agit d'un programme dont la conception comprend au moins deux niveaux de modélisation (niveau microscopique *et* niveau macroscopique). Pour la simulation des dynamiques urbaines, par exemple, le programme modélise à la fois le comportement des individus et celui des variables globales. Lors de l'exécution, ces deux modèles sont synchronisés pour simuler une activité urbaine multi-échelle[33]. Au contraire, une approche « moniste » limite la conception du système à ses parties microscopiques. Le niveau macroscopique n'est pas modélisé *a*

33. Les « systèmes multi-modèles » sont un bon exemple de systèmes dualistes. Plusieurs niveaux de modélisations sont synchronisés et maintenus cohérents pour simuler un système à plusieurs échelles. J. Gil-Quijano, G. Hutzler et T. Louail, « Accroche-toi au niveau, j'enlève l'échelle. Éléments d'analyse des aspects multiniveaux dans la simulation à base d'agents », *Revue d'Intelligence Artificielle*, vol. 24, 2010, p. 625-648. Les « systèmes à tableau-noirs » (*blackboard systems*) présentent un autre cas de dualisme. Des entités macroscopiques, en interaction avec les entités microscopiques du système, sont conçues pour implémenter des variables globales. R.K. Sawyer, « Simulating Emergence and Downward Causation in Small Groups », *Multi-Agent-Based Simulation*, vol. 1979, 2001, p. 49-67.

priori, mais élaboré *a posteriori* de l'exécution, lors de l'analyse[34]. Les phénomènes émergents, tels que le marché immobilier, sont alors conçus comme des épiphénomènes, *i.e.* des phénomènes sans puissance causale, qui existent relativement à un observateur ou à un processus d'abstraction. En interdisant la conception macroscopique des systèmes, le *monisme microscopique* rend possible une véritable « approche *bottom-up* » : il ne s'agit pas seulement de *simuler* les phénomènes émergents (en concevant un modèle *a priori* des variables globales), mais de les *émuler* véritablement, c'est-à-dire de reproduire leurs dynamiques émergentes dans leur intégralité à partir de leurs fondements microscopiques.

Non-éliminativisme. Le monisme méthodologique ne doit pas tomber dans les travers éliminativistes de son analogue philosophique. Ainsi, les méthodes d'analyse ne doivent pas se limiter à une description purement microscopique de l'exécution. Au contraire, nous souhaitons multiplier les points de vue sur le système[35]. En informatique, l'introduction de « modèles de l'observateur » permet d'engendrer des descriptions macroscopiques variées[36]. La tâche du scientifique n'est pas d'observer des phénomènes macroscopiques *per se*, mais de construire les abstractions qui seront utiles à la compréhension globale des systèmes. Ces abstractions *sont* les phénomènes émergents ; leur pertinence est toujours évaluée *en contexte*, c'est-à-dire relativement aux besoins particuliers de l'analyse et aux objectifs scientifiques préalablement fixés. Il n'y a pas de

34. Les « systèmes par auto-organisation » sont des systèmes monistes dans la mesure où leurs fonctionnalités émergentes ne sont pas explicitées lors de la conception. Celles-ci reposent uniquement sur l'implémentation de fonctions locales. G. Picard, *Méthodologie de développement de SMA adaptatifs et conception de logiciels à fonctionnalité émergente*, Thèse de doctorat de l'Université Paul Sabatier de Toulouse III, 2004.

35. Par exemple, les travaux qui définissent l'émergence en fonction de qualités intrinsèques aux systèmes sont éliminativistes. Ils n'autorisent qu'un seul niveau de description des phénomènes. V. Darley, « Emergent Phenomena and Complexity », *Artificial Life*, vol. 4, 1994, p. 411-416. M. Bedau, « Weak Emergence », *Philosophical Perspectives*, vol. 11, 1997, p. 379-399.

36. Par exemple, la conceptualisation de Bonabeau & Dessalles est non-éliminative. Elle définit l'émergence relativement à des hiérarchies de détecteurs. É. Bonabeau et J.-L. Dessalles, « Detection and Emergence », *Intellectica*, vol. 25, n°2, 1997, p. 85-94.

« bons phénomènes émergents » en-soi, mais seulement en fonction de ce que l'on veut en faire. Le *non-éliminativisme* favorise ainsi une conception pragmatiste des phénomènes émergents.

Ces deux contraintes (*monisme microscopique* et *non-éliminativisme*) établissent une approche cohérente pour simuler des phénomènes émergents. Elles bénéficient d'une conceptualisation solide de l'émergence, héritée de la philosophie, et importent ainsi l'épiphénoménisme et le pragmatisme en informatique (IA forte ⇒ IA faible). En pratique, elles permettent également de trier les formalisations de l'émergence et de travailler à partir de celles qui satisfont les exigences des spécialistes. Il est important de préciser cependant qu'il s'agit d'exigences *méthodologiques*. Elles n'imposent aucune contrainte *de principe* aux systèmes de simulation. Selon la critique de Dreyfus, le computationnalisme reste pertinent pour résoudre des problèmes particuliers bien délimités. De la même manière, les simulations dualistes ou éliminativistes peuvent se révéler efficaces en fonction des contraintes et des objectifs techniques de la simulation. Cependant, nous affirmons que, dans le cas de la simulation de systèmes distribués, complexes et de très grande taille, ces deux contraintes se révèlent nécessaires *en pratique*[37].

4. L'IA AU SERVICE DE LA PHILOSOPHIE

Une autre forme de collaboration entre IA et philosophie peut être dérivée du travail de Dreyfus. Sa critique de la mise en application du computationnalisme cristallise un point de désaccord avec la tradition philosophique. Elle a notamment permis de systématiser l'opposition au « Théâtre Cartésien » à partir de ses conséquences pratiques. Considérons la contraposée de l'implication précédente : « non IA faible ⇒ non IA forte ». Cela signifie que les échecs de l'IA faible témoignent de l'inadéquation des présupposés philosophiques dont elle hérite. Par exemple, l'échec du GPS peut

37. Pour plus de détails sur l'importance pratique de ces contraintes methodlogiques : R. Lamarche-Perrin, Y. Demazeau et J.-M. Vincent, « Observation macroscopique et émergence dans les SMA de très grande taille », *in* J.-P. Sansonnet et É. Adam (éd.), *19e Journées Francophones sur les Systèmes Multi-Agents,* Valenciennes, Cépaduès, oct. 2011, p. 53-62.

être interprété comme l'indice empirique des erreurs de la tradition cartésienne. Autrement dit, lorsque le computationnalisme échoue, son cadre philosophique est remis en cause.

Grâce au concours de l'IA, la philosophie de l'esprit peut ainsi devenir une *philosophie expérimentale*. L'IA est alors envisagée comme un banc d'essais, un atelier où le philosophe implémente ses modèles à partir de robots et de programmes. Il y observe ensuite le résultat de ses théories mises en pratique[38]. De cette manière, l'IA permet d'évaluer et de falsifier les modèles de l'esprit par des méthodes empiriques. On comprend enfin le renversement amorcé en introduction par Daniel Andler et qui fait de l'IA une véritable *science de la philosophie*[39]. Or, ce n'est pas la première fois que l'étude de machines concrètes illustre certaines options philosophiques. L'analyse comparée d'un régulateur symbolique et d'un régulateur dynamique amène par exemple Tim van Gelder à discuter de la pertinence philosophique des modèles qui leur sont associés[40] : de quel genre de processus mécaniques la cognition est-elle responsable ? À quel type de régulateur l'esprit est-il similaire ? De la même manière, les programmes de l'IA peuvent éclairer, à l'avenir, les modèles philosophiques et ainsi peser dans la balance des controverses.

38. Inman Harvey a pour cela une formule amusante : « faire de la philosophie de l'esprit à l'aide d'un tournevis. » I. Harvey, « Robotics: Philosophy of Mind Using a Screwdriver », *Evolutionary Robotics: From Intelligent Robots to Artificial Life*, vol. III, 2000, p. 207–230.

39. H. L. Dreyfus, *Intelligence Artificielle : mythes et limites*, *op. cit.*, p. XIV.

40. T. van Gelder, « Dynamics and Cognition », *in* J. Haugeland (ed.), *Mind Design II*, Bradford/MITP, 1996.

Recherches sur la philosophie et le langage 29 (2013)
192 p., ISBN : 978-2-7116-8410-6, p. 67-85, Vrin.

L'interaction entre science et philosophie en psychopathologie cognitive : expliquer et décrire l'expérience délirante[1]

Sarah TROUBÉ*

RÉSUMÉ

La question des rapports entre science et philosophie est abordée à partir de la psychopathologie cognitive contemporaine, révélatrice d'un renouvellement de leurs relations et de leurs rôles respectifs. La présentation d'un modèle pluridisciplinaire, proposant une explication ascendante du délire dans le syndrome de Capgras et dans la schizophrénie, met en évidence un rôle propre de la philosophie qui ne se limite pas à une réflexion épistémologique sur le statut des explications fournies par les protocoles scientifiques. En supposant à la source du délire une altération de l'expérience, causée par des dysfonctionnements d'ordre cérébral, ces modèles ascendants adressent en effet à la philosophie les tâches de clarifier la relation

* Sarah Troubé est ancienne élève de l'ENS Paris en philosophie, doctorante en psychopathologie et psychologie clinique à Université Paris-Diderot (CRPMS, EA 3522, Paris).

1. Ce travail a été présenté le 7 juin 2011 à l'Université Pierre-Mendès-France à Grenoble, lors du IIIe colloque des doctorants et des jeunes chercheurs, portant sur le thème « Repenser les rapports entre science et philosophie ». Je remercie les organisateurs du colloque, ainsi que les participants, pour leurs remarques et indications précieuses.

explicative entre expérience et croyance, d'analyser la dimension épistémique du délire, et de caractériser les composantes perceptives fondamentales supposées être altérées. Plutôt qu'une répartition des disciplines selon des niveaux d'explication distincts et hiérarchisés, la psychopathologie cognitive invite ainsi à concevoir une interaction entre sciences et philosophie à chaque niveau explicatif mis en jeu par ses modèles.

ABSTRACT

The paper explores the relations between science and philosophy through the perspective of contemporary cognitive psychopathology, which reveals a renewal of their interaction and of their respective tasks. A pluridisciplinary model is reviewed, which offers a « bottom-up » account of delusion in the Capgras syndrome and in schizophrenia. Considering this model, the paper claims that the task of philosophy is not limited to the one of proposing an epistemological understanding of the explanations at hand in scientific protocols. On the contrary, it is claimed that philosophy has a proper role to play. Assuming that delusion derives from an alteration of perceptual experiences, due to a supposed cerebral dysfunction, the model considered appeals for a philosophical clarification of the explanatory relation between experience and belief formation. Furthermore, this model requires a description of the perceptual components involved in those supposedly altered experiences. Rather than merely dividing the tasks respectively required from philosophy and science, at the different levels of explanation involved in these models, considering the case of cognitive psychopathology invites to conceive of an interaction between science and philosophy at each level of explanation.

INTRODUCTION

Aborder la question des rapports entre science et philosophie à partir de la psychopathologie pourrait paraître relever d'une approche indirecte du problème : en effet, la constitution même de la psychopathologie, de la psychiatrie et de la psychologie clinique comme disciplines propres s'est opérée, historiquement, par une autonomisation progressive tant vis-à-vis du champ de la philosophie que de celui de la science médicale organique[2]. Or, il s'agira ici de montrer que le problème des rapports de la science et de la philosophie se trouve au contraire au cœur de la psychopathologie. Celle-ci est en effet demeurée le lieu d'une interaction constante, parfois non explicite et polémique, entre les deux perspectives. L'influence de la philosophie sur la psychiatrie phénoménologique[3], d'une part, et, d'autre part, la persistance d'un courant de la psychiatrie dit « organiciste »[4], visant à rapporter les pathologies mentales à des causes cérébrales, en sont deux manifestations d'importance au cours du XXe siècle.

Il s'agira ici de questionner l'interaction entre science et philosophie au sein de la psychopathologie cognitive contemporaine, en interrogeant tout particulièrement la manière dont la perspective pluridisciplinaire des sciences cognitives peut renouveler, au sein de ce domaine, le problème des rapports et des tâches respectives de la science et de la philosophie. A première vue, la psychopathologie cognitive peut être située dans une certaine continuité vis-à-vis du courant de la psychiatrie organiciste, de par le projet de relier les grandes entités psychopathologiques à des bases cérébrales mises au jour par la neurobiologie et de questionner la pertinence de la distinction entre maladies psychiques et organiques. Cependant, tant les progrès considérables effectués dans les neurosciences, en particulier dans les techniques de mesure de l'activité cérébrale, que la perspective intégrative propre aux sciences cognitives, constituent

2. J. Postel et C. Quetel (dir.), *Nouvelle histoire de la psychiatrie*, Paris, Dunod, 2004.

3. Notamment l'influence de Husserl et de Heidegger chez K. Schneider, L. Binswanger ou encore W. Blankenburg. Voir A. Tatossian, *La phénoménologie des psychoses*, Puteaux, Le Cercle Herméneutique, 2002.

4. Représenté notamment au XXe siècle en France par G. G. de Clérambault.

une rupture vis-à-vis de la psychiatrie organiciste. C'est ce projet d'interaction et d'intégration de disciplines diverses qui pose de manière particulièrement révélatrice, dans la psychopathologie cognitive contemporaine, la question de l'articulation de différents paradigmes, méthodes et niveaux d'explication, notamment entre neurosciences, philosophie, et psychologies cognitive, sociale et clinique.

On cherchera à éclaircir ce renouvellement du problème de la délimitation des rôles respectifs de la science et de la philosophie dans la psychopathologie cognitive. Nous nous centrerons, pour se faire, sur un symptôme qui se situe au cœur de la littérature de ce domaine, le délire : nous présenterons un modèle aujourd'hui largement discuté, qui cherche à rendre compte de la formation du délire dans différentes pathologies, et dont l'originalité est de proposer ce qui sera nommé ici une hypothèse ascendante, directement basée sur des données neuroscientifiques. Ce modèle permettra de fournir un éclairage privilégié sur l'interaction entre science et philosophie, et de questionner la tâche pouvant incomber à chaque discipline. En effet, il peut sembler à première vue que le projet de rapporter le délire à des troubles directement issus de dysfonctions d'ordre cérébral amène à redéfinir les frontières entre science et philosophie en dépossédant la philosophie d'objets qui semblaient traditionnellement relever de son questionnement. L'assimilation traditionnelle du délire à la déraison, rapportant le délire à une violation manifeste du raisonnement et des croyances du sens commun, faisait en effet de ce dernier un défi pour le philosophe, relevant de la tâche philosophique de définition des règles de la rationalité et des normes du raisonnement. Une telle conception peut inviter à concevoir une dichotomie entre science et philosophie, la première recherchant des dysfonctionnements constituant une explication causale des symptômes, tandis qu'il reviendrait à la seconde de se pencher sur la dimension normative, inhérente à la qualification d'une croyance comme pathologique, et appelant une explication en termes de raisons irréductible à un dysfonctionnement de mécanismes cérébraux [5].

5. Pour une discussion de ces oppositions entre « fait » et « valeur », « descriptif » et « normatif », ou encore entre « expliquer causalement » et « rendre

On cherchera à montrer que c'est précisément ce type de dichotomie, assimilant d'un côté le rôle de la science au régime des causes explicatives, et, de l'autre, la philosophie au domaine des normes et des raisons, que les modèles dits ascendants du délire invitent à remettre en question dans la psychopathologie. Face à la tentation de penser une supériorité de la philosophie sur la science pour éclairer la question du délire, basée sur la tâche philosophique de définition des normes de la rationalité, peut alors apparaître la tentation opposée de poser une supériorité explicative de la science, basée sur la mise au jour par les neurosciences de troubles cérébraux causant les symptômes psychopathologiques. Il s'agira ici non pas d'opposer frontalement ces deux types de revendication dans leur radicalité, mais de questionner la tâche qui peut incomber à la philosophie dans ce contexte de renouvellement des oppositions traditionnelles entre régimes descriptif et normatif. Doit-on alors penser qu'il est fondé de confiner la philosophie à un rôle de clarification des concepts et du statut épistémologique des explications fournies par les modèles des sciences cognitives ? Ou bien faut-il opérer une répartition des rôles respectifs de la science et de la philosophie selon les niveaux d'explication mis en jeu par les modèles des sciences cognitives, en opposant ainsi des mécanismes dits « de bas niveau », relevant des neurosciences, à des processus dits « de haut niveau », relevant de la philosophie ? Nous nous opposerons à ces deux conceptions, en proposant de concevoir la tâche de la philosophie comme une participation active à l'élaboration des modèles de la psychopathologie cognitive, intervenant à chaque niveau explicatif mis en jeu par ces modèles.

1. LE MODÈLE ASCENDANT DANS LE SYNDROME DE CAPGRAS ET LA SCHIZOPHRENIE

Si le délire a été traditionnellement présenté comme un paradigme de la déraison, c'est qu'il apparaît d'emblée comme une croyance dont le contenu est en inadéquation avec la réalité, et dont

raison », et de leurs implications pour le rôle de la philosophie, voir P. Engel, *Philosophie et Psychologie*, Paris, Gallimard, 1996.

le mode d'affirmation, celui d'une certitude inébranlable, semble inadapté. Le DSM IV définit ainsi le délire comme une « croyance fausse, basée sur une inférence incorrecte concernant la réalité externe, et fermement soutenue en dépit de ce que presque tout le monde croit, et de ce qui constitue une preuve ou une indication indéniables et évidentes du contraire »[6]. Au vu de ces éléments, le délire a pu être assimilé à la manifestation d'une pensée primitive basée sur une causalité magique, à une altération du pouvoir de la raison par les passions, ou encore à un discours vide de sens. Le délire peut ainsi être conçu comme inaccessible à toute compréhension, comme pouvant être expliqué causalement, mais ne pouvant en aucun cas faire l'objet d'une justification en termes de rationalité : on retrouve là la radicalisation de l'opposition entre l'explicatif et le normatif, ou entre le régime des causes et le régime des raisons[7].

Or, c'est précisément ce type de conception du délire qui se trouve remis en cause par le modèle présenté ici, lequel regroupe un ensemble d'hypothèses portant sur des pathologies distinctes. Ces hypothèses ont pour point commun de rapporter le délire à des dysfonctionnements d'ordre cérébral, altérant l'expérience du monde ou de soi-même. Ce modèle est donc directement fondé sur les techniques d'exploration de l'activité cérébrale, plaçant au premier plan ce qui est souvent nommé l'activité de bas niveau, ou du niveau subpersonnel, inaccessible au contrôle et à la conscience du sujet. Il s'agit alors de supposer que le délire posséderait, par rapport à ces troubles de bas niveau, un caractère secondaire, au sens où il constituerait une expression, une explication ou une rationalisation du changement survenu dans l'expérience du fait de ces troubles. Ce type de modèle explicatif peut ainsi être qualifié de

6. American Psychiatric Association, *Diagnostic and Statistical Manual of mental disorders*, 4th ed., Washington, American Psychiatric Association, 1994. Il s'agit ici de ma traduction.

7. Au sein de la psychiatrie, l'idée d'une incompréhensibilité du délire provient notamment de K. Jaspers, *Psychopathologie générale* (1913), Paris, Alcan, 1928. Basée sur la distinction entre explication et compréhension proposée par Dilthey, l'incompréhensibilité du délire signifie qu'il est inaccessible à l'empathie et au régime des raisons psychologiques, et ne peut être expliqué que causalement par des mécanismes cérébraux.

modèle à deux étapes, au sens où l'étape de formation du délire succède à une première altération de l'expérience. Il relève également d'une démarche dite empiriste ou ascendante (*bottom-up*) [8], dans la mesure où les troubles de bas niveau expliqueraient le symptôme manifeste du délire [9]. On se centrera ici, au sein des nombreuses hypothèses pouvant être rapportées à ce modèle, sur deux d'entre elles, qui postulent à la source du délire une altération de l'expérience perceptive, dans deux pathologies distinctes : le syndrome de Capgras et la schizophrénie.

1. 1. Délire et reconnaissance des visages dans le syndrome de Capgras

Le syndrome de Capgras consiste dans la croyance délirante, pouvant surgir au sein d'une pathologie psychiatrique ou neurologique, que l'un des proches du patient a été remplacé par un sosie. Cette croyance étant souvent unique et circonscrite, notamment lorsque le délire est consécutif à des lésions cérébrales, ce syndrome appartient aux délires dits « monothématiques ». S'il s'agit d'un syndrome peu fréquent à l'état isolé, il a acquis, par la précision des hypothèses neuropsychologiques le concernant, un statut paradigmatique au sein de la psychopathologie cognitive [10].

8. Par opposition aux approches dites *top-down* ou rationalistes, plaçant au premier plan l'influence causale des croyances sur l'expérience : J. Campbell, « Rationality, meaning and the analysis of delusion », *Philosophy, Psychiatry, and Psychology* 8, 2/3 (2001), p. 89-100. Pour une discussion de ces deux types d'approches, voir T. Bayne et E. Pacherie, « Bottom-up or Top-down ? Campbell's Rationalist Account of Monothematic Delusions », *Philosophy, Psychiatry, and Psychology* 11, 1 (2004), p. 1-11.

9. Ce type de modèle définit le délire comme une croyance ou un ensemble de croyances, clairement différenciable de l'expérience qui le sous-tendrait, ce qui est par ailleurs objet de discussions : pour une critique de la définition du délire comme croyance, voir notamment G. Currie, « Imagination, Delusion and Hallucinations », *in* M. Coltheart & M. Davies (eds), *Pathologies of Belief*, Oxford, Blackwell, 2000, p. 167-182. Pour une discussion sur la difficulté de distinguer le délire proprement dit des expériences étranges vécues par le sujet, voir M. Spitzer, « On Defining Delusions », *Comprehensive Psychiatry*, vol. 31, n°5 (1990), p. 377-397.

10. Pour une présentation du syndrome de Capgras et des autres délires d'identification, ainsi qu'une revue des différentes hypothèses neurocognitives dont ils font l'objet, voir J. P. Luauté, « Neuropsychiatrie cognitive des délires d'identification des personnes. Une revue historico-critique », *L'Evolution psychiatrique* 74, 2009, p. 93-121.

En effet, des données neuroscientifiques ont mis en évidence, chez les patients atteints de ce syndrome, une altération du processus permettant la reconnaissance des visages des proches. Ces patients ne présentent pas la réaction affective implicite accompagnant normalement la perception du visage d'une personne familière, et pouvant être mesurée à partir des réponses électrodermales liées à l'activité cérébrale. Selon un modèle neurocognitif influent, la reconnaissance des visages des proches s'appuierait sur deux voies corticales : l'une, ventrale, dédiée à la reconnaissance explicite des traits du visage, l'autre, dorsale, dédiée à une réaction affective de familiarité[11]. C'est cette seconde voie qui dysfonctionnerait dans le syndrome de Capgras, ce qui semblerait pouvoir expliquer directement le contenu de la croyance délirante : le patient percevrait un visage en tout point semblable à celui de la personne proche, sans que ce dernier génère le sentiment habituel de familiarité, ce qui correspond à la définition d'un sosie[12]. La croyance délirante pourrait ainsi être conçue comme étant directement héritée du contenu perceptif altéré par le dysfonctionnement cérébral[13]. Elle constituerait une expression de l'expérience étrange résultant de cette altération.

1. 2. Etrangeté de la perception et délire schizophrénique

Si le caractère attrayant des hypothèses ascendantes portant sur le syndrome de Capgras réside dans la précision des données neuroscientifiques, le même type de démarche explicative avait été proposé antérieurement, sans atteindre ce degré de précision, pour la schizophrénie. A de nombreux égards, la schizophrénie s'oppose au syndrome de Capgras. Là où ce dernier consiste en une croyance

11. V. Bruce et A. Young, « Understanding face recognition », *British Journal of Psychology* 77 (1986), p. 305-327.

12. H. D. Ellis et A. W. Young, « Accounting for delusional misidentifications », *British Journal of Psychiatry* 157, 1990, p. 239-248.

13. C'est l'hypothèse d'un « endossement » direct du contenu perceptif dans la croyance délirante, qui s'oppose à l'hypothèse explicationniste, faisant de la croyance délirante une explication du contenu perceptif : voir E.Pacherie, « Perception, emotions and delusions : Revisiting the Capgras Delusion », *in* T. Bayne & J. Fernandez (eds), *Delusions and Self-Deception*, Hove, UK, Psychology Press, 2008, p. 105-123.

circonscrite et, bien qu'étrange, compréhensible logiquement, le délire schizophrénique consiste le plus souvent dans un enchevêtrement complexe de croyances et de thèmes délirants divers, contredisant parfois la conception commune de la causalité et de la physique[14]. Cela complexifie d'emblée le projet de recherche de correspondances entre les thèmes délirants et des altérations neurocognitives spécifiques.

Cependant, il a été postulé qu'une altération diffuse et globale de la perception pourrait rendre compte de ce qui a été nommé en psychiatrie l'atmosphère délirante. Cette dernière, fréquemment rapportée par les patients comme précédant l'apparition du délire, comporte de nombreux aspects touchant la perception : elle consiste notamment dans un sentiment d'étrangeté, de changement diffus et inexplicable, ou encore un sentiment de signification, l'impression que les choses sont des signes, des messages adressés personnellement au sujet, et qu'il lui revient de déchiffrer[15]. Plusieurs hypothèses ont été proposées pour relier ce changement survenu au sein de l'expérience perceptive à des troubles d'ordre cérébral. Selon l'une d'elles, cette expérience pourrait provenir d'une activation spontanée et inadéquate d'un signal d'erreur touchant la perception[16] : cette hypothèse se fonde sur une analogie avec la mise en évidence d'ondes cérébrales spécifiques survenant lors de la perception d'une incongruité sémantique ou syntaxique dans une phrase[17]. Le même phénomène pourrait survenir de manière inappropriée et toucher la perception dans son ensemble, provoquant au niveau expérientiel un sentiment d'étrangeté. Selon une autre hypothèse, qui n'exclut pas la première, l'impression d'étrangeté pourrait être rapportée à une difficulté neurocognitive touchant la hiérarchisation des stimuli dans un schéma de figure et de fond.

14. La croyance, par exemple, d'être contrôlé à distance par une entité extérieure dans le délire d'influence.

15. L'atmosphère délirante est notamment décrite par K. Jaspers, *Psychopathogie générale* (1913), Paris, Alcan, 1928.

16. B. A. Maher, « Anomalous experience in everyday life : its significance for psychopathology », *The Monist* 82, 1999, 4, p. 547-570.

17. Notamment l'onde N400 : voir M. Kutas, et S. A. Hillyard, « Reading senseless sentences : Brain potentials reflect semantic incongruity », *Science* 207, 1980, p. 203-205.

Cette difficulté conduirait à une saillance anormale de certains stimuli et à une intensité globale anormale de la perception, produisant une surcharge de données perceptives, à la source du sentiment angoissant d'une signification à déchiffrer[18].

Ces troubles supposés touchant le fonctionnement de la perception pourraient à leur tour être reliés aux données neurobiologiques indiquant une activité anormale de la dopamine chez les patients schizophrènes. L'activité anormalement élevée de ce neurotransmetteur pourrait être impliquée dans l'attribution d'une saillance anormale aux éléments de la perception : la perception actuelle différerait alors de la perception anticipée par le sujet[19], ce décalage étant source d'angoisse et d'étrangeté.

Tant la complexité du délire schizophrénique que le caractère global et diffus de ces altérations perceptives rendent difficile de penser que le contenu de la croyance délirante pourrait être directement hérité du contenu de l'expérience altérée. Ce dernier sous-détermine le contenu de la croyance délirante. Mais le délire peut néanmoins apparaître comme une tentative d'explication de cette bizarrerie perceptive, partant d'un besoin de rendre compte de cette expérience. Si le lien causal entre expérience altérée et délire est alors moins direct et plus problématique que pour le syndrome de Capgras, cette source expérientielle du délire peut conférer des raisons à l'étrangeté de son contenu, si l'on pense que l'étrangeté perceptive ne peut être expliquée que par une croyance elle-même étrange et extraordinaire, telle que l'idée d'une mission surnaturelle à accomplir ou d'un contrôle par des forces extérieures[20].

18. B. A. Maher, « Delusional thinking and perceptual disorder », *Journal of Individual Psychology* 30, 1 (1974), p. 98-113, et D. R. Hemsley, « The disruption of the "sense of self" in schizophrenia : potential links with disturbances of information processing », *British Journal of Medical Psychology* 71, 1998, p. 115-124.

19. S. Kapur, « Psychosis as a state of aberrant salience : a framework linking biology, phenomenology, and pharmacology in schizphrenia », *American Journal of Psychiatry* 160, 2003, p. 13-23.

20. B. A. Maher, « Delusional thinking and perceptual disorder », *op. cit.* Il s'agit là de l'hypothèse dite explicationniste.

2. L'INTERACTION ENTRE SCIENCE ET PHILOSOPHIE DANS LE MODÈLE ASCENDANT

Ce type d'hypothèse opère une requalification majeure du statut du délire dans sa dimension normative. Le caractère pathologique, qui dans les conceptions classiques était fondé sur la violation des normes de rationalité, est déplacé vers une expérience perceptive, ne pouvant être imputée à la responsabilité du sujet. Le statut du délire s'en trouve inversé : loin d'être le contraire de la raison et du sens commun, le délire est plutôt, dans un tel modèle, une tentative de la raison pour exprimer ou expliquer une expérience qui lui échappe et qui bouleverse ses cadres. Si le contenu de la croyance délirante est inadéquat, la démarche aboutissant à ce contenu n'en est pas moins conforme à une certaine rationalité épistémique guidant la formation des croyances : celle qui consiste à se fonder sur l'évidence perceptive pour former un jugement, ou à chercher une explication à une expérience répétée jugée inhabituelle et étrange. A l'opposé d'une conception du délire comme inaccessible à toute raison, postuler une expérience altérée sur la base de données scientifiques semble en mesure, dans ces hypothèses, de conférer au délire une certaine justification. La question centrale n'est plus de décrire en quoi le délire viole les règles de la raison, mais bien plutôt de se demander jusqu'à quel point l'altération de l'expérience précédant le délire permet de conférer à ce dernier des raisons.

Cette reformulation majeure de la question normative attachée au délire est directement ancrée dans l'interaction entre science et philosophie. Les hypothèses ascendantes sont d'emblée pluridisciplinaires, et visent une explication de la formation du délire articulant les niveaux de la neurobiologie, de la neuropsychologie, de la psychologie cognitive et de la philosophie. Plutôt qu'une position surplombante de fondation ou de critique, la philosophie peut alors sembler occuper une place circonscrite dans ce schéma explicatif, correspondant à l'étape de formation de la croyance, et visant à éclaircir le statut de cette croyance. On pourrait ainsi penser la complémentarité entre les différentes disciplines sur le mode d'une répartition des tâches, superposable aux différents niveaux d'explication : la mise au jour de dysfonctionnements de mécanismes cérébraux relèverait des neurosciences ; au niveau cognitif, la psychologie décrirait les implications de ces dysfonctionnements pour les fonctions perceptives et cognitives, et dégagerait des biais potentiels de raisonnement et d'attribution, pouvant s'ajouter aux altérations de l'expérience pour conduire à la croyance délirante. Enfin, il relèverait de la philosophie de dégager les critères permettant ou non d'assimiler le délire à un processus normal de formation de croyance, et de définir plus précisément le statut de cette croyance, expression ou explication, par rapport à l'expérience.

Or, il apparaît que si une telle conception de l'interaction pluridisciplinaire en psychopathologie cognitive n'est pas infondée et correspond à une certaine réalité au sein des protocoles de recherche, elle ne peut suffire à rendre compte de l'échange entre science et philosophie au sein de ce domaine. En effet, les données neuroscientifiques accessibles en psychopathologie illustrent tout particulièrement les questions qu'adressent au philosophe les mécanismes implicites qui conditionnent l'expérience consciente. Ces données invitent à se demander quelle description les concepts philosophiques peuvent permettre du fonctionnement de ce niveau. Si la question philosophique du rapport du délire aux normes épistémiques ne peut se poser indépendamment des résultats issus des explorations scientifiques, il ne s'agit pas d'une dépendance où la tâche philosophique ne consisterait qu'à établir les implications de ces résultats. Bien plutôt, une interaction entre science et philosophie semble nécessaire au niveau même de la description de l'altération de l'expérience. La question de savoir dans quelle mesure et en quel sens cette altération peut constituer une explication de la croyance délirante requiert en effet, au niveau épistémologique, de préciser le statut de cette expérience : s'agit-il d'une perception qui pourrait être qualifiée comme ayant un rôle causal dans la production d'une croyance qui en est directement héritée ? Ou bien faut-il réserver cette notion de causalité au rapport entre l'altération cérébrale et l'altération expérientielle, le rapport entre cette expérience et le délire ne pouvant être qualifié qu'en termes de raisons, de rapport épistémique d'explication ou de rationalisation ? Or, une telle question ne peut être éclaircie indépendamment d'une description expérientielle et phénoménologique de l'expérience consciente du sujet résultant des dysfonctions subpersonnelles.

Il s'agit donc, plutôt que d'une répartition des tâches selon les niveaux d'explication, d'une interaction à chaque niveau de description, les perspectives descriptive et normative ne pouvant plus être opposées l'une à l'autre, mais étant étroitement intriquées. Plusieurs champs de questionnements suscités par ces hypothèses ascendantes illustrent ainsi un rôle propre de la philosophie vis-à-vis des données scientifiques.

3. QUESTIONS PHILOSOPHIQUES : LE PASSAGE DE L'EXPÉRIENCE ALTÉRÉE AU DÉLIRE

La question philosophique de savoir dans quelle mesure la formation du délire correspond aux normes épistémiques de la formation de croyances exige une caractérisation de cette expérience étrange et altérée précédant le délire, qui ne peut consister uniquement en des données d'ordre neuropsychologique, si décisives soient-elles. Quelles caractéristiques cette expérience inhabituelle devrait-elle posséder pour justifier la formation et le contenu de la croyance délirante, et faire ainsi du délire non plus une violation, mais une illustration de la rationalité épistémique ?

Si la mise au jour des rôles joués dans la perception et la cognition par les mécanismes cérébraux subpersonnels relève bien du domaine de la neuropsychologie, l'analyse de la valeur de ces composantes pour l'expérience consciente appartient à la tradition de la phénoménologie et de la philosophie de la perception. La présence de termes renvoyant au registre de la valeur au sein même des descriptions issues des neurosciences, tels que « bizarrerie » ou « aberration » perceptives, invite à penser que les dimensions normative et descriptive sont intriquées dès ce niveau : dans la mesure où les mécanismes de la perception ne relèvent pas d'une activité volontaire et contrôlée, comment caractériser une perception dont le contenu n'est pas déformé, mais qui semble posséder une coloration ou une structure anormales ? Cette interrogation renvoie à la tâche philosophique de spécification des composantes fondamentales de l'expérience perceptive, et de clarification de la distinction entre mécanismes subpersonnels conditionnant la perception et éléments conscients de cette perception. Les notions de sentiment de présence et de familiarité semblent ainsi pouvoir désigner à la fois des mécanismes implicites et une coloration consciente de la perception. Les notions de hiérarchisation des stimuli, de contextualisation, de distinction entre figure et fond, apparaissant dans les travaux de la psychologie au titre de conditions de la perception, invitent de la même manière à préciser les conséquences de leur dysfonction potentielle dans le vécu perceptif du sujet.

La question du rapport entre l'expérience et le délire appelle également une confrontation avec les travaux expérimentaux de la psychologie cognitive et sociale. Par l'étude des biais de raisonnement et d'attribution pouvant s'intercaler entre l'expérience perceptive et la croyance, les protocoles expérimentaux de la psychologie permettent d'éclairer la question de savoir si la croyance délirante est formée selon les mêmes normes épistémiques que les croyances courantes[21]. Mais si la psychologie peut mettre au jour des biais particulièrement représentés chez les patients délirants, le statut à leur accorder dans le passage entre la perception et le délire dépend des questions philosophiques déjà mentionnées. Ces biais constituent-ils pour le délire un second facteur s'ajoutant aux troubles de bas niveau, ou bien ces troubles eux-mêmes, par l'expérience singulière qu'ils induisent, disposeraient-ils à des biais épistémiques spécifiques ? Cette question exige elle aussi une caractérisation des implications des troubles de bas niveaux sur l'expérience consciente. Seule une description phénoménologique de ce qui est vécu subjectivement peut permettre de savoir si le délire peut être rapporté à un besoin de donner sens à cette expérience, et s'il manifeste en cela une démarche épistémique habituelle. Le vécu angoissant d'une expérience inhabituelle et étrange n'altère-t-il pas les normes épistémiques habituelles du sujet, perturbant, malgré ses facultés intellectuelles intactes, sa capacité à suivre les règles de la

21. Il y aurait notamment, chez les sujets schizophrènes délirants, une représentation plus forte du biais de confirmation, ou biais nommé « jump-to-conclusion ». En ce qui concerne le syndrome de Capgras ainsi que les délires de persécution, un biais d'attribution, consistant à attribuer à une cause extérieure, plutôt qu'à une cause interne, les événements négatifs affectant le sujet, pourrait également jouer un rôle dans la formation et l'adoption de l'idée délirante. Sur ces conceptions dites « à deux facteurs », ajoutant à une altération expérientielle des biais d'ordre cognitif, voir P. Garety et D. Freeman, « Cognitive approaches to delusions : a critical review of theories and evidence », *British Journal of Clinical Psychology* 38, 1999, p. 113-154, et M. Davies, M. Coltheart, R. Langdon et N. Breen, « Monothematic delusions : Towards a two-factors account », *Philosophy, Psychiatry, and Psychology* 8, 2/3, 2001, p. 133-158.

rationalité[22] ? Ce type de questionnement invite à une interaction entre les études de la psychologie cognitive, les descriptions de patients issues de la clinique, et les outils de la philosophie phénoménologique[23].

4. DES CONCEPTS TRANSDISCIPLINAIRES ?

Que chaque niveau de description du processus menant au délire appelle une interaction entre protocoles et données scientifiques d'une part, questionnement et réflexion philosophique d'autre part, ne résout pas la question de savoir dans quelle mesure cette interaction peut se faire au moyen de concepts en eux-mêmes pluridisciplinaires. Les questions mentionnées ci-dessus témoignent d'un rôle propre de la philosophie dans la compréhension des étapes menant au délire, lié à l'éclaircissement de la nature de la croyance, de la perception, et des normes épistémiques. Elles invitent à décrire les interfaces et les passages entre chaque niveau, à l'aide de concepts dont la richesse semble résider, entre autres, dans leur capacité à être employés par les différentes disciplines, tout en recevant de chacune un éclairage spécifique.

Les notions de sentiment de familiarité et d'étrangeté appartiennent à ce type de concept. Le rôle crucial joué par ces sentiments tient au fait qu'ils se situent à l'interface entre le niveau subpersonnel et implicite de la perception et le processus de formation de la croyance : dans le cas du syndrome de Capgras, le dysfonctionnement neuronal donnerait lieu, dans l'expérience consciente, au sentiment d'une absence de familiarité, appelant la

22. Il ne s'agit pas ici de traiter des diverses conceptions des règles de la rationalité, et l'on désigne ainsi par le terme de rationalité épistémique l'ensemble des principes prescriptifs impliqués dans la formation et la fixation des croyances, touchant notamment à la non contradiction, à la consistance et à la cohérence des croyances, dans une perspective holiste. Voir P. Engel, « Peut-on parler de croyances délirantes ? », *in* J. Chemouni (dir.), *Clinique de l'intentionnalité*, Paris, In-Press, 2001, p. 157-173.

23. Pour une analyse phénoménologique de l'altération expérientielle dans la schizophrénie, voir L. Sass, *The Paradoxes of Delusion : Wittgenstein, Schreber, and the Schizophrenic Mind*, Ithaca, N.Y., Cornell University Press, 1994.

notion de « sosie »[24]. Dans la schizophrénie, les anomalies perceptives causées par des troubles de bas niveau se traduiraient dans l'expérience vécue par un sentiment d'étrangeté, appelant un besoin d'explication et la formation d'une croyance elle-même étrange. Ce type de sentiment accompagnant la perception joue ainsi dans ces hypothèses à la fois le rôle de charnière causale et de justification rationnelle à la formation du délire. Or, sous l'appellation commune de sentiment de familiarité et d'étrangeté, peuvent prendre place des descriptions appartenant aux différents niveaux et disciplines : de la description neuronale de la familiarité par la voie dorsale de reconnaissance des visages à la description phénoménologique de l'expérience consciente de familiarité, il s'agit d'une notion commune et transversale, permettant d'effectuer la jonction entre différents niveaux d'explication.

Cette notion peut être rapprochée de celle de sentiment épistémique qui, de la même manière, se trouve à l'interface entre perception, affect et cognition, et entre niveau subpersonnel et conscience. En tant qu'un sentiment épistémique, tel le sentiment de savoir ou de douter, porte sur le statut d'une perception ou d'une cognition, il possède une dimension métacognitive ou métaperceptive. Il contient une dimension d'évaluation de ses propres états mentaux, pouvant guider et justifier les démarches épistémiques du sujet : par exemple, refuser un jugement formé sur la base d'une connaissance accompagnée d'un sentiment d'incertitude, ou, dans le cas de la psychopathologie, chercher une croyance explicative face à l'étrangeté perceptive. Il peut ainsi être tentant de voir dans cette notion de sentiment épistémique une notion jouant le rôle de jonction entre le régime des causes, en tant qu'un tel sentiment semble pouvoir être directement causé par un mécanisme de bas niveau ou par son dysfonctionnement, et le régime des raisons, au sens où il renvoie à la dimension normative des justifications et des raisons de la formation des croyances[25].

24. Pour une analyse phénoménologique de ce sentiment et de son rapport à la conscience dans le syndrome de Capgras, voir M. Ratcliffe, « The phenomenological role of affect in the Capgras delusion », *Continental Philosophy Review* 41, 2, 2008, p. 195-216.

25. R. De Sousa, « Epistemic feelings », *in* G. Brun, U. Doguoglu, & D. Kuenzle (eds), *Epistemology and Emotions*, Aldershot, Ashgate, p. 185-204;

La question d'éventuels troubles de la métacognition dans la schizophrénie donne lieu à de nombreux travaux pluridisciplinaires, et la notion d'évaluation, à laquelle elle est liée, se pose à tous les niveaux d'analyse. Le mode d'affirmation de la croyance délirante, caractérisé par le sentiment métacognitif de certitude, est l'un des éléments les plus frappants pour le clinicien : l'irrationalité d'une telle évaluation de la vraisemblance de la croyance est d'autant plus difficile à expliquer pour les hypothèses ascendantes présentées ici, que ces hypothèses mettent l'accent sur le sentiment d'étrangeté et de perplexité au niveau perceptif. Comment une évaluation de la perception en termes de perplexité peut-elle donner lieu à une certitude inébranlable au niveau de la croyance ?

Si aucune hypothèse ne semble aujourd'hui apporter une solution tout à fait satisfaisante à ce paradoxe, il suscite un ensemble de propositions qui visent à construire un schéma explicatif du délire schizophrénique sur le mode d'un continuum hiérarchique : la notion d'évaluation y joue un rôle transversal entre les différents niveaux. Ainsi, dès le niveau neurobiologique, le dysfonctionnement de l'activité dopaminergique peut être caractérisé en termes d'évaluation, au sens où cette activité serait impliquée dans l'attribution de la saillance aux stimuli, selon leur pertinence pour le sujet. Le dysfonctionnement se traduirait par une attribution abusive et inadéquate de saillance, qui ne serait plus guidée par le contexte ou les croyances d'arrière-plan. Or, un mécanisme analogue semble pouvoir être décrit au niveau cognitif, où une attribution abusive de saillance à certaines représentations pourrait entrainer un biais de confirmation et un sentiment de certitude, entrainant l'adoption de la croyance délirante[26].

Bien loin d'opposer une tâche d'explication causale scientifique à une question normative philosophique, ce type d'hypothèse révèle

A. Koriat, « Metacognition and Consciousness », *in* P. D. Zelazo, M. Moscovitch, et E. Thompson (eds), *Cambrigde Handbook of Consciousness*, New York, Cambridge University Press, 2006.

26. P. R. Corlett, C. D. Frith, P. C. Fletcher, « From Drugs to Deprivation : a Bayesian Framework for Understanding Models of Psychosis », *Psychopharmacology* 206, 4, 2009, p. 515-530. Fletcher et Frith, « Perceiving is Believing : a Bayesian Approach to Explaining the Positive Symptoms of Schziophrenia », *Nature Reviews Neuroscience* 10, 2009, p. 48-58.

l'intrication de ces dimensions où la dimension normative n'est plus limitée au niveau de la rationalité consciente, mais se retrouve dès le niveau de l'évaluation implicite des éléments perceptifs. Il semble aussi que ces concepts transversaux à différents niveaux, du niveau cérébral à la métacognition consciente, interpellent la philosophie également dans sa tâche critique traditionnelle de clarification conceptuelle. En effet, que ces hypothèses soient le fruit d'une interaction entre science et philosophie n'éclaire pas en soi le statut de ce type d'usage transversal des concepts. Doit-on penser ces usages comme la nécessité pragmatique d'un langage commun aux différentes disciplines, ou comme le signe d'une intégration réussie entre différents niveaux explicatifs, ou encore comme une homonymie source de malentendus ? Il semble relever de la philosophie de questionner les conditions d'applicabilité des concepts aux différents niveaux d'explication : qu'ont en commun la saillance perceptive générée par l'activité d'un neurotransmetteur et la saillance affective attachée à une représentation ? Des termes possédant une dimension normative ou métacognitive, et traditionnellement employés par la philosophie pour caractériser des activités de la raison, peuvent-ils être employés pour désigner des activités subpersonnelles ? Si de tels usages transversaux de concepts semblent nécessaires pour établir des schémas d'explication suivant un continuum hiérarchique, la réflexion épistémologique est requise pour dégager les possibles risques de confusion, entre les usages pragmatiques et les implications ontologiques de tels usages.

CONCLUSION

Il semble que la psychopathologie, malgré l'évolution des conceptions qui la constituent, ait conservé une dimension de défi pour la philosophie. Là où ce défi était traditionnellement de rendre compte des rapports d'exclusion entre folie et raison, il prend la forme, dans la psychopathologie cognitive contemporaine, d'une nécessité de décentrement, le philosophe étant amené à se confronter aux données cliniques et scientifiques de la psychologie, de la psychiatrie et des neurosciences. On a cherché à montrer que la tâche de la philosophie au sein de cette interaction conservait une dimension de clarification épistémologique et conceptuelle, et restait attachée de manière privilégiée à l'objet de la raison, notamment par l'analyse du processus normatif de formation de croyances rationnelles. Mais ces questionnements s'ancrent dans une reconfiguration des espaces propres de la science et de la philosophie : plutôt qu'une répartition des disciplines selon des niveaux ontologique et épistémologique hiérarchisés, l'interaction entre analyses philosophiques et scientifiques s'opère à chaque niveau de caractérisation des processus. Les hypothèses que l'on a présentées, qui sont le fruit de cette interaction, montrent par ailleurs que la question des rapports entre science et philosophie ne se situe pas uniquement au niveau épistémologique, mais renvoie à des enjeux pratiques, à travers, notamment, la transformation de la conception commune du délire.

Recherches sur la philosophie et le langage 29 (2013)
192 p., ISBN : 978-2-7116-8410-6, p. 87-113, Vrin.

Rapports entre éthique et science dans la pensée de James Rachels

Florian COUTURIER*

RÉSUMÉ

Prendre la théorie de l'évolution darwinienne au sérieux, affirme James Rachels, implique que nous réexaminions aujourd'hui nos croyances et principes moraux hérités des siècles antérieurs. Afin d'éclairer cette position, nous considérerons dans cet article le lien entre les raisons qui sous-tendent le jugement moral et la conception du monde en arrière-plan que les sciences contribuent à dégager. Nous distinguerons ainsi un naturalisme réducteur, cible (à juste titre) de nombreuses critiques tout au long du XXe siècle, qui fait de la nature un modèle pour la vie morale ; et un naturalisme d'ordre méthodologique, inspiré de Quine, qui défend « seulement » la recherche d'une cohérence globale entre les divers domaines de production de connaissances. Suivant cette seconde approche, le « darwinisme » chez Rachels s'entend comme une étape décisive

* Florian Couturier est diplômé de l'Institut National Polytechnique de Grenoble et doctorant au laboratoire *Philosophie, Langages et Cognition* de l'Université Pierre-Mendès-France. Ses travaux, dans le cadre de l'éthique animale et des éthiques dites « de l'environnement », portent sur la prise en considération morale des formes de vie non-humaines et la contribution du darwinisme à ce problème. Il s'intéresse à l'œuvre du philosophe américain James Rachels, notamment l'un de ses principaux ouvrages : *Created from Animals* (1990).

dans l'évolution de notre conception du monde et de son origine – en particulier le monde vivant – et, à ce titre, comme une contrainte additionnelle forte que le philosophe moral se doit d'intégrer à sa réflexion. Une authentique « implication morale du darwinisme », selon notre auteur, sera ainsi une nouvelle façon d'appréhender le statut moral des êtres humains et des autres formes de vie, davantage attentive au caractère significatif et à la variété tant des circonstances que des caractéristiques et capacités de chaque individu.

ABSTRACT

According to James Rachels, taking the Darwinian evolutionary theory seriously implies that today we reassess our beliefs and moral principles inherited from earlier centuries. In order to clarify this perspective, we shall examine in this article the link between reasons underlying moral judgments and the conception of the world that sciences contribute to drawing in the background. Then we shall distinguish between a reductive naturalism, repeatedly (and quite rightly) criticized throughout the 20th century, which takes nature as a model for moral life, and a methodological naturalism, inspired by Quine, which "only" defends the search for coherency among the various fields of knowledge production. According to this second approach, "Darwinism" in Rachels' work has to be understood as a decisive step in the evolution of our conception of the world and its origin – in particular, the living world – and, as such, as a strong additional constraint that moral philosophers must take into account in their views. Thus a genuine "moral implication of Darwinism", according to our author, would be a new way to apprehend the moral status of human beings and other forms of life, paying closer attention to the significant nature and variety of circumstances together with the characteristics and capacities of each individual.

INTRODUCTION

Le XXe siècle fut une période de grande méfiance vis-à-vis de la tendance à puiser l'inspiration philosophique dans les sciences. Le rapport de l'éthique aux disciplines scientifiques, notamment la biologie, fut conçu comme étant le plus problématique de tous, pour ne pas dire le plus dangereux : « darwinisme » est devenu un mot presque tabou, relayé en philosophie par les objections de Moore et celles inspirées de Hume.

En 1990, l'auteur américain James Rachels choisissait pourtant de se pencher sur les « implications morales du darwinisme » en publiant son *Created from Animals*[1]. L'ouvrage, qui s'inscrit dans la continuité de nombreux travaux en éthique appliquée et éthique de l'environnement[2], semble en marquer sinon un aboutissement, du moins une étape décisive. En sélectionnant un titre si explicite, l'auteur affirme sans détour la pertinence des dernières découvertes biologiques pour (re)penser l'homme, le vivant et les rapports moraux, et ce faisant, il dénonce les excès d'une philosophie qui a cru possible de se couper de tout rapport au réel.

1. *Created from Animals. The Moral Implications of Darwinism*, Oxford, Oxford University Press, 1990.

2. L'ouvrage de Rachels s'inscrit dans la perspective de ce que dans la littérature anglo-saxonne on nomme « éthique animale », laquelle vise à établir le statut moral des animaux dit « sensibles », c'est-à-dire capables de faire l'expérience du plaisir et de la souffrance, et les obligations particulières que les agents moraux ont à respecter à leur égard.

Par « éthique de l'environnement » j'entends, suivant l'acception de Luc Bégin, une catégorie plus large, qui comprend la réflexion zoocentriste ainsi que toute autre réflexion portant sur le statut moral des entités non humaines : biocentrisme, écocentrisme… (*cf.* G. Hottois, J-N. Missa (dir.), *Nouvelle Encyclopédie de Bioéthique*, Bruxelles, De Boeck Université, 2001, entrée : « Éthique environnementale ».)

Enfin, par « éthique appliquée » je renvoie sans plus de détermination à un vaste domaine, développé dans les pays anglo-saxons dans la 2de moitié du XXe siècle, où la réflexion philosophique est portée sur des problèmes d'éthique concrets et divers, notamment en bioéthique (avortement, euthanasie, manipulations génétiques…) et éthique de l'environnement, mais aussi pour ce qui concerne le racisme, la distribution des richesses au sein des populations humaines, etc.

Dans cet article, nous nous consacrerons donc à ce rapport entre descriptif et prescriptif qui intéresse directement les éthiques de l'environnement ; autrement dit, il s'agit d'établir le lien, et de préciser sa nature, entre les raisons qui sous-tendent le jugement moral et la conception du monde en arrière-plan que les sciences contribuent par ailleurs à dégager. Nous serons ainsi amenés à ménager une distinction cruciale entre d'une part une perspective fortement réductrice qui fut (à juste titre) cible de nombreuses critiques tout au long du XXe siècle, et d'autre part une perspective naturaliste très différente, d'ordre méthodologique, inspirée de W. V. O. Quine et de son « réseau de croyances » ; nous présenterons ensuite la proposition de Rachels pour étendre cette conception holiste de la connaissance au terrain éthique. Les travaux de Darwin, et les prolongements récents de sa pensée, interviennent dans ce tableau en raison de leur contribution décisive au XXe siècle pour l'évolution de notre conception du monde et de son origine ; ce constat est la source même du « darwinisme » dont il est ici question. Dans les dernières pages, nous nous efforcerons de mieux cerner la nature du rapport, et le degré d'influence exact de la science darwinienne sur le travail philosophique, et je donne l'exemple de ce que je conçois, chez Rachels, comme étant une contribution majeure, significative, de cette perspective féconde.

L'ŒUVRE DE JAMES RACHELS

La carrière du philosophe américain James Rachels représente une contribution importante, pour l'essentiel sur le terrain de la philosophie morale, dans le domaine de ce qu'il est convenu maintenant d'appeler « l'éthique appliquée ». Suivre sa pensée au travers des nombreux articles et ouvrages de sa main qui furent publiés depuis les années 1970 réclame de prendre connaissance d'un point fondamental :

> Richard Hare a dit que c'était son désir de résoudre des problèmes pratiques qui l'avait d'abord mené à s'intéresser à la philosophie ; pour moi ce fut l'inverse – j'étais attiré par l'étude de sujets

> pratiques parce qu'ils impliquent des questionnements philosophiques fascinants[3].

En éclairant ainsi sa démarche, Rachels distingue la simple application de « recettes » philosophiques d'une éthique appliquée réellement productrice, discipline à part entière de la philosophie[4]. D'où l'intérêt de porter une grande attention à l'évolution de son œuvre.

Ses premiers textes dans les années 1970 se caractérisent par une volonté de maintenir l'expertise philosophique dans les limites de la seule analyse et clarification des concepts ; un exemple typique est son célèbre article *Active and Passive Euthanasia* de 1975 où, sans prendre encore parti, il entend montrer que la distinction entre euthanasie active ou passive est sans fondement[5]. Mais Rachels entendra bientôt défendre sur le terrain éthique un point de vue plutôt qu'un autre. Aussi lui faut-il en amont s'intéresser à la conception du monde qui sous-tend les positions défendues, confère à certains faits le statut particulier de « raisons » et leur donne par-là un poids dans le jugement ; ainsi l'ouvrage *The End of Life* de 1986, qui reprend ses divers articles autour de l'euthanasie, replace-t-il les divers arguments dans un cadre historique, culturel et religieux. Par là, très naturellement, Rachels en vient à promouvoir l'importance d'une information sur les faits dans l'élaboration du jugement moral correct, et donc un rôle (encore à déterminer) pour la science.

Il est évident qu'une information trop locale ne saurait avoir qu'une influence minime sur nos croyances morales. Par conséquent, *si* de quelque façon la science doit venir influencer la réflexion éthique, ce ne sera que par le biais de modifications profondes et sûres de notre conception de l'homme, du vivant, du

3. Rachels, *Can ethics Provide Answers? And Other Essays in Moral Philosophy*, Totowa, N.J., Roman and Littlefield, 1997 (préface).

4. « The relation between applied ethics and ethical theory is not that one "applies" the theory to the practical issue. Rather, it is that in dealing with practical problems, one encounters all sorts of theoretical issues that must be addressed before one can make progress » (*ibid.*).

5. Sur la distinction entre « tuer » et « laisser mourir », voir chez Rachels, *Euthanasia, Killing, and Letting Die* (1979), *Killing and Starving to Death* (1979), *Euthanasia* (1980), *Barney Clark's Key* (1983), etc.

monde en général. C'est pourquoi Rachels en vient-il peu à peu à concevoir la révolution scientifique commencée au XVIIe siècle comme une dynamique de pensée nouvelle dont l'influence sera ressentie jusque dans la philosophie et l'éthique.

Un élément crucial de cette évolution dans notre représentation du monde, par exemple, se rapporte à l'importance *cosmique* de l'être humain :

> De bien des manières nous nous sommes faits à l'idée que la terre n'est pas le centre de l'univers et que nous autres humains sommes une race parmi d'autres qui se sont ici développées. Mais en ce qui concerne l'éthique, nous nous accrochons encore à l'idée que l'humanité serait le centre du cosmos. L'idée selon laquelle la vie humaine serait sacrée a été remplacée par son équivalent séculier, à savoir l'idée que toute vie humaine présente une valeur et une dignité spéciales en vertu seulement du fait d'être humaine[6].

Cette dénonciation, aux accents très humiens, se verra confortée par les progrès majeurs des sciences naturelles aux XIXe et XXe siècles. Enfin Rachels, dans la seconde moitié de sa carrière, en fera le fondement de sa pensée, relevant le défi de concevoir une « éthique débarrassée de *l'hubris*, de l'idée que nous nous faisons de la spécificité de l'humain »[7].

Une telle éthique, en définitive, rassemble les conclusions de ses divers travaux sur l'euthanasie, l'expérimentation sur le fœtus, l'éthique animale, *etc.*, les rend solidaires et les conforte. Privé d'une conception de l'origine du monde qui donnait corps à cette *hubris*, en effet, il n'est ainsi plus possible de comprendre pourquoi l'argument « toute vie est sacrée » (on entend alors que c'est la seule vie *humaine* qui possède une valeur infinie[8]) est une raison recevable pour prohiber l'euthanasie mais non pas pour empêcher l'industrie

6. Rachels, « Can Ethics Provide Answers ? » (1980), in *Can Ethics Provide Answers ? And Other Essays in Moral Philosophy*, *op. cit.*.

7. Cf. *The Elements of Moral Philosophy*, 1986 (1st ed.), chap. 12, section 1: « Morality Without Hubris ».

8. L'« équivalent séculier » de l'idée selon laquelle la vie humaine serait sacrée, c'est bien entendu, au premier plan, la conception kantienne de la dignité humaine : « ce qui en revanche est au-dessus de tout prix, et par conséquent n'admet nul équivalent, c'est ce qui possède une dignité » (*Fondation de la métaphysique des mœurs*, Paris, Flammarion, 1994, p. 115).

de la chair des animaux non-humains. Désormais, c'est en raison de la souffrance infligée et éprouvée que Rachels tout en même temps souscrit à une légalisation de la pratique de l'euthanasie et condamne les traitements auxquels sont soumis les animaux des élevages industriels[9]. Il est alors manifeste que c'est en vertu d'un arrière-plan tout différent – une conception différente du monde ainsi que de son origine – que de telles considérations pour la souffrance, ou autres considérations semblables, en viennent à obtenir ce rôle si prépondérant pour le jugement moral qu'auparavant on leur refusait.

Le poids des arguments avancés dans un débat éthique ne semble pas, en fin de compte, pouvoir être compris indépendamment d'une représentation du monde en arrière-plan qui leur donne sens et les institue en tant que raisons, mais un arrière-plan qui a lui-même évolué considérablement au fil des siècles. Rachels présente cette transition, dans les grandes lignes, comme abandon d'une conception aristotélicienne (ou scolastique) du monde au profit d'une représentation plus conforme aux découvertes scientifiques récentes et aux travaux de Darwin notamment. Mettre en lumière l'évolution de cet arrière-plan, et la cohabitation d'arrière-plans hétérogènes dans les débats contemporains, permet ainsi de rendre compte de certains désaccords moraux qui persistent. Cela permet en outre de cerner le paysage global – incluant donc des croyances sur le monde physique – auquel nous nous rattachons, si nous tenons à être cohérents, lorsque nous abordons ces questions d'éthique.

Sur un plan plus général, nous entr'apercevons ici une manière de concevoir l'articulation de l'éthique et de la science qui s'inscrit dans le courant de philosophie « naturaliste » hérité de Quine, et qui s'oppose au naturalisme dénoncé par Moore.

9. Cf. *Created from Animals, op. cit.*, chap. 5: « Morality without the Idea that Humans are Special ». (La question de l'euthanasie est évoquée p. 203-205.)

Y A-T-IL UNE OBJECTIVITE MORALE ? ESQUISSE DE DEUX NATURALISMES

L'évolution de la pensée éthique sur le dernier siècle montre une perte et un renouveau de la pensée objectiviste en éthique, non sans lien avec l'évolution récente et relativement brutale de notre représentation de la nature en occident, elle-même largement impulsée par les travaux de Darwin[10]. Il sera ici question de livrer quelques traits seulement de ce mouvement de grande ampleur, pour voir émerger deux conceptions du naturalisme quasiment opposées.

Le questionnement assez radical qui eut lieu en éthique au XXe siècle, autour de l'articulation entre éthique et sciences naturelles notamment, présente parmi ses principales causes le rejet d'une conception fort ancienne de la nature, conçue comme substantielle et normative. Les valeurs sont alors des quasi-faits que l'on peut lire dans le livre de la nature et dont on déduit directement les prescriptions. Cette dimension fortement normative, mise en avant par les scolastiques, est tributaire d'une perspective téléologique, une conception aristotélicienne ou quasi-aristotélicienne du monde[11] expliquant les phénomènes en ayant recours à des causes finales.

Faute d'alternative, ces vues sur la compréhension du vivant ont persisté jusqu'au XIXe siècle – en fait, jusqu'à Darwin et la biologie moderne (nous reviendrons sur ce point plus loin). Ainsi au tournant du XXe siècle, l'épistémologie propre au positivisme logique va-t-elle promouvoir une conception du monde radicalement

10. *Cf.* Rachels, « Can Ethics Provide Answers », *op. cit.*, et « Moral Philosophy in the Twentieth Century » (1995). Pour approfondissement, voir l'essai sur le réalisme moral de S. Virvidakis : *La Robustesse du bien*, Nîmes, J. Chambon, 1996. On trouvera également une étude fouillée du débat oppéosant naturalisme et réalisme dans R. Ogien, *Le Réalisme moral,* Paris, PUF, 1999. Enfin, pour une mise en perspective de la philosophie en général, et de l'éthique en particulier, avec l'évolution des conceptions de la nature en occident, *cf.* B. Lustig, B. Brody, G. McKenny (éds), *Altering Nature. Vol. I : Concepts of 'Nature' and 'The Natural' in Biotechnology Debates*, Springer, 2008.

11. « All those Aristotelian and quasi-Aristotelian views of the world in which a teleological perspective provided a context in which evaluative claims functioned as a particular kind of factual claim » (A. MacIntyre, *After Virtue,* 2007, cité dans *Altering Nature. op. cit.*, p. 66).

opposée à la conception classique, un monde désormais dépouillé de toute valeur intrinsèque ou prescriptive (on peut y voir l'apogée d'une tendance apparue avec la conception mécaniste de la nature introduite au XVIIe siècle). La morale ne peut plus être éclairée par aucun fait de la nature, ni de prétendues causes finales, ni même des faits purement matériels [12].

D'où la critique du « sophisme naturaliste » de Moore dans les *Principia Ethica* : il s'agit de dénoncer en priorité la tentative « naturaliste » de *définir* le bien en l'identifiant à des faits de nature (le bien = l'agréable, l'utile, *etc.*), et plus largement, la *réduction* du discours éthique aux seules considérations d'ordre scientifique ; pour Moore, en effet, le bien est une propriété inanalysable des choses.

S'il existe encore une alternative au début du XXe siècle en éthique, c'est donc entre deux extrêmes [13]. Il faut compter, en premier lieu une conception intuitionniste à la Moore : les propriétés morales sont alors des propriétés non-naturelles, irréductibles à des propriétés non-morales. Thomas Baldwin, dans son introduction aux *Principia Ethica*, estime que Moore embrasse ici :

> une conception quasi-platonicienne des valeurs conçues comme des objets abstraits, détachés de la réalité empirique mais néanmoins tout aussi réelles que n'importe quel objet empirique [14].

L'argument de l'étrangeté de Mackie [15] pointe deux types de difficultés liées à cette conception singulière : dans sa version métaphysique, il souligne que s'il existait des valeurs objectives ainsi

12. « The positivist's criterion of cognitive meaningfulness had consequences for normative as well as metaphysical statements. Statements of value were to be understood as expressions of feeling, not as saying anything substantive about the world. From the positivist point of view, then, there can be no connection between assertions of fact and normative assertions because no logical relations can be drawn between them and *a fortiori*, no implicative relations established between conceptions of nature (to the extent that they are cognitively meaningful) and claims about what ought to be done. » (*Altering Nature*, *op. cit.*, p. 91-92)

13. *Cf.* T. Baldwin, *G. E. Moore*, London, Routledge, 1990, p. 66.

14. G. E. Moore, *Principia Ethica* (1903), édition révisée par T. Baldwin, Cambridge, Cambridge University Press, 1993, p. xii (introduction). *Cf.* § 66 des *Principa Ethica*.

15. J. L. Mackie, *Ethics : Inventing Right and Wrong*, London, Penguin, 1977, p. 38.

conçues, ce seraient alors « des entités ou des qualités ou des relations d'un type très étrange, entièrement différentes de toute autre chose dans l'univers » ; dans sa version épistémologique, il met l'accent sur le fait que même si nous parvenions à accéder à de telles valeurs objectives, ce serait « grâce à une faculté spéciale de perception ou d'intuition morale, entièrement différente de nos moyens ordinaires de connaitre quelque chose ». Une autre difficulté à surmonter est d'ailleurs de parvenir à expliquer comment les faits moraux saisis par l'intuition pourraient bien être motivants et susciter chez nous l'action[16].

Même si Moore concevait que les propriétés morales étaient en lien avec le monde physique par une relation de survenance, cela n'en rendait pas moins mystérieuse l'existence de telles propriétés « non naturelles ». Ainsi jusque dans les années 1960 environ, on convint généralement que Moore avait porté à la perspective naturaliste un coup décisif ; mais on considéra également que la conception qu'il lui substituait était elle-même intenable.

Comme solution alternative à la position de Moore pourrait être proposée une conception purement *subjectiviste* des jugements moraux développée par les émotivistes. Pour un émotiviste, un jugement moral ne se distingue pas d'une information sur le *sentiment* d'un individu vis-à-vis d'un évènement donné ; il ne se distingue pas d'un moyen d'influencer le comportement d'autrui dans le sens induit par ce sentiment[17].

Bien que sophistiquée, étayée par une analyse approfondie des diverses fonctions du langage, la conception émotiviste est en revanche incapable de rendre compte de certains aspects conséquents de la phénoménologie morale. Il faut entendre ici que *toutes* les attitudes ne sont pas propres à servir de base à un authentique jugement moral : il semble bien exister des raisons meilleures que d'autres à l'appui de tels jugements[18]. De même que Hume l'avait

16. R. Ogien, *Le Réalisme moral*, *op. cit.*, p. 79.

17. *Cf.* A. J. Ayer, *Language, Truth, and Logic*, 1936 (en particulier le chap. 6) et C. L. Stevenson, *Ethics and Language,* New Haven, Yale University Press, 1944.

18. Ce qui s'oppose à l'affirmation de C. Stevenson selon laquelle « *any* statement about *any* fact which *any* speaker considers likely to alter attitudes may be adduced as a reason for or against an ethical judgment » (*Ethics and Language, op. cit.,*

remarqué dans son *Enquête*, seuls les sentiments d'approbation ou de désapprobation préalablement filtrés, enrichis, transformés par un examen attentif et impartial des faits peuvent remplir cet office[19]. Deuxièmement, nos attitudes, remarque-t-on, ne nous sont pas données une fois pour toutes et figées dans le temps ; elles sont perméables aux informations sélectionnées ou produites par le processus délibératif.

De là un renouveau à la fois de la pensée objectiviste et « naturaliste » à compter de la seconde moitié du XXe siècle et jusqu'à nos jours, sur le plan métaéthique, et dont procède également l'éthique appliquée en tant que discipline philosophique. Rachels construit sa propre conception de l'objectivité *via* la réponse de J. Dewey, qu'il traduit ainsi :

> « *X* est désirable » signifie « *X* est tel qu'il sera désiré par quelqu'un qui aura considéré, intelligemment et sans préjugé, la nature de *X* et ses conséquences. […] Il est clair je pense qu'il [Dewey] définirait « *X* est bon », « *X* est juste » et « *X* devrait être accompli » sensiblement de la même manière[20].

Ainsi Rachels rend-il compte de l'objectivité des jugements moraux non pas sur le fond d'une position fortement réaliste postulant des faits moraux qui feraient partie de « la trame du monde »[21], mais en affirmant que les vérités morales relèvent essentiellement des raisons valables susceptibles de les étayer (*truths of reason*)[22].

p. 114). Ce passage de son œuvre, désormais fameux, donne crédit à l'idée que l'émotivisme réduit ultimement tout débat moral à une affaire de propagande où l'efficace des arguments prime sur leur qualité.

19. Hume, *Enquête sur les Principes de la Morale,* trad. fr. P. Béranger et P. Saltel, Paris, Flammarion, 1991, p. 73 et Appendice I.

20. Rachels, « John Dewey and the Truth about Ethics », *in* Steven M. Cahn (ed.), *New Studies in the Philosophy of John Dewey*, Hanover, New Hampshire, University Press of New England, 1977, p. 161. Voir aussi : John Dewey, *The Quest for Certainty* (1929).

21. « part of the fabric of the world » : l'expression est de J. L. Mackie, dans *Ethics : Inventing Right and Wrong, op. cit.*, p. 15 ; trad. fr. du texte de Mackie *in* A. C. Zielinska (éd.), *Textes-clés de métaéthique*, Paris, Vrin, 2013.

22. Rachels, « Subjectivism », *in* P. Singer (ed.), *A Companion to Ethics*, Oxford, Blackwell, 1991, p. 432-441.

Dans ce cadre, le problème initial de la dichotomie entre être et devoir être peut être réglé avec une plus grande facilité non par un appel à la déduction *logique* de normes, mais par un simple recours aux meilleures raisons d'accepter ou de refuser un jugement moral donné. Et ce rôle conféré à la raison critique, quand bien même elle est informée par les faits, s'inscrit donc en opposition complète avec le premier naturalisme plus classique : la nature a perdu son rôle directement prescriptif et l'autonomie du domaine éthique vis-à-vis des faits est préservée.

LE NATURALISME DE QUINE SUR LE TERRAIN ÉTHIQUE

Dans les grands traits, donc, le naturalisme en philosophie se rattache au succès spectaculaire des sciences constaté sur les derniers siècles. Mais ce constat grossier dissimule au moins deux grands types de naturalisme très différents l'un de l'autre : le premier, que nous qualifierons de « nécessairement réducteur » ; le second, de « contemporain ».

Le partisan du premier naturalisme se distingue en ce qu'il ne reconnaît pas la valeur de l'explication morale[23]. Autrement dit, il tend à s'opposer à l'idée d'un domaine moral conçu comme autonome et à l'idée corrélative selon laquelle l'éthique serait « une investigation théorique que l'on peut aborder par des méthodes rationnelles *et qui possède des critères internes de justification et de critique* »[24]. Ce premier naturalisme est « nécessairement réducteur » puisqu'il constitue, par définition, un parti-pris métaphysique sur le monde ; les concepts cruciaux que sont le « bien » et le « juste » sont alors définis en termes soit de propriétés métaphysiques, rattachées à une conception préalable du monde et de la « nature humaine », soit de propriétés physiques, par référence aux notions et explications mises en œuvre par les sciences naturelles, qui de fait acquièrent une

23. C'est la définition du naturalisme qu'adopte R. Ogien dans *Le Réalisme moral* (voir notamment p. 25).

24. T. Nagel, *Mortal Questions*, Cambridge, Cambridge University Press, 1979, p. 142 (je souligne).

dimension directement normative. Cette tendance, telle que je l'entends, recouvre tant le perfectionnisme moral que l'on trouve dans la *Somme Théologique* de Thomas d'Aquin que l'éthique évolutionniste de H. Spencer au XIXe siècle[25] ou encore, plus récemment, la suggestion globale du sociobiologiste E. O. Wilson de « biologiciser » l'éthique[26], qui est peut-être l'élément le plus représentatif – parce que le plus explicite – de cette perspective réductrice.

Il est incontestable, cependant, que le naturalisme réducteur ouvre la voie à une reprise idéologique et à une variété de dérives et d'excès (sous la forme tout d'abord du darwinisme social, puis de l'entreprise eugéniste nazie notamment) qui, au tournant du XXe siècle, ont conduit ainsi la communauté philosophique à un rejet global, et peu nuancé, du naturalisme. Cela s'est traduit par conséquent en la thèse radicale inverse, selon laquelle la philosophie se suffirait à elle-même – et en particulier, que l'éthique et la science n'ont rien à voir l'une avec l'autre – discours relayé par le positivisme logique. En matière de philosophie, c'est là une opinion qu'embrassent des auteurs aussi influents que Russell, Husserl ou Wittgenstein[27] ; lorsqu'il s'agit plus particulièrement d'éthique, on se réclame plus volontiers de Moore et de Hume.

La « loi » de Hume est ainsi devenue une « guillotine » très redoutée, bien qu'elle fut interprétée pourtant comme une dichotomie *radicale* que le texte d'origine ne semble pas porter[28]. On ne saurait en effet effacer une réelle dimension naturaliste dans la

25. H. Spencer, *The Data of Ethics* (1879).

26. E. O. Wilson, *Sociobiology : The New Synthesis*, Cambridge, Ma., 1975, p. 562.

27. Dans *Philosophy and the Darwinian Legacy* (1996), Suzanne Cunningham montre en s'appuyant sur Russell, Moore et Husserl que les courants majeurs de la philosophie du XXe siècle – la phénoménologie et la philosophie analytique – ont considéré que la théorie biologique de l'évolution n'est pas pertinente pour la philosophie. Certains passages du *Tractatus* ont fait de Wittgenstein une figure de proue de cette attitude puriste envers la philosophie : aphorismes 4.1111 et en particulier 4.1122 : « La théorie de Darwin n'a pas plus à voir avec la philosophie que n'importe quelle autre hypothèse des sciences de la nature. »

28. *Cf.* V. Nurock, « Faut-il guillotiner la loi de Hume ? », *in* J.-P. Cléro, P. Saltel (dir.), *Lectures de Hume*, Paris, Ellipses, 2009.

pensée même du philosophe écossais[29]. Á se référer au texte fameux du tome III du *Traité de la nature humaine*[30], on y lira donc, plutôt qu'une stricte séparation faits/normes, le problème de la motivation voire de la justification du jugement moral. L'objection de la dichotomie entre faits et valeurs ne présenta pas moins au XXe siècle un obstacle conséquent pour les partisans d'une conception naturaliste de la connaissance morale sur le terrain métaéthique, mais aussi, de la même façon, pour les philosophes critiques de l'anthropocentrisme de la tradition morale occidentale (critique dont procèdent les éthiques de l'environnement) qui, de plus en plus nombreux, tiraient beaucoup de profit des récents progrès des sciences de la nature[31].

29. Voir l'introduction de Philippe Saltel au tome III du *Traité de la nature humaine* de Hume (Paris, Flammarion, 1993), en particulier p. 12.

30. Hume, *Traité de la nature humaine III,* 1, §1.

31. « The objection is that ethics does not depend *logically* on facts about human nature and the world. William Frankena argues ethical judgment comes about because of an additional, non-factual premise. There is always a *tacit* value postulation (the definition of "good"). Thus, from the mere *fact* that *X* injures someone, we do not get an ethical judgment. If we say "*X* is wrong" because *X* injures someone, there is a tacit premise or "bridge principle" in the logic – that injuring someone is wrong. In this sense, Frankena concludes, "those who insist that we cannot go from Is to Ought or from Fact to Value are correct" [W. Frankena, *Ethics*, 1973 (2nd ed.), p. 97]. The conclusion is, then, ethical norms and values cannot be justified by grounding them in "the nature of things" » (*Altering Nature*, *op. cit.,* p. 116).

Alors que des auteurs tels que W. Frankena discutent l'argument de la dichotomie de Hume pour lui-même (*cf.* « Que reste-t-il de la dichotomie du fait et de la valeur ? », *in* R. Ogien, *Le Réalisme moral*, *op. cit.,* chap. 16), un autre terrain de discussion qui doit attirer notre attention est celui-là même de l'éthique environnementale, anxieuse de désarmer cette critique qui la touche de près. On peut noter ainsi que les auteurs biocentristes et écocentristes ont généralement cherché à montrer en quelles conditions il pouvait être pertinent de dériver une théorie de la valeur des objets naturels à partir de l'information de l'écologie scientifique (J. B. Callicott, « Hume's *Is/Ought* Dichotomy and the Relation of Ecology to Leopold's Land Ethic », in *In Defense of the Land Ethics* (1989) ; Holmes Rolston III, *Environmental Ethics : Values in and Duties to the Natural World* (1988)) La tâche des partisans d'une éthique animale s'avérait plus aisée ; ils ont en général pris le parti de montrer comment la biologie évolutionniste et la sociobiologie pouvaient nourrir la réflexion sans pour autant signifier qu'il existe une implication *logique* entre les faits et les valeurs (Rachels, *Created from Animals, op. cit.*, chap. 2 : « How

Il y a manifestement quelque chose d'absurde, pourtant, à se priver de cet enseignement. Ainsi le naturalisme « contemporain » se présente-t-il, quant à lui, comme réaction aux excès du début du XXe siècle qui ont entériné une séparation radicale de la science et de la philosophie, et il n'est pas étonnant de voir Rachels s'en rapprocher.

Un tel naturalisme est, par contraste avec le premier, « non-nécessairement » réducteur : son objet n'est pas un postulat métaphysique ; il défend seulement la multiplicité des sources et la recherche de cohérence globale entre les divers domaines de production de savoir. En d'autres termes, nous avons affaire à un naturalisme *méthodologique,* qui par définition ne dépend d'aucune idée préconçue sur « la nature »[32].

Deux autres points caractéristiques de ce naturalisme hérité de Quine nous intéressent : une conception faillibiliste de la connaissance et le refus d'une philosophie première[33]. Ces deux aspects sont condensés dans une image célèbre que Quine reprend tout d'abord dans *Word and Object*[34] :

> Neurath a comparé la science à un bateau qui, si nous avons à le réparer, doit être reconstruit planche après planche tout en restant à flot. » Sauf que, pour Quine, « le philosophe et le scientifique sont sur le même bateau. » En d'autres termes, nul ne peut se prévaloir d'une position ferme et assurée depuis laquelle il serait possible de fonder et (re)construire l'édifice entier des connaissances et ainsi viser la certitude. « Le philosophe naturaliste commence à raisonner au sein de la théorie du monde dont il a hérité, déjà constituée et en vigueur. Il croit en cette théorie de manière provisoire, mais croit aussi que certaines parties, qui restent à identifier, sont fausses. Il

Evolution and Ethics May Be Related », notamment p. 92-98 ; P. Singer, *The Expanding Circle* (1981), chap. 3 : « From evolution to ethics ? »)

32. L'un des plus éminents représentants contemporains de ce naturalisme méthodologique est le philosophe américain Daniel Dennett. John Symons lui a consacré un petit ouvrage fort instructif, pour partie portant sur la philosophie de l'esprit, pour partie sur la méthode naturaliste en général : *Dennett. Un naturalisme en chantier*, Paris, PUF, 2005. Voir p. 17 et 19 pour le point qui nous occupe.

33. *Ibid.*, p. 13-16 : « La nature, l'analyse conceptuelle et l'œil de Dieu ».

34. *Word and Object*, MIT Press, 1960, p. 3 (*Le mot et la chose*, trad. fr. J. Dopp et P. Gochet, Paris, Flammarion, 1977).

> tâche d'améliorer, de clarifier et de comprendre le système de l'intérieur. Il est le marin affairé, voguant à la dérive sur le bateau de Neurath[35].

Ce qui nous importe ici, c'est que l'éthique partage avec l'épistémologie ce problème fondamental consistant à identifier un point de départ et une assise solides pour construire la connaissance scientifique ou morale. Le problème initial, comme l'a remarqué Hume dans son *Enquête sur l'entendement humain*, est que toute chaine d'arguments dépend d'un premier principe qui est lui-même invérifiable. Il faut pourtant bien commencer quelque part : soit l'on se fonde sur des axiomes dont on dérive ensuite les jugements particuliers (l'utilitarisme en est le parfait exemple), soit l'on prête confiance à certaines de nos croyances les plus solides et l'on remonte aux principes qui les expliquent (typiquement, la démarche de « l'équilibre réflexif » élaborée par Rawls dans *A Theory of Justice*). Mais dans les deux cas le point de départ repose sur une « intuition » invérifiable, suggère Rachels, et aucune des deux approches ne parait complètement satisfaisante.

Rachels suggère ainsi dans un article de 1993, *Moral Philosophy as a Subversive Activity,* de mobiliser une seconde image proposée par Quine, celle du « réseau de croyances » (*web of belief*), et de la réinterpréter en lui intégrant également, outre la connaissance factuelle, les principes et croyances morales. Sur cette toile, les principes et croyances les plus au centre sont tenus pour relativement plus certains que ceux en périphérie[36] ; toutefois, chacun des points de la toile peut être à tout instant révisé, voire abandonné. Si certains points sont reliés logiquement, d'autres croyances en revanche sont soutenues par un ensemble de raisons plutôt que des implications logiques. L'ensemble de ces croyances et de ces raisons forme un seul réseau cohérent et satisfaisant.

35. « Five Milestones of Empiricism » in *Theories and Things*, Cambridge, Harvard University Press, 1981, p. 72.

36. Rachels choisit sur ce point de s'écarter de la caractérisation proposée par Quine concernant ce qui est au centre ou sur les franges de la toile (cf. *From a Logical Point of view*, 2nd ed., Cambridge, Mass., Harvard University Press, 1961, p. 42). Mettons bien au clair, par ailleurs, que Quine ne s'est jamais dans ses travaux préoccupé d'éthique.

Ce faisant, Rachels affirme que l'objectivité morale ne saurait être atteinte que par le truchement d'un processus particulièrement critique de confrontation régulière de nos croyances morales et des raisons qui les soutiennent. Ce processus inclut en outre nos meilleures théories scientifiques sur le monde physique et biologique. Cela ne signifie pas que les hypothèses explicatives avancées par les scientifiques doivent être rattachées sans discussion à un ensemble de *valeurs*, mais elles ne peuvent pas non plus être purement et simplement *ignorées* par le philosophe. Un apport de connaissance peut bien ainsi modifier l'issue d'une évaluation morale, simplement en nourrissant par une information pertinente les principes moraux prescriptifs conçus séparément.

Il devient ainsi concevable de parler des « implications morales du darwinisme » sans suggérer pour autant que les valeurs soient données à lire dans la nature : ce sont toujours les *raisons,* au travers du processus de délibération, qui sont réellement normatives, non pas les faits en eux-mêmes, même si ceux-ci sont autant d'éléments du réel envers lesquels nous ne sommes pas neutres. Auquel cas, il faut comprendre que Rachels est un naturaliste qui fait de la morale, bien plus qu'il n'est un naturaliste moral (si l'on entend bien sûr par « naturalisme moral » une thèse nécessairement réductrice, sur l'invitation de Moore).

JUSTIFIER LE TERME « DARWINISME »

Le naturalisme est donc une position philosophique, objet de débats, sur les rapports qu'entretiennent science et philosophie. Le darwinisme constitue quant à lui un aspect déterminant d'une réflexion philosophique d'emblé engagée dans la perspective naturaliste contemporaine, dans la mesure où l'importance des découvertes de Darwin pour la pensée y est immédiatement reconnue. Il serait en effet malaisé pour quiconque, à l'heure actuelle, de dénier le profond bouleversement qu'ont représenté les travaux de Darwin à de nombreux niveaux sur le premier terrain de la science, par la constitution de tout le champ de la biologie évolutionniste proprement dite, mais aussi au niveau épistémologique, modifiant la pratique scientifique elle-même (rejet des explications supranaturelles et du finalisme) et, au-delà, contribuant à l'évolution de notre compréhension théorique de ce qu'est la science[37] ; enfin, instituant une philosophie de la biologie propre[38]. Tout ceci ne pouvait aller sans marquer, sur un plan plus général, la façon dont nous nous représentons le monde, à commencer par une compréhension nouvelle de la complexité du monde vivant ainsi que de la place l'homme au sein de celui-ci.

Aussi nous pouvons considérer avoir ici le cas exemplaire d'un naturalisme que l'on dira « fort » : il s'agit d'une modification majeure et bien identifiée de notre représentation du monde, qui par son envergure atteint non pas seulement nos croyances et jugements locaux, mais jusqu'à nos catégories et nos concepts pour décrire le monde. (L'une des manifestations les plus évidentes de cette influence sur le terrain philosophique fut le repli de la pensée essentialiste qui, jusqu'alors, tirait avantage de la conception typologique des espèces[39]). Par là il semble juste de nommer « darwinisme » ce qui procède alors, dans une mesure appréciable, de changements impulsés par les travaux de Darwin et leur suite.

Dans la pensée de Rachels, le « darwinisme » est donc déjà quelque chose de plus que la seule théorie transformiste des espèces ; il se présente comme un arrière-plan scientifique et métaphysique cohérent qui donne donc le change à la conception aristotélicienne du monde physique qui a longtemps prévalu. Et de ce basculement, il devrait s'ensuivre également des modifications sur le terrain éthique : le darwinisme renouvelle la réflexion sur la genèse de la moralité[40] et nourrit d'autant les questions d'épistémologie morale et métaphysiques sur le terrain métaéthique[41]; il alimente la

37. *Cf.* D. Hull, *Darwin and his Critics. The Reception of Darwin's Theory of Evolution by the Scientific Community* (1973).

38. Voir E. Mayr, *Toward a New Philosophy of Biology* (1988). Sur l'influence globale des travaux de Darwin, voir aussi son article « Darwin's Influence on Modern Thought » (1999).

39. Voir par exemple E. Sober, « Evolution, Population Thinking, Essentialism », in *From a Biological Point of View* (1994).

40. Pour un tour d'horizon, voir C. Clavien, « Évolution, société, éthique : darwinisme social *versus* éthique évolutionniste », in T. Heams, P. Huneman, G. Lecointre, M. Silberstein, *Les Mondes darwiniens. L'évolution de l'évolution*, Syllepse, 2009, notamment p. 891-898.

41. L'ouvrage de Michael Ruse, *Taking Darwin Seriously* (1998), figure parmi les principaux en ce domaine, même s'il convient de noter par ailleurs l'amplitude des

réflexion en éthique appliquée en renouvelant notre compréhension du vivant et de l'homme ; et par là-même il est susceptible de contribuer, comme suggéré d'entrée, à la réflexion théorique dans le cadre de l'éthique normative. Les deux derniers points sont ceux qui nous intéressent ici – ceux qui donnent à l'ouvrage *Created from Animals* sa structure : puisque les valeurs de la morale traditionnelle ont perdu leurs étais, il est au minimum légitime de demander à ceux qui les défendent de produire de nouveaux arguments pour leur justification, sinon de les rejeter.

Remarquons toutefois que, pour autant que sont mobilisés des éléments relatifs à la théorie de l'évolution, il reste une manière de contester que le darwinisme ait réellement part à ces divers travaux. Après tout, ne pourrait-on admettre le point de vue de Rachels, c'est-à-dire considérer qu'il y a des conclusions morales à tirer de ce nouveau regard sur le monde, et émettre néanmoins des réserves lorsqu'il s'agit semble-t-il de créditer Darwin de découvertes *philosophiques* ? Ne serait-ce pas alors un abus de parler, comme le fait Rachels, des « implications morales du darwinisme » ?

Il y a du vrai en ceci : premièrement, parler de « darwinisme » ce n'est pas parler de Darwin, mais de son héritage scientifique, lequel s'étend loin au-delà des seuls ouvrages qu'a écrits le naturaliste anglais. Deuxièmement, il demeure que la connaissance scientifique ne peut signifier aucune implication *logique* sur le terrain des valeurs. L'usage du terme « *darwinism* » dans le sous-titre de *Created* s'apparente donc plutôt à une *extension*, sur le terrain de la philosophie, d'un terme appartenant en toute rigueur au vocabulaire des sciences – un usage relativement impropre du terme mais que l'on peut parfaitement tolérer, parce qu'il signifie non pas une *incursion* de la science sur le terrain de la philosophie, ni une *absorption* de celle-ci par la science, mais le seul fait d'une *contrainte additionnelle* : il indique que le philosophe de la morale s'engage à la compatibilité et la cohérence de sa réflexion et de ses conclusions philosophiques avec les traits fondamentaux propres à la théorie de l'évolution darwinienne.

positions métaéthiques défendues à l'aide d'arguments évolutionnistes. Pour un regard à la fois synthétique et critique sur ces diverses positions, *cf.* C. Clavien, « Le Réalisme métaéthique face à la science : un rapport conflictuel », *Klesis*, n°9, 2008.

OU SONT LES IMPLICATIONS POUR LA PENSEE DE JAMES RACHELS ?

La réflexion philosophique n'a nul besoin de se risquer et de se perdre dans le détail des hypothèses scientifiques[42] ; s'il existe une influence du biologique sur l'éthique, elle sera portée pour l'essentiel par quelques grands traits caractéristiques de la théorie synthétique de l'évolution, marquant l'évolution de notre compréhension d'un monde où la vie apparaît et se diversifie selon un continuum, où les propriétés des êtres vivants issus de ce processus, y compris l'homme, ne varient qu'en termes de degrés et sont largement partagées entre les espèces[43].

Ignorer le changement impulsé par les travaux de Darwin, ce serait se mettre en porte-à-faux vis-à-vis de découvertes scientifiques nombreuses qui conditionnent notre compréhension du monde aujourd'hui. Mais prendre en compte ce changement, comme le montre Rachels, c'est s'engager également à réexaminer sérieusement les croyances et principes moraux qui sont les nôtres, encore largement teintés de notre compréhension pré-darwinienne du monde. Une telle idée se retrouve ainsi dans la démarche des éthiques de l'environnement, tous terrains confondus, lorsqu'elles prennent comme point de départ la remise en cause (par les travaux de Darwin, notamment) de l'idée d'une « exception humaine » et nous incitent – à raison, semble-t-il – à reconsidérer le choix consistant à réserver le bénéfice de considérations morales directes aux seuls êtres humains (de même lorsqu'il s'agit, par exemple, de reconsidérer la position occidentale traditionnelle envers l'euthanasie). C'est là l'un des aspects essentiels par lesquels, à mon sens,

42. P. Kitcher, « Giving Darwin is Due », *in* J. Hodge, G. Radick (eds), *The Cambridge Companion to Darwin*, Cambridge University Press, 2003. Voir notamment p. 406.

43. Pour approfondissement signalons, outre les ouvrages de E. Mayr déjà cités; Richard Dawkins, *Le Gène égoïste* (1976) ; les « réflexions sur l'histoire naturelle » de Stephen J. Gould, une sélection d'articles parus mensuellement dans la revue *Natural History* puis compilés en une série de dix ouvrages : *Darwin et les grandes énigmes de la vie* (1977), *Le Pouce du panda* (1980), etc. ; Ernst Mayr, *Darwin et la pensée moderne de l'évolution* (1991) ; ou encore le *Darwin's Dangerous Idea* (1995) de Daniel Dennett…

les travaux en éthique animale depuis les années 70 rendent manifeste une influence croissante de la science sur l'éthique, bien que dans un climat de profonde méfiance et donc en faisant preuve le plus souvent d'une discrétion de circonstance.

Nous reconnaissons là également l'approche privilégiée par Rachels, en particulier dans *Created from Animals*. Toutefois, si de telles considérations semblent suffisantes pour ouvrir des pistes de réflexion multiples, dignes d'être explorées, elles sont encore trop vagues et générales, trop peu substantielles, pour qu'on puisse y voir en toute rigueur une implication du *darwinisme*. Les diverses thèses défendues selon cet axe de recherche sont en outre amenées par des voies bien éloignées de tout ce qui concerne Darwin, où les éléments de biologie ne jouent qu'un rôle somme toute périphérique ; dire par exemple que le darwinisme établirait le bien-fondé d'un acte d'euthanasie, ce serait non pertinent et abusif – pour tout dire, ce serait même une phrase tout à fait privée de sens eu égard à notre compréhension de ce qu'est le darwinisme.

La question se pose donc encore de savoir quelle place plus concrète tient le darwinisme dans la réflexion de Rachels, et par quels aspects originaux sa pensée se distingue de celle d'autres auteurs, notamment en éthique de l'environnement. L'espace qu'il nous reste sera consacré à traiter de l'un de ces aspects, que je formulerai ainsi : la démarche adoptée par Rachels semble en particulier remettre en cause la tentative, conforme à l'approche privilégiée en occident, de rapporter l'appartenance à la communauté morale à un unique critère ou jeu de critères que remplit ou non l'individu (posséder la raison, le sens moral ou autres ; la sensibilité, mise à l'honneur par la « libération animale », ne me semble pas se dérober à cette objection). Cette perspective globale forme, à mon sens, la colonne vertébrale des travaux de Rachels saisis dans leur ensemble.

Sur le plan des rapports inter-espèces, la tentative de définir un ou plusieurs critères *généraux*, c'est-à-dire servant de justification pour *tout* type de traitement (telle la rationalité), est identifiée très tôt, chez Rachels, sous le nom de « stratégie kantienne »[44]. Dans ses premiers articles, Rachels se contente de suggérer qu'une telle stratégie serait bien improbable. Il argumente donc en faveur d'une *multiplicité de critères* (en nombre indéfini), chacun n'étant pertinent que pour un type de traitement bien précis. Que lui fasse défaut la parole, ou la raison, n'est pas une bonne justification pour battre un animal. C'est en revanche une raison suffisante pour refuser de lui payer des études à l'université ou de lui accorder le droit de vote. Ainsi *l'Individualisme Moral* – point de vue défendu dans *Created* – est-il la conception selon laquelle ce qui importe pour le jugement moral relève des caractéristiques pertinentes des individus impliqués (non des espèces auxquelles ils appartiennent) eu égard aux traitements envisagés.

Le darwinisme est venu par la suite consolider ce discours. Rejetant l'idée selon laquelle il existe des types biologiques (ou essences), il a mis en lumière le caractère crucial des petites différences individuelles pour la survie et la reproduction ; l'Individualisme Moral présente un parallèle frappant lorsqu'il opère ce décentrement sur le plan de l'éthique. De surcroît, la question de savoir qui, entre toutes formes de vie, peut être objet de considérations morales, dépend étroitement, dorénavant, d'une toute nouvelle perspective sur la vie et les espèces :

> Si Darwin a raison, il n'existe aucune différence absolue entre les humains et les membres de toutes les autres espèces – en fait, il n'existe aucune différence absolue entre les membres d'une quelconque espèce et ceux d'une autre. Plutôt que des ruptures brutales entre espèces, nous trouvons à la place une incroyable profusion de similitudes et de différences, avec les caractères propres à une espèce devenant graduellement les caractères propres à une autre sans qu'il soit possible de dire à quel endroit précis l'on passe de l'une à l'autre. Comme le dit Darwin, il n'existe que des

44. Rachels, « Do Animals Have Rights ? », in *Can Ethics Provide Answers? And Other Essays in Moral Philosophy*, *op. cit.*. Cet article représente la dernière version publiée de « Do Animals Have a Right to Liberty ? », d'abord paru dans le collectif *Animal Rights and Human Obligations* (T. Regan & P. Singer (eds), 1976). Toutefois la partie I, rebaptisée « The Kantian Strategy », est issue d'un second article, « Do Animals Have a Right to Life ? », paru dans *Ethics and Animals* (H. B. Miller & W. H. Williams (eds) 1983).

> différences de degré – un motif complexe de similitudes et de différences qui reflète une ascendance commune, ainsi que des variations aléatoires parmi les individus au sein d'une seule espèce[45].

Il en résulte que la stratégie kantienne est infondée et impropre, puisque la notion de rupture ne fait pas même partie du maillage conceptuel du nouveau paradigme régissant notre compréhension du vivant. En effet, sur quoi reposera donc un traitement moral différencié si des distinctions nettes entre les formes de vie ne peuvent être reconnues au préalable ? Pour le dire de façon plus brutale, prétendre aujourd'hui qu'une propriété ou un ensemble de propriétés chez une espèce puisse justifier *toutes* les différences de traitement revient à se mettre en porte-à-faux avec le darwinisme[46].

Plusieurs années après la parution de *Created*, il faut noter un article remarquable, *Drawing Lines* (2004), où l'auteur poussera plus loin sa réflexion et rendra explicites certains aspects de la question déjà sensibles ici. En fin de compte, la conception du vivant sur laquelle s'appuie Rachels, et dont nous avons livrés ci-dessus quelques grands traits, permet difficilement de discerner des classes, d'établir des séparations strictes, de fixer des frontières (sinon pour des raisons d'ordre purement pratique[47]). Or Rachels repère dans les travaux des philosophes certaines propriétés ou jeux de propriétés régulièrement mis en avant et censés distinguer *a priori* les êtres vivants méritant un traitement respectueux ainsi que des considérations morales de ceux qui ne sauraient en bénéficier en aucun cas. Pour Rachels, de telles « superqualités » n'existent pas (et il précise, point important, que la sensibilité même ne peut être regardée comme une superqualité[48]) :

45. Rachels, « Why Darwin Is Important for Ethics », *in* D. Weissbord (ed.), *Mind, Value, and Culture: Essays in honor of E. M. Adams,* Atascadero, Cal., Ridgeview Publishing Company, 1989, p. 321.

46. Je renvoie pour le détail de l'argumentation à mon article : « Contributions du darwinisme au statut éthique des animaux », *in* J.-B. Jeangène-Vilmer (éd.), *Humanité et animalité*, Klesis, n°16, 2010.

47. Voir par exemple Rachels, « Drawing Lines », in *The Legacy of Socrates : Essays in Moral Philosophy*, New York, Columbia University Press, 2007, p. 45.

48. À la différence de P. Singer, l'importance de la sensibilité n'est reconnue chez Rachels qu'*a posteriori*. En d'autres termes, comme le remarque également M. Nussbaum, il se trouve que les êtres susceptibles d'être lésés de multiples façons

> Voilà la mauvaise façon de penser les relations entre les caractéristiques d'un individu et la manière de le traiter. A la place, nous avons un éventail de caractéristiques et un éventail de traitements, chaque caractéristique étant pertinente pour justifier de certains types de traitements et non d'autres.

En définitive, la communauté des patients moraux, constate Rachels, est tout sauf définie avec des frontières bien nettes ; par là il s'oppose à une tendance forte de la tradition morale occidentale, tout à fait explicite chez Kant par exemple, mais dont bon nombre d'auteurs en éthique de l'environnement semblent également avoir hérité :

> A la question « envers qui est-il approprié d'observer des considérations morales de base ? », nous pourrions répondre : envers tout individu qui présentera tout item figurant en une liste indéfiniment longue de ces caractéristiques qui constituent les raisons moralement bonnes pour lesquelles il ou elle devrait ou ne devrait pas être traité en quelqu'une des diverses manières selon lesquelles sauraient être traités des individus [49].

Rachels se prononce donc, ultimement, en faveur de la disparition du statut de « patient moral », insistant en contrepartie sur l'importance des circonstances : « il n'existe rien de tel qu'un statut moral pur et simple. Considérons plutôt qu'il est question toujours d'un statut moral eu égard à un genre particulier de traitement. » Et donc : « cela ne ferait pas de mal, toutefois, et aiderait à clarifier les choses, de renoncer entièrement à la notion de « statut » (*standing*) et la remplacer par quelque chose de plus simple » [50]. Plutôt que d'un statut moral unique, indépendant des circonstances, dit-il, il conviendrait plutôt d'évoquer en chaque

sont aussi, du fait de l'évolution, des êtres capables de faire l'expérience du plaisir et de la souffrance ; on peut donc *a posteriori* assimiler la classe des patients moraux à l'ensemble des êtres sensibles (*cf.* M. Nussbaum, *Frontiers of Justice. Disability, Nationality, Species Membership*, Harvard University Press, 2007, chap. 6, section vi, où M. Nussbaum critique les thèses de Rachels mais reprend également certaines de ses analyses).

49. « Toward any individual who has any of the indefinitely long list of characteristics that constitute morally good reasons why he or she should or should not be treated in any of the various ways in which individuals may be treated ».

50. « Drawing Lines », *op. cit.*, p. 40 et 41 (pour les quatre dernières citations).

situation trois éléments dont résulte le jugement moral correct : ce que l'on fait à l'individu, ou la manière dont on prévoit de le traiter (par exemple, dans le cadre d'un protocole expérimental) ; les raisons d'agir ou ne pas agir ainsi, qui lient l'action envisagée aux conséquences en termes de bénéfice ou préjudice pour l'individu impliqué ; les faits pertinents à propos de cet individu permettant d'expliquer pourquoi il est susceptible de ce bénéfice ou de ce préjudice.

Somme toute, il faut en conclure à l'impossibilité de tracer une ligne unique qui séparerait les êtres vivants ayant un statut moral de ceux n'en ayant pas. Il faut également, et surtout, renoncer à l'idée qu'il y a une manière particulière de traiter un individu auquel l'on reconnaît le statut de patient moral, censée le distinguer sans doute d'un individu auquel l'on ne reconnaîtrait pas cette dignité :

> Entre autres choses, cela signifie que la question « où tracer la ligne ? » est malavisée. Comme nous l'avions noté tout au début, cette question peut être entendue de deux façons : (1) Où tracer la ligne eu égard aux types d'animaux envers qui nous aurions des devoirs ? (2) Où tracer la ligne eu égard aux devoirs que nous aurions à observer ? Mais en aucun cas il n'existe un unique emplacement pour tracer la ligne. Il y a seulement une longue série de lignes en nombre indéfini[51].

Une telle conception ouvre ainsi la voie à n'en pas douter à un traitement plus gradué, plus attentif à la variété des circonstances, des diverses formes de vie non humaines mais aussi des nombreux cas marginaux de l'humanité que sont les fœtus et nouveau-nés, les vieillards séniles, les « fous », les personnes avec un handicap, *etc.* C'est là un aspect original de la pensée de notre auteur appelé à être mieux compris et, je pense, repris et développé. Cet aspect est à mon sens amené par le darwinisme, non pas dans le sens où la théorie de l'évolution darwinienne jouerait le rôle de modèle pour l'élaboration d'une théorie éthique, mais plutôt (et seulement) dans

51. *Ibid.*, p. 44. Il convient je crois d'entendre la formule « drawing lines » qu'emploie Rachels dans cet article à la fois au sens figuré – « fixer des limites » – et au sens propre – tracer des lignes pour séparer, pour faire des catégories –, d'où la formulation neutre privilégiée dans ma traduction (nous aurions pu également parler de « frontières »).

le sens où elle oriente la réflexion en introduisant une contrainte forte que le philosophe se doit de comprendre et intégrer.

CONCLUSION

Dans le courant des XIXe et XXe siècles, les sciences naturelles ont été sollicitées de nombreuses fois sur le terrain de la philosophie et des valeurs, et il faut bien le dire de façon parfois erronée et potentiellement dangereuse. Pourtant de telles erreurs, et le développement des idéologies dans leur prolongement, étaient en un sens prévisibles. Que tout l'édifice de nos connaissances se trouvât ébranlé par la publication de *l'Origine des espèces* sans que rien ne change de nos idéaux ni de nos mœurs, ou tout au moins de nos discours à visée normative, voilà qui aurait été autrement improbable. Si des révolutions[52] d'une si grande ampleur ouvrent assurément la voie à des erreurs et à des excès, cela ne doit pas, pour autant, nous mener à nier par la suite la réalité ni l'importance des changements qui semblent devoir s'opérer. L'attitude de méfiance envers le naturalisme et le darwinisme, que nous avons héritée du début du XXe siècle, doit donc être reconsidérée ; il nous faut envisager de nouveau, avec le recul qui faisait absolument défaut à l'homme du XIXe siècle, que la réflexion philosophique puisse être nourrie des travaux relatifs à la théorie de Darwin, et ainsi s'en trouver transformée.

Le naturalisme réducteur est certes particulièrement vulnérable à la critique, sinon pour la reprise idéologique auquel il s'expose, du moins pour sa méthode, qui consiste somme toute à faire de la nature, d'une partie de la nature ou des processus à l'œuvre dans la nature (comme l'évolution) un modèle pour la vie morale. Les réflexions rassemblées par Rachels dans *Created* participent en revanche d'une perspective toute différente : un naturalisme « contemporain », qui défend la multiplicité des sources et la recherche de cohérence globale entre les divers domaines de production de savoir. Ainsi sont concevables des changements relatifs à notre

52. Le terme est d'Ernst Mayr. Voir par exemple *Darwin et la pensée moderne de l'évolution* (1991).

conception du monde et de son origine, si amples et si profonds qu'ils viendront imposer leur marque, influencer, des champs de la réflexion auxquels ils sont par ailleurs étrangers. Et dans ce cadre, exemple par excellence, la théorie darwinienne de l'évolution, tant est vaste son impact sur notre connaissance du monde vivant en général et de l'homme en particulier, devient source d'un naturalisme fort, un « darwinisme ». En cela, elle représente une contrainte additionnelle forte que le philosophe se doit de comprendre et intégrer à sa réflexion, du fait non pas d'hypothèses scientifiques de détail, toujours sujettes à révision, mais plutôt des traits caractéristiques qui la distinguent radicalement de la conception pré-darwinienne du monde ayant longtemps prévalu.

Ainsi ce que l'on trouvera de remarquable dans *Created from Animals* tient-il non seulement au fait que Rachels insiste sur la variété et le caractère significatif tant des circonstances que des caractéristiques et capacités de chaque individu pour la simple prise en considération morale[53] (ce dont procède, ultimement, la suggestion de renoncer entièrement à la notion de « statut moral »), mais aussi, et surtout, au fait que ces aspects cruciaux de la réflexion sont chez lui introduits, articulés et défendus au titre d'« implications morales du darwinisme » : le point de vue défendu n'en est rendu que plus solide, car désormais toute remise en cause des implications concrètes, toute proposition de dépassement, même sur le plan théorique et normatif, doit en principe constituer en même temps une solution plus complète, plus précise et toujours plus cohérente avec cette conception du monde au sein de laquelle la morale est désormais pensée.

53. Voir *Created from Animals, op. cit.*, en particulier p. 194 : « The Connection Between Darwinism and Moral Individualism ».

Recherches sur la philosophie et le langage 29 (2013)
194 p., ISBN : 978-2-7116-8410-6, p. 115-134, Vrin.

Contributions de la philosophie morale aux recherches sur la qualité de vie liée à la santé[1]

Julien BLANC*

RÉSUMÉ

Un projet de recherche pluridisciplinaire sur le concept de qualité de vie des personnes atteintes de maladie chroniques, impliquant philosophes, médecins, et chercheurs de santé publique a soulevé des problèmes spécifiques de convergence entre approche philosophique et approche scientifique. En ce qui concerne la conceptualisation de la qualité de vie en vue de sa mesure cette convergence ne va pas de soi. En particulier, il y a un fossé apparent entre une démarche de mesure empirique qui prétend être

* Julien Blanc est docteur en éthique appliquée aux sciences de la vie et de la santé. Après s'être intéressé dans ses premières recherches philosophiques aux rapports entre théorie et pratique, il vient d'achever une thèse sur les enjeux conceptuels de l'évaluation de la qualité de vie en santé, réalisé parallèlement dans un laboratoire de santé publique et une équipe de philosophie et d'éthique de la médecine, à Marseille. Son travail porte principalement sur la rencontre entre enjeux épistémologiques et enjeux éthiques, sur le rôle des normes dans la production des données à la base des décisions.

1. Une version antérieure de ce travail a été présentée en juin 2011 au 3e colloque des doctorants et des jeunes chercheurs, Université Pierre-Mendès-France à Grenoble, *Repenser les rapports entre science(s) et philosophie*. Que les différents participants soient remerciés ici pour leurs remarques et leurs encouragements. Je remercie également les deux rapporteurs anonymes de la revue.

axiologiquement neutre et la réflexion philosophique qui porte sur la vie bonne ou le bonheur, et qui ne prétend justement pas toujours à un idéal de neutralité axiologique. Cependant cet écart n'est qu'apparent. Après avoir décrit brièvement un type répandu d'instrument de mesure psychométrique de la qualité de vie liée à la santé, basé sur le point de vue des patients, nous montrons à travers des problèmes particuliers posés par la mesure, qu'au moins trois types de contribution de la philosophie morale peuvent être envisagés : un élargissement du champ conceptuel et problématique ; une analyse, voire une dissolution par des méthodes philosophiques, des problèmes rencontrés par les scientifiques ; et l'usage des ressources théoriques philosophiques pour imaginer de nouvelles hypothèses ou applications.

ABSTRACT

A multidisciplinary research project on the concept of the quality of life of chronically ill people, involving philosophers and public health physicians and researchers, has raised specific issues of convergence of the philosophical and the scientific approaches. Regarding the conceptualization of a measurable construct of quality of life, this convergence is not clear. There is an *apparent* gap between an empirical process of evaluation, which claims to be normatively neutral, and the philosophical reflections on happiness and the good life, which do not always claim to follow an ideal of normative neutrality. But this gap is only apparent. After the brief description of a common type of health-related quality-of-life psychometric instrument, based on the patients' point of view, we show, through specific problems raised by the measure of quality of life, that at least three types of contribution of moral philosophy to health-related quality-of-life research can be advanced: the extension of the conceptual and problematic field; the analysis, or even the dissolution of, issues faced by scientists; and the use of theoretical materials of philosophy in order to imagine new hypotheses or applications.

INTRODUCTION

Un projet de recherche pluridisciplinaire intitulé « Concepts, usages et déterminants de la qualité de vie des personnes atteintes de maladie chronique » rassemble des philosophes, des sociopsychologues et des médecins-chercheurs en santé publique[2]. Alors que l'usage du concept de « qualité de vie » est de plus en plus fréquent dans la littérature médicale et semble parfaitement aller de soi, le but de ce projet est, à rebours, de tâcher d'y voir plus clair dans les enjeux épistémologiques et éthiques[3] de la définition de la qualité de la vie, de sa mesure et des usages pratiques de cette mesure. C'est la raison pour laquelle des jeunes chercheurs[4] en philosophie y ont été impliqués. S'établissent ainsi des rapports de collaboration entre les sciences de la santé publique et la philosophie. C'est le mode de rapport particulier de la *contribution* sur lequel nous nous pencherons ici en nous demandant comment la philosophie (et en particulier la philosophie morale) peut participer aux recherches empiriques sur la qualité de vie.

Trois types de contribution peuvent être envisagés :

– un élargissement du champ conceptuel et problématique ;

– une analyse des problèmes rencontrés par les scientifiques et selon les cas, une dissolution de ces problèmes ;

– l'usage des ressources théoriques de la philosophie pour imaginer des hypothèses ou des applications.

Après avoir exposé rapidement en quoi consiste la mesure de la qualité de vie, nous discutons à travers des cas ces trois contributions.

2. Laboratoire « Evaluation des systèmes de soins et santé perçue », Faculté de médecine de la Timone, Marseille.

3. Plus particulièrement sur la problématique éthique, un tel travail critique a été initié en France par A. Fagot-Largeault, « Réflexions sur la notion de qualité de la vie », *Archives de philosophie du droit*, vol. « Droit et science », 36, 1992, p. 135-153.

4. J'y ai préparé une thèse de philosophie : *Enjeux conceptuels de l'évaluation de la qualité de vie en santé*, thèse d'Aix-Marseille Université, soutenue en décembre 2012. J'y discute en détail toutes les questions soulevées ici.

1. MESURER LA QUALITÉ DE LA VIE

Dans ce projet de recherche les disciplines empiriques qui s'occupent de la qualité de vie sont, pour simplifier, la psychométrie, pour tout ce qui concerne la conceptualisation de la qualité de vie et sa mesure, et l'épidémiologie pour tout ce qui concerne l'identification des facteurs qui influent sur la qualité de vie et en général les rapports entre cette dernière et les états de santé. Le statut des sciences de la santé publique est problématique : l'identification de leurs objets, qu'ils relèvent ou non du pathologique, dépend de considérations pratiques (médicale et/ou politique) et le mode de théorisation de ces objets lui-même peut être dépendant des perspectives d'usage décisionnel des données[5]. Cette intrication particulièrement marquée en santé publique de l'épistémologique et du pratique soulève des problèmes théoriques qui constituent la toile de fond des rapports entre santé publique et philosophie morale. Comme nous le montrons ici, ces problèmes sont pour ainsi dire « concentrés » lorsqu'il s'agit des mesures de la qualité de vie[6].

Le laboratoire « Evaluation des systèmes de soins et santé perçue» s'est spécialisé dans l'étude de la qualité de vie « subjective », qui part du « point de vue » des individus sur ce qui est important dans l'existence et sur leurs jugements propres portés sur leur état. Documenter le point de vue des individus, et des patients en particulier, a pour but de mieux connaitre l'histoire naturelle des états de santé (leurs causes et leurs effets), et d'informer des décisions thérapeutiques ou préventives en tenant compte des attentes et du vécu de ceux à qui elles s'appliquent.

5. A. Ehrenberg, « Épistémologie, sociologie, santé publique » Tentative de clarification, *Mouvements*, 2007/1, n° 49, p. 89-97. L'auteur soutient à propos d'enquêtes relatives aux troubles du comportement d'enfants et d'adolescents qu'une approche holistique des facteurs est impérative pour que les données puissent informer une décision efficace.

6. Pour une approche exhaustive des enjeux éthiques en santé publique et des éléments sur les aspects épistémologiques, R. Massé, *Ethique et santé publique, Enjeux, valeurs et normativité*, Presses Université de Laval, 2003.

Durant les quatre dernières semaines,						
		Jamais Pas du tout	Rarement Un peu	Parfois Moyennement	Souvent Beaucoup	Toujours Enormément
27	avez-vous manqué d'énergie ?	❒	❒	❒	❒	❒
28	avez-vous été en bonne forme physique?	❒	❒	❒	❒	❒
29	vous êtes-vous senti(e) faible, fatigué(e)?	❒	❒	❒	❒	❒
30	vos parents vous ont-ils donné des conseils ?	❒	❒	❒	❒	❒

Figure 1 : *Exemple de questions composant le questionnaire VSP-A*

Les instruments de mesure de la qualité de vie se présentent sous la forme de questionnaires (fig. 1). C'est le cas du questionnaire *Vécu Santé Perçue des Adolescents*, VSP-A[7], développé au laboratoire « Evaluation des systèmes de soins et santé perçue ». Il relève de la psychométrie, ou mesure des états mentaux. La qualité de vie n'y est cependant pas nécessairement assimilée à un état mental. L'instrument repose sur l'inférence d'une valeur d'une variable latente ou cachée (la QV) à partir de déclarations relatives à une expérience passée (les quatre dernières semaines) ou en cours : il évalue donc la vie vécue, et non pas les jugements des personnes sur des scénarii ou états de santé hypothétiques[8]. Les modalités de

7. C. Sapin, M.-C. Simeoni, P. Auquier *et al.*, « Reliability and Validity of the VSP-A, a Health-related Quality of Life Instrument for Ill and Healthy Adolescents », *Journal of Adolescent Health*, 36, 2005, p. 327-336.

8. Sont ainsi établis des index des états de santé pondérés par les préférences. Ces mesures dites économétriques reposent explicitement sur des théories de

réponse aux questions sont des adverbes de fréquence (« toujours ») et de quantité (« énormément ») et se présentent sous la forme d'une échelle dite de Likert[9]. Ces réponses ont pour fonction de *décrire* ce que la personne a fait, vécu ou ressenti dernièrement, et par-là même, d'enregistrer son jugement à l'égard de cette expérience. En effet, les états décrits dans les questions, comme « pouvoir se retrouver en bande avec des copains » sont supposés être prudentiellement bons, ou importants pour les personnes : plus cet état est réalisé, meilleur c'est[10]. Les réponses ne donnent cependant pas une information objective : « souvent » peut renvoyer à une fois par mois pour un individu et quatre fois par mois pour un autre. On suppose en revanche que les réponses expriment la même satisfaction à l'égard de l'état de chose perçu. Les réponses expriment donc des jugements implicites relativement à certains états de chose. A chaque modalité de réponse est attaché un score. Les questions sont regroupées dans des « dimensions » ou domaines de l'existence, comme le bien-être psychologique, la vitalité, les relations amicales ou les performances à l'école. Les réponses apportent une information sur ces domaines d'importance de l'existence.

Les états vécus par l'individu (ou *items,* formulés ici en questions) et les dimensions explorés par le VSP-A sont sélectionnés à partir d'entretiens avec un groupe représentatif de la population à qui est destiné l'instrument. Il représente donc le point de vue « subjectif » des principaux concernés relativement à ce qui a de l'importance ou est bon prudentiellement, en particulier ce qui « touche » à la santé, soit relativement à des symptômes (la fatigue), au vécu des symptômes ou de la maladie et à leurs conséquences (altération des capacités physiques ou sociales, inquiétudes). L'instrument est donc

l'utilité en terme de satisfaction des préférences. Parmi les plus connus l'EuroQol et le Health Utilites Index, respectivement : M. L. Essink-Bot *et al.* « Generalizability of Valuations on Health States Collected with the EuroQol Questionnaire », *Health Economics* 2, 1993, p. 237-246 et G. W. Torrance *et al.* « Multiattribute utility function for a comprehensive health status classification system. Health Utilities Index Mark 2 », *Medical Care* 34 (7), 1996, p. 702-722.

9. R. Likert, « A Technique for the Measurement of Attitudes », *Archives of Psychology*, 140, 1932, p. 44-53.

10. De manière exactement inverse, moins l'état « être stressé » s'est réalisé, meilleur c'est.

en un sens doublement subjectif : d'une part parce que la liste des items est produite à partir du point de vue des principaux concernés et d'autre part parce que c'est leur jugement sur ces états importants qu'expriment les réponses. Ces jugements peuvent être interprétés comme reflétant le niveau de satisfaction de désirs ou comme faisant référence à un état vécu comme plus ou moins bon. Compte tenu de la conception des instruments, il n'est pas possible de trancher en faveur de l'une ou l'autre interprétation[11].

2. TROIS CONTRIBUTIONS

2. 1. Elargir le champ conceptuel et problématique

Dans le projet, les philosophes travaillent sur un axe « concept ». L'objectif général est de clarifier, explorer et critiquer des fondements théoriques des instruments de mesure de la qualité de vie liée à la santé, si fondements il y a. Les philosophes sont d'abord amenés à répondre à des demandes des médecins de santé publique quant à la tradition philosophique elle-même : un point de vue assez répandu consiste à opposer la démarche de mesure de la qualité de vie et l'activité de définition philosophique, la première n'ayant pas pour but de dire quelle est la *nature* de la qualité de la vie. Chercher à déterminer ce *qu'est* la qualité de vie, c'est-à-dire ce qu'est une vie de *bonne* qualité dans un sens potentiellement normatif, serait justement dévolu à la philosophie[12].

Un des objectifs du projet est de voir justement si ce point de vue est consistant, en se demandant si tout ce que le corpus philosophique a à dire sur le bien-être n'est que normatif, si la démarche empirique de mesure est neutre axiologiquement et fondamentalement si toute normativité peut être bien exclue de l'approche empirique de la qualité de vie. Dans le cas des instruments de mesure constitués à partir du point de vue de personnes comme le VSP-A, la question de la conceptualisation de la qualité de la vie

11. L'interprétation du concept sous-jacent aux instruments et de la nature de la « réalité » mesurée est particulièrement problématique. Pour une discussion plus étendue, je renvoie le lecteur à ma thèse.

12. A. Leplège, *Les mesures de la qualité de vie*, Paris, PUF, 1999.

semble réglée : le concept reflèterait fondamentalement ce que pensent effectivement les individus. Mais en réalité, même dans ce cas de figure, le concept sous-jacent repose sur des présupposés discutables. Le concept de qualité de vie vécue sous-jacent au VSP-A s'appuie sur le présupposé selon lequel les principaux concernés ne peuvent pas commettre d'erreur quant à ce qui constitue et détermine la qualité de leur vie, autrement dit qu'ils sont les mieux placés pour en juger. Cela constitue donc une position sur la *nature* de la qualité de la vie. Or justement, de la doctrine socratique de la vie d'examen aux théories du bien-être comme satisfaction de préférences *rationnelles*[13] ou améliorées, il existe une grande diversité de doctrines philosophiques de la valeur prudentielle qui contestent ce présupposé et tentent au contraire d'en surmonter la difficulté inhérente[14]. Par conséquent, même dans le cas des instruments de mesure intégralement subjectifs comme le VSP-A, les questions de conceptualisation et de normativité en général ne sont pas entièrement réglées. La réflexion sur la *nature* de la qualité de la vie ne peut être dissociée de sa mesure. Cette opposition entre la science qui mesure et la philosophie qui spécule est renforcée par l'idée que représenter le point de vue des individus permet de garantir la *neutralité* de l'offre de soin et de prévention eu égard aux conceptions de la vie bonne[15].

Nous supposons donc que les traditions philosophiques de conceptualisation de *l'eudaimonia*, du bonheur, de la vie bonne, du

13. Par exemple, R. B. Brandt, *A Theory of Good and Right*, Oxford, Clarendon Press, 1979.

14. Cette difficulté est formulée avec précision par J. Griffin : si d'un côté nous avons individuellement autorité pour déterminer ce qui améliore notre bien-être, cependant, « notoirement, nous méconnaissons notre propre intérêt ». J. Griffin, *Well-Being, its Meaning, Measurement and Moral Importance*, Oxford, Clarendon Press, 1986, p. 10 (je traduis).

15. Il peut y avoir une superposition et un renforcement mutuel entre la neutralité comme valeur propre à la recherche et comme valeur morale et politique. Sur la neutralité à l'égard de la vie bonne comme critère du libéralisme R. Dworkin, « Liberalism », *in* S. Hampshire (éd.), *Public and Private Morality*, Cambridge, Cambridge University Press, 1978.

bien-être ou de la qualité de vie[16], constituent des ressources mobilisables pour la compréhension de la nature de la qualité de la vie ou pour critiquer certains présupposés. Un travail en cours consiste ainsi à mettre en perspective les concepts sous-jacents aux instruments de mesure avec les doctrines philosophiques de la vie bonne. L'histoire de la philosophie est mobilisée, de la pensée socratique aux positions développées par Griffin ou Nussbaum[17], en passant par les éthiques classiques comme celle de Spinoza, qui sont relativement méconnues par les développeurs d'instruments de mesure. Ainsi par exemple, l'« adaptation » des individus aux circonstances de l'existence et en particulier aux maladies est perçue assez largement comme un mécanisme qui induit un biais de la mesure et qu'il faut pondérer. Des arguments principalement issus des doctrines philosophiques antiques en faveur du rôle de l'adaptation pour le bonheur peuvent être mobilisés pour discuter les présupposés et faire apparaître les enjeux éthiques, et pas seulement métriques, du statut de l'adaptation[18].

16. Il y a un flottement dans les différentes littératures entre bonheur-vie heureuse, qualité de vie, bien-être. Pour réduire cette confusion, on recourt la plupart du temps à des définitions nominales, pas toujours explicites, ce qui fait enfler les discussions. Bien que l'usage ordinaire ou les choix techniques puissent assigner des significations différentes aux termes, chaque auteur peut préférer parler de bonheur, de qualité de vie ou de bien-être pour désigner la même chose, l'état global de l'existence, susceptible de plus ou de moins en valeur. Comme nous ne traitons ici d'aucun auteur en particulier, nous parlons de bonheur, de qualité de vie et de bien-être indistinctement. Pour désigner les choses de manière plus générale, nous usons des concepts de prudence et de valeur prudentielle qui par opposition à la morale et aux valeurs morales en vient à désigner ce qui concerne l'intérêt, le bonheur, le bien-être, *etc.*

17. J. Griffin *op. cit.*, M. Nussbaum « Capabilities as Fundamental Entitlements : Sen and Social Justice » *Feminist Economics*, 9 (2-3), 2003, p. 33-59.

18. En psychologie, le concept d'adaptation (ou ajustement ou *coping*) désigne un ensemble de mécanismes précis, parfois distingués des mécanismes de défenses ou de la perception de son état (d'une maladie par exemple). R. S. Lazarus & S. Folkman, *Stress, Appraisal and Coping*, Springer, New York, 1984. Mais par « adaptation » en philosophie morale on peut désigner un ensemble plus large qui va de la modification des désirs aux modifications des perceptions et des croyances en passant par la suspension ou l'annulation des jugements de valeur *etc.* et qui peut être « traduit » par les concepts psychologiques d'adaptation, de perception de soi ou autres. Des règles de traduction restent à établir. En retour, ceci présente

2. 2. Dissolution des problèmes

Un deuxième mode de contribution possible de la philosophie a trait directement aux problèmes de recherche spécifiques à la psychométrie ou à l'épidémiologie de la qualité de vie. Nous pouvons voir dans un cas comment une réinterprétation des données et de leur statut épistémique peut alors conduire à reconsidérer le problème, voire à le dissoudre.

Une des limites à la validité des tests est l'ensemble de phénomènes rangés sous le nom de *responseshift*, c'est-à-dire du changement de la réponse ou du sens de la réponse que les sujets donnent aux tests. Face aux anomalies que présentent les données, on suppose alors que le concept de qualité de vie de la personne n'est pas (ou plus) en adéquation avec le concept sous-jacent à l'instrument, qui donc ne représente plus ce qu'il est censé représenter. Ainsi, par exemple, avant et après un événement médical (chimiothérapie), les scores de qualité de vie de la personne restent identiques, alors qu'on pourrait s'attendre au contraire à une diminution (en raison par exemple de l'amoindrissement de ses capacités). On suppose que l'événement médical a modifié la conception de qualité de vie de l'individu. Mais doit-on pour autant supposer que les résultats sont faux, dénués de sens, et est-il nécessaire de trouver une stratégie de correction ?

Le *responseshift* se décompose en trois mécanismes principaux : la reconceptualisation, la repriorisation et la recalibration[19]. Nous discutons ce dernier mécanisme seulement, qui fait l'objet d'un nombre important de publications[20]. Pour détecter et corriger métriquement les effets de la recalibration on recourt principalement à la méthode du *then-test* : les sujets sont testés à t0 puis à t1. On leur demande alors à t1 de réévaluer *a posteriori* leur état tel qu'il était à t0 ; appelons les résultats *a posteriori* t0'. Pour mesurer le changement

l'intérêt d'amener les questions psychologiques d'adaptation dans le champ des questions de valeur prudentielle, et d'en discuter la signification éthique.

19. C. Schwartz & M. Sprangers, « Methodological approaches for assessing response shift in longitudinal health-related quality-of-life research », *Social Science & Medicine*, 48 (11), 1999, p. 1531-1548.

20. C. Schwartz *et al.* « The clinical significance of adaptation to changing health : a meta-analysis of response shift », *Quality of Life Research*, 15 (9), 2006, p. 1533-1550.

dans le temps de la qualité de vie on fait la différence entre t0' et t1, si t0' diffère de t0. Si les modalités de réponse du test sont des adverbes de fréquence ou de quantité, comme c'est souvent le cas, on suppose ainsi que « souvent » ou « énormément » ne *signifiaient* pas la même chose à t0 et à t1 et qu'ils ne sont donc pas comparables. Or la signification est bien au cœur du dispositif, et donc du problème, puisqu'il y va de la nature du rapport entre les énoncés manifestes, les réponses, et la variable latente qui fait l'objet de l'enquête.

L'utilisation du *then-test* repose, nous semble-t-il, sur la supposition que le sens des modalités de réponse est de faire *référence* soit à un état intérieur du sujet comme un degré de satisfaction, soit à ce qui est le cas dans l'histoire du sujet. Sur une échelle qui va de « jamais » à « toujours », le sens de « souvent » serait ainsi de référer à un degré de satisfaction proche de la satisfaction complète ou à la fréquence d'un état de chose proche de la saturation. Mais il n'est pas du tout évident que la signification de ces adverbes fonctionne uniquement par *référence*. Ils fonctionnent plutôt comme des *expressions* d'attitudes évaluatives du sujet à l'égard de son expérience[21], et il n'y a pas de raison de penser que le sens de cette expression se modifie ou se recalibre dans le temps. Ainsi, lorsqu'on lui demande à quelle fréquence il a manqué d'énergie (*cf.* fig. 1), le sujet peut être enclin à répondre « souvent » à t0, alors qu'il aura manqué disons 10 fois d'énergie dans le mois passé, et également « souvent » à t1 après une dégradation de son état de santé, alors qu'il aura manqué 20 fois d'énergie. Mais « souvent » exprime dans les deux cas la même attitude et signifie la « même chose », bien que ce qui a été effectivement le cas diffère : la vérité de la réponse ne dépend donc pas uniquement de ce qu'a vécu « réellement » le sujet. Par conséquent, il n'y a pas de raison de considérer que le score *a posteriori* t0' est plus « vrai » que le score initial t0, et on peut penser

21. Les analyses wittgensteiniennes des différences entre la grammaire de la référence et la grammaire de l'expression, ainsi que de la grammaire des concepts psychologiques nous semblent particulièrement pertinentes ici pour interroger les présupposés des théories psychométriques quant à la signification des réponses. Sur les attitudes, leurs expressions et l'implication de l'agent dans ce qu'il dit, S. Laugier, *Wittgenstein, le mythe de l'inexpressivité*, Paris, Vrin, 2010, *esp.* chap. 2

que la recalibration ne rend donc pas les scores faux ou dénués de sens. De ce point de vue le problème qu'elle pose se dissout.

2. 3. Imaginer de nouvelles hypothèses…

On trouve deux éléments dans les définitions de la valeur prudentielle d'une vie : un aspect formel qui explique comment un *X* est ou a une valeur prudentielle ; et un aspect substantiel : la liste des *X* qui ont une valeur prudentielle (on appelle les théories uniquement substantielles des théories à « liste objective »[22] ou « théories substantielles du bien »[23]).

Les débats entre les théories du mécanisme formel de la valeur prudentielle (l'identification du *value maker*) portent principalement sur le réalisme des valeurs. Les débats entre les théories substantielles sont issus de la question du réalisme des valeurs prudentielles, et tournent principalement autour du présupposé individualiste et de l'idiosyncrasie des valeurs prudentielles et de l'ordre d'importance établi entre elles par l'individu[24].

Les théories philosophiques de la qualité de vie peuvent être convoquées pour discuter ou enrichir les modèles disponibles en qualité de vie liée à la santé selon ces deux aspects distincts, formel et substantiel.

2. 3. 1 … à partir des théories formelles

On peut considérer qu'il existe fondamentalement cinq types d'explication du mécanisme de la valeur prudentielle[25]. Selon

22. D. Parfit, *Reason and Persons*, Oxford, Oxford University Press, 1984. On parlera aussi de « conception substantielle du bien », R. Dworkin, *op. cit.*, de « l'idéal de la vie bonne », J. Raz, 1986. *The Morality of Freedom*, Oxford, Clarendon Press, 1986.

23. T. Scanlon, « Value, Desire, and Quality of Life », *in* M. Nussbaum et A. Sen, éd., *The Quality of Life,* Oxford, Clarendon Press, 1993, p. 185-200.

24. Voir par exemple l'ouvrage collectif : R. Crisp & B. Hooker *éd.*, *Well-Being and Morality, essays in honor of James Griffin*, Clarendon Press, Oxford, 2000

25. Je n'aborde pas ici les différentes positions relatives à *ce dont il doit y avoir* égalité dans une perspective de justice et dans le cadre d'une philosophie politique générale. Voir J. Rawls, *A Theory of Justice*, Oxford, Oxford University Press, 1971 (trad. fr. C. Audard, *Théorie de la justice*, Paris, Seuil, 1987), et J. Rawls, « The Priority of Right and Ideas of the Good », *Philosophy & Public Affairs*, 17 (4) 1988, p. 251-276 ; (trad. fr. A. Tchoudnowsky et C. Audard, « La priorité du juste et les

l'explication de type hédoniste, la qualité de la vie est fonction d'états mentaux qui accompagnent ou sont causés par les circonstances de l'existence, et qui ont une valeur *per se*, comme le plaisir et l'absence de peine[26]. Selon l'explication de type préférentialiste, la qualité de vie est fonction de la satisfaction des désirs ou préférences d'un individu[27]. Selon une explication de type perfectionniste, la qualité de la vie dépend de la réalisation d'une forme de vie qui représente la norme de la vie humaine[28]. Selon l'explication par les « capabilités », la qualité de vie est fonction de la liberté réelle qu'a un individu de faire des choix parmi des états de choses accessibles[29]. Et enfin, il existe un cinquième type d'explication, moins connu, développé par J. Griffin, selon lequel la qualité de la vie dépend de la satisfaction des désirs informés, l'information portant sur ce qui améliore effectivement la vie, c'est-à-dire la réalisation de valeurs prudentielles que l'on peut lister[30].

À la différence des outils économétriques qui sont globalement préférentialistes, les outils psychométriques utilisés pour évaluer la qualité de vie en lien avec la santé sont relativement indifférents à ces théories formelles qui réduisent la valeur prudentielle à *un* mécanisme homogène principal. Comme le relève E. Picavet, ils

conceptions du Bien », *Archives de Philosophie du Droit* 33, 1988, p. 39-59) ; R. Nozick,. *Anarchy, State and Utopia*, New-York, Basic Books, 1974 ; A. Sen, « Equality of What ? », *in* S. McMUrrin (ed.), *Tanner Lectures on Human Values*, Cambridge, CUP, 1980, R. Dworkin, « Equality of Welfare », *Philosophy and Public Affairs* 10, 1981 ; G. A. Cohen, « On the Currency of Egalitarian Justice », *Ehtics*, 99, 1989.

26. C'est la position épicurienne ou benthamienne classique. Pour une référence récente d'une approche pluridisciplinaire : D. Kahneman, E. Diener & N. Schwarz (eds), *Well-Being : The foundations of Hedonic Psychology*, Russell Sage Foundation, New York, 1999.

27. J. Harsanyi, *Essays on Ethics, Behavior, and Scientific Explanation*, Reidel, Dordrecht, 1976.

28. La doctrine aristotélicienne peut passer pour le modèle des théories perfectionnistes, J. Griffin, *op. cit.*, p. 56-64.

29. A. Sen, *Commodities and Capabilities,* North-Holland, Amsterdam, 1985, en particulier les chapitres 2 et 4.

30. Par exemple des relations personnelles riches, l'autonomie ou l'accomplissement de soi, J. Griffin *op. cit.* p. 67.

reposent plutôt sur un concept hétérogène[31]. En revanche, ces théories formelles ont des implications notamment quant à la nature de l'agent qui évalue la qualité de sa vie, et celles-ci peuvent être transformées en implications empiriquement testables au niveau psychologique. C'est une démarche en un sens plus humble que celle qui consisterait à tirer un concept opérationalisable et un instrument de mesure d'une construction conceptuelle[32]. Dans la mesure où le concept sous-jacent aux instruments existants semble compatible avec plusieurs théories formelles, il s'agit plutôt d'explorer certaines implications d'une théorie *choisie* pour compléter la connaissance des phénomènes impliqués dans la qualité de la vie.

Ainsi un travail est en cours dans l'équipe de santé publique de la Timone[33] sur l'impact des troubles cognitifs sur la validité des questionnaires de qualité de vie pour les patients atteints de scléroses multiples. Les troubles cognitifs explorés ont trait aux fonctions exécutives. Mais les patients atteints de scléroses multiples peuvent présenter d'autres types de troubles cognitifs, ce que relève l'auteur, et l'on peut supposer par ailleurs que d'autres fonctions cognitives peuvent être impliquées dans l'évaluation par un individu de son propre état et donc que d'autres dysfonctionnements non étudiés pourraient altérer, s'ils étaient avérés, la confiance dans les résultats de test de qualité de vie. Parmi les cinq théories formelles résumées ci-dessus, celle de J. Griffin présente une solidité conceptuelle et une vraisemblance qui, à notre connaissance, n'a pas été sérieusement mise en défaut[34], à la différence des quatre autres. C'est donc un bon candidat pour imaginer des implications testables. Selon J. Griffin le bien-être est fonction de la satisfaction

31. E. Picavet, « Le concept de qualité de vie (entre besoins, satisfaction psychologique et faculté de choix) », *Cités*, n° 4, 2000, p. 111-120.

32. C'est à l'inverse le cas de la démarche de Kahneman (*op. cit.*) et de la psychologie positive qui part de présupposés hédonistes forts.

33. K. Baumstarck *et al.* « Is the concept of quality of life relevant for multiple sclerosis patients with cognitive impairment? Preliminary results of a cross-sectional study », soumis le 23 juin 2011.

34. En tant que théorie du bien-être basée sur la satisfaction d'une certaine classe de désirs, les désirs *informés*, la théorie de Griffin présente la même faiblesse que les autres théories basées sur les désirs, à savoir le caractère vague de la limite dans le temps et l'espace des objets de désirs pertinent pour le bien-être. Voir L. Sumner « Something in Between », *in* R. Crisp & B. Hooker (eds), *op. cit.*, p. 1-19.

de préférences informées quant à ce qui vaut d'être préféré prudentiellement. Ainsi poursuivre son intérêt et évaluer son propre état dépendent notamment de la capacité à percevoir les fins générales de la vie humaine, c'est-à-dire les valeurs prudentielles, de la capacité à les désirer, par suite de la capacité à percevoir quelles valeurs sont réalisées dans les actions particulières, et de la capacité à entretenir un projet de vie et à contrôler ses désirs de premier ordre de manière à ce qu'ils soient conformes à des désirs plus généraux. Il s'agit donc de capacités évaluatives et de capacités relatives à l'agentivité. Or ces capacités peuvent recevoir une description de manière à être empiriquement détectables. On envisage ainsi, en prolongement de l'étude sur les troubles cognitifs des scléroses multiples d'étudier l'impact de leur dysfonctionnement sur les évaluations de la qualité de vie. Une piste, documentée par ailleurs dans une étude en cours sur la qualité de vie et la schizophrénie[35], consisterait ainsi à explorer les fonctions réflexives ou métacognitives impliquées dans la conscience que le sujet a de lui-même, dans la capacité à adopter sa propre perspective ou plus généralement dans l'agentivité.

2. 3. 3.… à partir des théories substantielles de la qualité de la vie

Il est concevable qu'il y ait une « expertise » philosophique relative aux aspects formels des théories de la valeur prudentielle car

35. Une étude en cours met en évidence chez les patients atteints de schizophrénie des corrélations entre les résultats des tests de qualité de vie et l'irrigation du sillon temporal supérieur. Or cette zone du cerveau est connue par ailleurs pour être impliquée dans les capacités métacognitives de conscience de soi et d'auto-perspective, ainsi que dans la théorie de l'esprit et de l'intention des autres. L. Boyer *et al.* « Functional involvement of superior temporal sulcus in quality of life of patients with schizophrenia », *Psychiatry Research Neuroimaging*, en cours de publication.

Les aspects conceptuels sont discutés dans ma thèse. Je plaide en particulier pour l'idée que la réflexivité, que l'on peut rapprocher des fonctions métacognitives, est une condition formelle générale de la qualité de vie : les personnes dont les capacités métacognitives sont altérées ne pourraient pas être dites avoir une qualité de vie au même titre que les personnes dont les capacités sont intactes. Cette thèse a des implications importantes qui vont contre le présupposé très répandu selon lequel il peut suffire d'évaluer la qualité de vie à partir de la qualité des états mentaux et/ou des satisfactions des attentes manifestes des personnes.

ces derniers relèvent principalement de l'analyse conceptuelle. Bien que l'homogénéité conceptuelle des théories philosophiques s'oppose à l'hétérogénéité des concepts sous-jacents aux instruments de mesure effectifs, les deux domaines ne sont pas imperméables et les discussions peuvent s'engager entre eux.

Mais en ce qui concerne les aspects substantiels des théories ou les théories substantielles du bonheur, il est plus délicat d'affirmer qu'il y a une expertise philosophique : c'est tout le problème de la normativité inhérente aux conceptions philosophiques substantielles de la vie bonne. Ce problème est renforcé, relativement aux approches psychométriques, par le fait qu'il n'y a pas de procédure empirique explicite par laquelle une doctrine philosophique quelconque rendrait compte de sa conception substantielle de la vie bonne. Cette normativité apparaît par contraste de la neutralité *affichée* des démarches empiriques. Evidemment, à l'intérieur du champ philosophique même l'idée de donner une définition substantielle de la vie bonne est très controversée[36]. Un des arguments avancés en faveur de la construction des instruments de qualité de vie à partir du recueil du point de vue « subjectif » des principaux concernés est justement d'éviter le dogmatisme et le paternalisme qu'une définition de la qualité de vie spéculative ou à partir de valeurs dont l'objectivité, loin d'être évidente, est en fait controversée, comme la satisfaction des besoins[37], pourrait présenter.

Les doctrines philosophiques substantielles du bonheur présentent un aspect dogmatique, au sens où elles contreviennent à la quasi-intuition qu'il y a autant de conceptions du bonheur que d'individus, et ce parce qu'elles cherchent à déterminer quel est le type de vie *véritablement* heureux plutôt qu'à décrire le détail de ce qui, de fait, est l'objet du goût, des préférences et des volontés diverses et parfois contradictoires des hommes. Les réflexions philosophiques sur le bonheur sont largement fondées sur l'opposition entre bien réel et bien apparent : ceci est bien sûr vrai pour les doctrines antiques perfectionnistes qui décrivent une forme de vie

36. Sur les différents types de justifications de la neutralité à l'égard des conceptions de la vie bonne : Ch. Korsgaard, « Commentary », *in* M. Nussbaum et A. Sen (eds), *op. cit.*, p. 54-61.

37. E. Picavet, *op. cit.*

bonne comme les doctrines socratiques, aristotéliciennes ou stoïciennes, mais c'est également vrai pour l'utilitarisme hédoniste classique ou pour les théories plus récentes des préférences *améliorées*. Lorsque de surcroît une doctrine prudentielle philosophique consiste, pour dire les choses simplement, à postuler que la condition du bonheur est l'activité philosophique elle-même, comme c'est le cas dans l'éthique stoïcienne par exemple, on voit l'écart qu'il peut y avoir entre les théories prudentielles substantielles et les démarches empiriques.

Mais l'écart est-il si grand ? Les mesures *subjectives* de la qualité de vie *subjective* sont supposées être neutres moralement et laisser une place à la diversité des formes de vie tout en permettant d'obtenir des résultats qui sont valides pour plusieurs individus différents. En réalité sous un aspect fondamental les échelles de mesure de la qualité de vie décrivent implicitement *une* forme de vie *bonne*. Dans le cas du VSP-A, les adverbes de fréquence qui constituent les modalités de réponse expriment des jugements de valeur implicites et l'échelle comporte un minimum et un maximum, ce qui signifie que le score maximum décrit une forme de vie *bonne*. Par inférence, cette forme de vie est en effet désirable et potentiellement recommandable.

De plus, comme nous l'avons signalé, l'instrument se décompose en dimensions sous lesquelles sont regroupées les questions. L'instrument permet d'obtenir un score pour chaque dimension, ce qui dessine un « profil », et également un score global appelé « index ». Or les dimensions ne sont pas hiérarchisées les unes par rapport aux autres : on ne peut poser un ordre entre les dimensions qui serait valable pour toute personne passant le test. Par conséquence, la dimension « bien-être physique » est supposée avoir ni plus ni moins d'importance que la dimension « relations amicales ». Mais le score global, ou « index », est obtenu en faisant la moyenne des scores des dimensions. Par conséquent, malgré sa neutralité affichée, l'instrument décrit implicitement *une* forme de vie bonne, où toutes les dimensions de l'existence sont d'égale importance.

D'autre part la méthode de « délibération » sur les valeurs prudentielles que propose Griffin pour établir la liste des valeurs prudentielles communément partagées ou la recherche spéculative des « vrais biens » entretiennent un air de famille avec les démarches de recherche qualitative destinées à faire émerger les items qui composeront les questionnaires de qualité de vie et à regrouper ces items sous des dimensions. Il s'agit en effet d'analyser le contenu d'interviews semi-dirigées sur la qualité de la vie avec des groupes de taille restreinte[38], de repérer les éléments récurrents, puis de regrouper ces éléments dans des ensembles signifiants qui sont porteurs de l'importance ou de la valeur. La dimension « relation avec les amis » qui constitue explicitement le « concept » de l'instrument, est ainsi ce qui a de la valeur aux yeux des individus. Par analogie, la dimension est à l'égard des items qui la composent ce qu'une fin est à ses moyens. En un sens, cette dimension relative aux amis n'est pas autre chose que la formulation dans une expression « neutre » d'une valeur prudentielle que l'on retrouve chez Griffin : avoir des relations personnelles *riches* et *profondes*. La méthode qui consiste à faire émerger le contenu du concept empirique de qualité de vie à partir de discours et de discussions entre individus, et la méthode d'analyse rationnelle philosophique ne sont donc pas si hermétiquement séparées que cela. Simplement, le pas supplémentaire à franchir en approche empirique serait d'inclure une forme de réflexion et de délibération dans ces groupes sur ce qui a, généralement, de la valeur prudentielle. Il ne s'agirait pas nécessairement d'une intervention extérieure paternaliste puisqu'il est possible d'instaurer des formes de débats et de délibération entre les membres d'un groupe[39] sans altérer la valeur des données obtenues.

38. La méthode employée pour le VSP-A est notamment celle des *focus groups*, dans l'objectif est de susciter la plus grande diversité possible de points de vue. Sur la méthode des *focus groups* en sciences sociales et psychologiques : David L. Morgan « Focus Groups », *Annual Review of Sociology*, vol. 22 (1996), p. 129-152.

39. Sur la diversité des méthodes de révélations des préférences et des jugements en recherche empirique en éthique de la santé, voir V. Clément et D. Serra , « L'équité en matière de santé : qu'en pense l'opinion publique ? Une revue de l'éthique empirique dans le champ de la santé », *Revue de philosophie économique*, 2009/1, vol. 10, p. 55-77. Les auteurs insistent sur l'intérêt des méthodes faisant appel à des *délibérations* de groupes *informés* qui permettent d'obtenir des jugements motivés et réfléchis : R. Cookson, « Incorporating psycho-social considerations into health valuation: an experimental study », *Journal of Health Economics*, 19, 2000, p. 369-401. Si les études disponibles portent sur les préférences *sociales* et non pas personnelles, et sur des jugements moraux relatifs notamment à des problèmes de justice distributive, il y a tout lieu de penser cependant que de telles méthodes

CONCLUSION

On peut remarquer d'une manière générale qu'un des enjeux centraux de la recherche empirique en qualité de vie liée à la santé rejoint un des problèmes majeur des théories philosophiques du bien-être : identifier les valeurs et les « biens réels », c'est-à-dire ce qui améliore *effectivement* la qualité de vie, mais qui soient effectivement les biens prudentiels *propres aux personnes*, et non pas des valeurs dogmatiquement ou paternellement imposées depuis l'extérieur (par des médecins ou des philosophes, même bienveillants). A ce titre, la distance entre philosophie et recherche empirique sur le thème de la qualité de vie, n'est pas si grande qu'on peut le penser à première vue. Nous montrons ainsi que des contributions positives de la philosophie morale sont possibles, par la confrontation des concepts et l'élargissement des problématiques, la critique des présupposés et l'imagination de nouvelles hypothèses et applications.

Si, comme nous le pensons, l'intrication du normatif et du descriptif propre au concept de qualité de vie justifie la circulation entre philosophie et approche empirique, alors, logiquement, une piste qui reste à explorer est de déterminer, dans ce qui fait varier la qualité de vie mesurée des patients, ce qui est le plus proche des activités décrites dans les doctrines philosophiques substantielles du bonheur. On peut ainsi penser à tout ce qui peut être décrit comme de l'adaptation, de la modification des préférences[40], des réévaluations de l'importance des domaines de l'existence ou la recherche de la connaissance *per se* qui apparaissent classiquement dans les doctrines philosophiques du bonheur. Dans la mesure où la qualité

seraient fructueuses pour les problèmes prudentiels, dans la mesure où comme le montre Griffin (*op. cit.*) les valeurs prudentielles ne sont pas purement individuelles et idiosyncratiques mais au contraire exprimées dans un langage commun, inscrites dans une forme de vie, et où les jugements que nous faisons sur notre bien-être sont formulés dans un langage « interpersonnel » : J. Griffin « Comment comparer la qualité de vies différentes ? » *in* M. Canto-Sperber (dir.), *La philosophie morale britannique*, Paris, PUF, 1994, p. 171-196.

40. Sur les enjeux des interventions sur la formation des préférences, T. Otterholt, « 'The Taste Approach' Governance Beyond Libertarian Paternalism », *Revue de philosophie économique* 11 (1), 2010, p. 57-80.

de vie a une place grandissante comme résultats des interventions de santé où la qualité de la vie est un concept en partie normatif qui est un objet propre de la réflexion philosophique, alors des applications préventives ou thérapeutiques indirectes des doctrines prudentielles philosophiques sont imaginables.

Recherches sur la philosophie et le langage 29 (2013)
194 p., ISBN : 978-2-7116-8410-6, p. 135-155, Vrin.

La mathématisation au cœur d'un différend entre science et philosophie

Raphaël SANDOZ*

RÉSUMÉ

C'est au sein de la philosophie que, durant des siècles, l'étude de la nature avait trouvé sa place : il eût donc paru logique qu'elle restât dans le giron de la communauté qui l'avait cultivée. Dès lors, on peut s'interroger au sujet des raisons ayant conduit la science à s'éloigner du creuset intellectuel qui l'avait engendrée. À cet égard, l'histoire nous révèle un élément qui n'est sans doute pas étranger à cette séparation, en nous apprenant que, dès la Renaissance, de profondes dissensions d'ordre méthodologique divisent les savants au sujet de la possibilité même de mathématiser les phénomènes empiriques.

Nous chercherons dans un premier temps à retracer les principaux traits de la polémique ayant accueilli l'introduction des mathématiques dans l'étude de la nature, en montrant comment elle a pu contribuer à aiguiller la science moderne sur une voie clairement distincte de celle que suivra la philosophie. Puis nous nous demanderons si cette démarche de mathématisation, si évidente

* Raphaël Sandoz est assistant à l'Université de Genève, et ses recherches portent sur les interrogations philosophiques liées à l'applicabilité des mathématiques aux sciences empiriques. Sa thèse de doctorat se propose de retracer l'histoire de cette problématique, en poursuivant l'objectif de clarifier le champ conceptuel propre à sous-tendre la réflexion contemporaine sur ce terrain.

pour le scientifique contemporain, ne serait pas néanmoins, aujourd'hui encore, en quête d'une légitimité plus difficile à conquérir sur le terrain philosophique.

ABSTRACT

For centuries, the study of nature had its place within philosophy: so, it would not have been surprising if theses activities had remained the privilege of the community who gave birth to them. Therefore, why did science part from its mother philosophy? In this respect, history gives us an interesting clue: as far back as the Renaissance, profound disagreements brought scholars into a methodological controversy about the possibility to mathematize natural phenomena and the relevance of such an approach.

At first, I plan to relate the main features of this much debated reception of the idea to import mathematics in the field of natural philosophy. My goal is to show that this controversy should have significantly contributed to methodologically separate science from philosophy. After that, I will ask if the mathematization way, although being an intrinsic part of contemporary sciences, couldn't nevertheless still remain in search of a philosophical justification, one that is not so obvious.

INTRODUCTION

Il ne saurait être question de réduire la ligne de démarcation, aujourd'hui très nette, qui distingue les activités du scientifique de celles du philosophe à la limite imprécise d'une simple frontière disciplinaire qui n'aurait d'autre origine que la spécialisation des savants. Car, loin de se distribuer de manière complémentaire dans un corps unifié de connaissances, la science et la philosophie entendent au contraire dans une large mesure circonscrire les spécificités et l'indépendance de leurs territoires respectifs à travers une opposition méthodologique réciproque. Celle-ci conditionne notamment, tant l'absence de tout recours aux mathématiques et à l'expérimentation dans la démarche des philosophes, que la réticence des scientifiques à s'intéresser aux questions métaphysiques liées à leurs investigations au sujet des phénomènes naturels.

Pourtant, c'est au sein même de la philosophie que, durant des siècles, l'étude de la nature avait trouvé sa place : nous aurions donc pu nous attendre à ce qu'elle restât dans le giron de la communauté qui l'avait cultivée, à l'instar de l'éthique ou de la métaphysique par exemple. Pourquoi la science a-t-elle été conduite à s'éloigner aussi résolument du creuset intellectuel qui l'avait engendré ? Si les raisons ayant été avancées pour rendre compte de cette divergence sont multiples, l'histoire nous révèle à cet égard un élément qu'il nous paraît important de prendre en considération, et méritant une analyse plus approfondie : dès la Renaissance, une polémique tournant autour de la possibilité de mathématiser les phénomènes naturels opposera deux communautés de savants se disputant le terrain de l'étude de la nature. En effet, au sein des institutions académiques, les professeurs de philosophie auront à faire face à la concurrence des mathématiciens, qui, empruntant à l'ingénierie certaines méthodes empiriques, prétendront établir un savoir au sujet des phénomènes naturels. Le différend méthodologique qui s'ensuivra alors entre les savants contribuera dans une large mesure à amorcer une opposition durable entre la philosophie naturelle et ce qui deviendra par la suite les sciences exactes, en les orientant sur des voies distinctes.

1. LES MATHÉMATIQUES ET L'ÉTUDE DE LA NATURE

Si elles nous paraissent aujourd'hui intervenir de manière parfaitement légitime dans les sciences expérimentales, les mathématiques n'ont historiquement trouvé leur place dans l'étude de la nature qu'au prix d'un effort soutenu de la part d'une communauté de savants ayant eu à défendre leur démarche face à de nombreux opposants, en particulier durant la Renaissance et les premiers siècles qui suivront.

Car, durant l'Antiquité, les activités amenant les mathématiques à entrer en contact avec les phénomènes physiques étaient essentiellement étrangères à l'étude scientifique de la nature. En effet, ni les premiers calculs astronomiques visant à utiliser le mouvement des astres comme horloge ou comme calendrier, ni les travaux des grands ingénieurs de l'antiquité comme Archimède ou Héron d'Alexandrie, n'avaient pour objectif d'expliquer les phénomènes naturels, visant plutôt à résoudre des problèmes concrets[1]. Ces pratiques utilitaires restaient principalement l'apanage des artisans, architectes et commerçants, lesquels avaient parfois recours à des calculs mathématiques ou à des considérations géométriques, qui pour fabriquer des pièces mécaniques, qui pour élever des monuments, et qui encore afin de déterminer le volume de ses tonneaux.

De ces pratiques utilitaires, il n'était donc pas question d'espérer tirer un savoir au sens noble du terme : c'est au contraire à la philosophie naturelle que revenait l'étude et l'explication des phénomènes physiques. Et celle-ci restera essentiellement qualitative, car selon la tradition aristotélicienne, qui dominera la pensée antique et médiévale, les mathématiques constituent un domaine du savoir indépendant de la philosophie naturelle, laquelle n'y aura guère recours pour expliquer les phénomènes[2].

1. De sorte que ce n'est que *méthodologiquement*, et non pas *téléologiquement*, que leur démarche peut s'apparenter à certaines pratiques du scientifique contemporain.

2. Comme l'indique notamment Sabine Rommevaux, la tradition aristotélicienne préconise une « séparation stricte entre les mathématiques et la philosophie naturelle, chacune devant s'appuyer sur ses propres principes et développer ses propres modes de validation », cf. *Mathématiques et connaissance du monde réel avant Galilée*, Montreuil, Omniscience, 2010, p. 9.

Ce n'est qu'à la Renaissance que la situation évoluera de manière significative, lorsque certains mathématiciens, ayant recours à des pratiques empiriques et expérimentales utilisées par les ingénieurs, prétendront instituer une science de la nature fondée sur la mathématisation des phénomènes, en s'appuyant sur des résultats issus de la mesure de grandeurs physiques. Initialement, ce sont surtout des raisons d'ordre sociologiques qui motiveront une telle démarche : en effet, à la Renaissance, les mathématiques souffrent d'un prestige inférieur à celui de la philosophie naturelle, ayant perdu durant le Moyen-Age une grande partie de la noblesse que la pensée antique leur avait conférée, en étant trop éloignées des préoccupations de la théologie. D'autre part, les premiers expérimentateurs, en général des ingénieurs ou des artisans, étaient pour ainsi dire exclus du monde savant. Dès lors, c'est essentiellement la perspective d'une promotion sociale et institutionnelle qui catalysera ce mouvement par lequel une partie importante de la communauté des mathématiciens sera progressivement conduite à se rapprocher sensiblement du terrain de l'expérimentation pour chercher à instituer en tant que science de la nature des activités qui seront par la suite regroupées sous le nom de *mathématiques mixtes*[3], fondées sur des calculs et des démonstrations impliquant des résultats de mesure en provenance de la mécanique, de l'optique et de l'astronomie.

Combinant astucieusement la rigueur démonstrative des mathématiques pures à des données issues de l'expérience, la méthode envisagée par ces *mathématiques mixtes* s'avérera idéale pour promouvoir les activités qui l'encadrent : en se rapprochant mutuellement, ces dernières pourront s'apporter un soutien réciproque qui contribuera à les affranchir de certains défauts qui leur étaient reprochés. Tandis que les mathématiciens tenteront de montrer que leurs travaux, à l'instar de ceux de la philosophie naturelle, peuvent conduire à l'acquisition de connaissances au sujet des phénomènes physiques, les expérimentateurs entendront, pour leur part, trouver dans la rigueur démonstrative des mathématiques de quoi conférer à leurs pratiques un caractère de certitude et de fiabilité qui leur était jusque-là contesté.

3. *Cf.* P. Dear, *Discipline and Experience : The Mathematical Way in the Scientific Revolution*, Chicago, University of Chicago Press, 1995.

S'il faudra attendre le début du XVIIe siècle pour que les *mathématiques mixtes* soient pleinement reconnues au niveau institutionnel, ce champ disciplinaire commence déjà à se former à la Renaissance, héritant des acquis de nombreux travaux bien antérieurs à la « révolution scientifique »[4]. Dès lors, ce ne sont pas tant les pratiques sur lesquelles repose ce domaine du savoir qui seront révolutionnaires, que l'idée qu'elles puissent sous-tendre une science visant à comprendre la nature[5], un objectif qui placera les *mathématiques mixtes* en rupture avec la démarche prônée par la philosophie naturelle inspirée de la tradition aristotélicienne. Appliquer les mathématiques à des problèmes concrets issus du monde physique n'est guère nouveau ; en revanche, c'est en détournant aux fins d'une étude scientifique de la nature des activités y étant auparavant étrangères, et en les introduisant au programme des institutions académiques, que ce domaine du savoir va se constituer de manière novatrice.

Car c'est bel et bien un statut semblable à celui des philosophes de la nature que vont revendiquer les partisans des *mathématiques mixtes*, qui promouvront intensément leurs activités, initialement surtout au sein des collèges jésuites. Au *Collegio Romano*, Christophe Clavius (1538-1612) est l'un des premiers à réclamer l'introduction de ce domaine de la connaissance au programme de l'enseignement, dans la perspective de l'instituer comme un champ disciplinaire autonome[6], bénéficiant d'un statut comparable à celui de la philosophie. À sa suite, nombreux seront ceux qui prendront la défense de cette branche du savoir : mentionnons en particulier Francis Bacon (1561-1626), dont l'ouvrage *Of the Proficience and Advancement of Learning* (1605)[7] baptise cette discipline au moyen de l'expression

4. *Cf.* W . R. Laird & S. Roux, *Mechanics and Natural Philosophy before scientific Revolution*, Londres, Springer, 2008.

5. Une idée néanmoins déjà défendue auparavant par quelques précurseurs isolés, tels que Roger Bacon, et assez courante chez les savants arabes médiévaux, en particulier Al-Biruni.

6. *Cf.* C. Clavius, « In disciplinas mathematicas prolegomena », *Opera mathematica*, Mayence, 1612.

7. F. Bacon, *Of the Proficience and The Advancement of Learning* (1605), éd. J. F. Dove, 1828. *Cf.* en particulier Livre II, VIII.

« mixed mathematics »[8], ou encore John Wilkins (1614-1672), qui en fait l'éloge dans son *Mathematical Magick* (1648)[9].

2. LA *QUAESTIO DE CERTITUDINE MATHEMATICARUM*

Or, ce n'est pas sans réagir que les philosophes de la nature accueilleront la prétention des mathématiciens et des ingénieurs à marcher ainsi sur leurs plates-bandes : dès la fin du XVIIe siècle, un débat polymorphe particulièrement virulent se développe autour des *mathématiques mixtes*, dont on attaque à la fois la pertinence, la fiabilité, la méthodologie et les fondements philosophiques. Dépassant rapidement une simple lutte de pouvoir entre des communautés s'affrontant pour promouvoir le statut de leurs activités, cette polémique, connue sous le nom de *Quaestio de certitudine mathematicarum*[10], s'étendra à de nombreuses questions ontologiques et épistémologiques tournant autour de la possibilité d'appliquer les mathématiques à l'étude de la nature. Les arguments philosophiques qui accompagneront ce mouvement de « scepticisme mathématique »[11], particulièrement subtils et acérés, exerceront en fin de compte sur la science moderne naissante une influence bénéfique, la contraignant à méditer sur ses fondements.

La controverse se focalisera en particulier sur les caractéristiques de la démonstration mathématique, et de l'usage qu'entendaient en faire les partisans des *mathématiques mixtes*. Prétendant intégrer des données empiriques à leurs démonstrations, leur démarche allait en effet à l'encontre des préceptes méthodologiques aristotéliciens. Car

8. Une terminologie qui sera employée jusqu'au XIXe siècle. *Cf.* G. Brown, « The Evolution of the Term *Mixed Mathematics* », *Journal of the History of Ideas*, vol. 52, n°1, 1991, p. 81-102.

9. J. Wilkins, *Mathematical Magick, or the Wonders that may be Performed by Mechanical Geometry* (1648), in *Mathematical and Philosophical Works of John Wilkins*, London, C. Whittingham, 1802.

10. *Cf.* P. Dear, *op. cit.* & P. Mancosu, *Philosophy of mathematics and mathematical practice in the seventeenth century*, Oxford, Oxford University Press, 1996.

11. *Cf.* L. Floridi, « Mathematical Skepticism », *in* J. R. M. Neto & R. H. Popkin (eds), *Skepticism in Renaissance and Post-Renaissance Thought : New Interpretations*, New York, Prometheus, 2004.

même si le Stagirite n'exclut pas que les mathématiques puissent parfois servir d'auxiliaire dans l'étude de la nature, ce n'est en aucun cas de la façon préconisée par les *mathématiques mixtes*. En particulier, il ne saurait être question d'espérer établir un savoir à partir de résultats numériques issus de la mesure de grandeurs observables : la science ne s'acquiert en aucun cas par la considération de particuliers. Ce n'est qu'à travers l'étude de la *forme* des corps (par opposition à leur *matière*) que les mathématiques peuvent être amenées à jouer, dans l'étude de la nature, un rôle tout à fait subalterne, et indépendant de l'expérience concrète : « Jusqu'à quel point le physicien doit-il connaître la forme ? N'est-ce pas dans la mesure où le médecin connaît les tendons ? »[12]. De même que l'anatomie, n'indiquant pas comment soigner les maladies, ne saurait être substituée à la médecine, les mathématiques, incapables d'expliquer les phénomènes, constituent un domaine d'étude distinct de la philosophie naturelle.

Car Aristote considère que l'explication des phénomènes ne peut passer que par des démonstrations procédant des causes aux effets, mais jamais l'inverse. Cette prescription méthodologique découle de son importante distinction entre le « syllogisme du fait » (τοῦ ὅτι) et le « syllogisme du pourquoi du fait » (τοῦ διότι) : tandis que le premier se contente d'établir comment les choses sont, le second, sur lequel repose la science, a pour vocation de nous expliquer le *pourquoi* des phénomènes. Or, c'est l'ordre dans lequel la cause et l'effet prennent place au sein de la démonstration qui détermine son statut :

> Dans les cas où les moyens termes ne sont pas réciproques et où le terme plus connu est celui qui n'est pas cause, c'est le fait qui est démontré, et non le pourquoi. […] Exemple : quand on démontre la sphéricité de la Lune par les accroissements de sa lumière. Si, en effet, ce qui augmente ainsi est sphérique, et si la Lune augmente, il est clair qu'elle est sphérique. Énoncé de cette façon, on obtient un syllogisme portant sur le fait, mais si la position du moyen est renversée, on aura un syllogisme du pourquoi : car ce n'est pas en

12. Aristote, *Physique*, livre II, 194b, trad. A. Stevens, Paris, Vrin, 1999.

raison de ses accroissements que la Lune est sphérique, mais c'est parce qu'elle est sphérique qu'elle prend de tels accroissements[13].

De sorte qu'il n'est pas question d'inférer à partir de données mesurées des lois mathématiques censées fournir l'explication des phénomènes physiques. Certes, il restera possible, notamment en astronomie, de déduire des conséquences mesurables à partir de prémisses faisant intervenir des considérations mathématiques, en s'appuyant par exemple sur la circularité, reconnue parfaite, des orbites des corps célestes – accrochés à leurs sphères de cristal – pour calculer la position des astres lors d'une éclipse. Par contre, le processus inverse ne sera en aucun cas légitime, et il ne sera pas question, par exemple, de chercher à déterminer la forme de la trajectoire des planètes à partir d'un ensemble de mesures empiriques de leurs positions respectives, comme le fera Kepler bien plus tard. C'est pourquoi la physique aristotélicienne restera essentiellement qualitative, privilégiant dans sa démarche les démonstrations τοῦ διότι orientées vers la recherche des quatre causes.

La classification aristotélicienne des mécanismes démonstratifs sera élargie par la suite par Averroès, qui introduira, à côté des syllogismes du fait et du pourquoi du fait (que les médiévaux nommeront *demonstratio quia* et *demonstratio propter quid*), un nouveau type de preuve : la démonstration *potissima*, qui réunit les deux autres en fournissant à la fois la connaissance du fait et des raisons qui le sous-tendent (*simul et quia et propter quid*)[14]. Ce dernier type de démonstration, le plus complet, deviendra progressivement un idéal pour les savants médiévaux, et restera jusqu'à la Renaissance un incontournable canon de la méthode scientifique, par sa capacité à fournir le plus haut degré de certitude tout en étant capable d'exhiber la cause formelle des phénomènes.

Or, c'est autour de cette pierre angulaire méthodologique que se focaliseront les critiques des détracteurs des *mathématiques mixtes* qui, niant le caractère *potissima* des démonstrations de cette discipline, lui

13. Aristote, *Seconds Analytiques*, I, §13, 78b, trad. J. Tricot, réimpr. Paris, Vrin, 2000.

14. *Cf.* R. Glasner, *Averroes' Physics. A Turning Point in Medieval Natural Philosophy*, Oxford, Oxford University Press, 2009, voir en particulier le chapitre 8.6 : « The divorce between mathematics and physics », p. 162.

contesteront le statut d'une science à part entière. Parmi eux, Alessandro Piccolomini (1508-1579), professeur de philosophie à l'*Accademia degli Infiammati* de Padoue, affirme que les mathématiques, tant *pures* que *mixtes*, sont étrangères au régime des causes, et par conséquent tout à fait incapables d'expliquer les phénomènes réels : « le mathématicien n'est pas en mesure de démontrer les causes efficientes et finales »[15]. Ceci provient essentiellement du fait que les mathématiques n'entretiennent aucun rapport avec les substances, la quantité n'étant, suivant l'interprétation averroïste, qu'un simple 'accident' de la matière :

> La matière est par sa propre nature dépourvue de toute forme substantielle, et néanmoins elle peut recevoir toutes les formes possibles : donc aucune quantité ou figure déterminée n'y est intrinsèquement attachée[16].

Si les mathématiques parviennent à un tel degré de certitude, c'est précisément parce que les entités sur lesquelles elles portent sont séparées des substances. Mais c'est aussi ce qui les distingue des objets et phénomènes étudiés par la philosophie naturelle, dont les causes restent hors de portée des mathématiques, tant *pures* que *mixtes*. À côté de ce problème, les *mathématiques mixtes* rencontrent une difficulté plus aiguë encore, qui leur est spécifique : en entendant déduire des vérités universelles (lois mathématiques des phénomènes) à partir de faits particuliers (résultats de mesure), elles reposent sur une démarche opposée à celle de la démonstration *potissima*, dont les prémisses doivent au contraire être plus générales que les conclusions, et devant procéder par inférence des effets à partir des causes, et jamais l'inverse comme c'est le cas avec les *mathématiques mixtes*. Piccolomini reconnaît toutefois l'utilité de ce domaine du savoir ; c'est sur la scientificité des pratiques auxquelles il a recours que porte sa critique.

S'opposant radicalement aux critiques de Piccolomini, le mathématicien Pietro Catena (1501-1576) envisagera pour défendre sa discipline une stratégie inspirée par une lecture platonicienne des *Seconds analytiques* d'Aristote, qu'il développera dans trois ouvrages

15. A. Piccolomini, *Commentarium de Certitudine Mathematicarum Disciplinarum*, Rome, Asulanum, 1547, f. cIIv.

16. A. Piccolomini, *Parte Prima della Filosofia Naturale*, Venice, 1576, p. 42.

touchant aux statuts hiérarchiques respectifs des mathématiques et de la philosophie, et aux relations entre ces disciplines : *Universa loca in logicam Aristotelis in mathematicas disciplinas*, *Super loca mathematica contenta in Topicis et Elenchis Aristotelis* et *Oratio pro Idea Methodi.* Niant que la connaissance puisse être obtenue par abstraction à partir de particuliers, il considère qu'elle préexiste dans notre intellect, envisageant dès lors les entités mathématiques comme des universaux[17]. Selon lui, alors qu'il est possible de prendre connaissance des phénomènes physiques par le moyen des sens, les entités mathématiques, relevant exclusivement du domaine de l'âme, ne peuvent être connues que par la raison[18]. Adhérant à la théorie platonicienne de la réminiscence, Catena réduit le rôle que peut jouer la perception sensorielle dans l'acquisition du savoir mathématique à celui de la réactivation d'une connaissance préexistante dans l'intellect[19].

Chaque particulier participe dès lors à une nature mathématique universelle, sans pour autant s'y réduire, car il contient en plus de cette essence universelle des caractères spécifiques par lesquels il s'en distingue en tant que particulier. La science réside alors essentiellement dans l'*application d'universels intelligibles à des particuliers*, une opération par laquelle on transforme la *re*connaissance en connaissance véritable. Pour illustrer sa position, Catena s'appuie sur un exemple que l'on trouve chez Aristote, celui du triangle de bronze : il est possible de reconnaître la participation de cet objet à l'universel triangle en remarquant que la somme de ses angles est égale à deux droits. Pour ce faire, l'esprit exclut graduellement certaines de ses propriétés (par exemple le fait qu'il soit en bronze) jusqu'à ne garder que ce sans quoi cette propriété de la somme des angles disparaît. Ce qui reste nécessaire pour que soient conservées les propriétés du triangle constitue alors l'universel lui-même, considéré comme une pure forme mentale.

Dès lors, Catena est en mesure de défendre l'intérêt des *mathématiques mixtes* pour connaître la nature. D'une part, les universaux que constituent les entités mathématiques s'avèrent

17. P. Catena, *Universa loca in logicam Aristotelis in mathematicas disciplinas*, 1556, p. 197.

18. *Ibid.*, p. 191.

19. *Ibid.*, p. 200.

nécessaires pour nous mener à une connaissance véritable des particuliers, et c'est en cela que les mathématiques sont utiles à la découverte de connaissances nouvelles au sujet du monde réel. Et d'autre part, il est possible de reconnaître à partir des particuliers, par le truchement de la réminiscence, des vérités générales et universelles. Dès lors, le recours à l'expérience se justifie puisqu'elle peut jouer un rôle important dans la mise en place de théories rationnelles. Elle est utile à la connaissance sur un plan heuristique : elle intervient dans la redécouverte, via la réminiscence, d'un savoir scientifique général et universel préexistant dans l'intellect.

Appuyant Catena dans sa défense des *mathématiques mixtes*, l'architecte italien Giacomo Barozzi[20] (1537-1604) considère également que la plupart des démonstrations mathématiques sont *potissimae*, tout en reconnaissant néanmoins que certaines ne le sont pas, en particulier les preuves par l'absurde. En adhérant lui aussi à une conception néo-platonicienne mettant les entités mathématiques au nombre des idées parfaites pré-existant dans l'entendement, il place la science qui les étudie au dessus de la philosophie, en considérant, à l'instar de Proclus, que l'organisation hiérarchique des différentes branches du savoir doit refléter la perfection de leurs objets d'étude respectifs. Dès lors, au sein de ce classement, « la théologie tient la première place, les mathématiques la seconde et la philosophie naturelle la troisième »[21]. Barozzi revendique ainsi pour les mathématiques, tant *pures* que *mixtes*, un statut hiérarchique supérieur à celui de la philosophie naturelle.

La réponse des philosophes à cette provocation passera par une argumentation visant à nier purement et simplement la scientificité des mathématiques, tant *pures* que *mixtes*. En particulier, le métaphysicien jésuite Benito Pereira (1535-1610), soutenant Piccolomini, affirme que les mathématiques ne constituent pas une science véritable :

> À mon avis, les disciplines mathématiques ne sont pas véritablement des sciences. [...] Avoir la science de quelque chose, c'est avoir connaissance de la cause qui rend compte de l'existence

20. Davantage connu sous le nom de Vignole.

21. F. Barozzi, *Opusculum, in quo una Oratio, & duae Quaestiones: altera de certitudine, & altera de medietate Mathematicarum continentur*, Padoue, 1560, c. 38v, p. 129.

> de cette chose ; la science repose sur la démonstration des effets à partir des causes. Or, la démonstration (je parle de la démonstration la plus parfaite) doit se fonder sur les choses étant en elles-mêmes propres à produire l'effet démontré ; en effet, les choses accidentelles sont exclues des démonstrations parfaites. Mais le mathématicien ne considère ni l'essence de la quantité, ni ne traite des attributs qui procèdent de son essence, ni ne les déclare causes sur la base de ce en quoi ils appartiennent à la quantité, et ses démonstrations ne reposent pas sur des prédicats essentiels, mais accidentels. De sorte que la doctrine mathématique n'est pas à proprement parler une science[22].

De plus, considérant que l'existence et la nécessité des sens contredit de manière évidente la théorie de la réminiscence platonicienne, Pereira s'oppose aux conceptions défendues par Catena et Barozzi, niant que les entités mathématiques puissent être innées[23]. Dès lors, suivant une voie aristotélicienne, Pereira considère que seule une physique qualitative est à même de fournir des démonstrations *potissimae*. En effet, abstraites à partir de la matière sensible, les entités mathématiques sont complètement disjointes des essences métaphysiques, dont la recherche est pourtant le propre de la philosophie naturelle. La quantité et la substance sont donc deux choses très différentes, et l'étude de la première ne saurait être assimilée à la recherche des causes, qui appartient à la seconde. Dès lors, les démonstrations mathématiques, incapables d'expliquer le pourquoi des phénomènes, ne peuvent en aucun cas être qualifiées de *potissimae*, comme l'illustre Pereira au moyen d'un exemple tiré de la géométrie :

> Le géomètre prouve que le triangle a trois angles égaux à deux droits sur la base du fait que l'angle extérieur résultant de la prolongation des côtés de ce triangle est égal aux deux angles opposés du même triangle. Qui ne voit pas que ce n'est pas la cause (l'explication) de cette propriété qui est démontrée ?[24]

22. B. Pereira, *De communibus omnium rerum naturalium principiis et affectionibus libri quindecim*, Rome, 1576, p. 24.

23. *Ibid.*, 86 col. b, De Pace, p. 94, §166.

24. *Ibid.*, 26 cols. a-b, De Pace, p. 90, §154.

En d'autres termes, les démonstrations mathématiques ne nous indiquent pas plus la cause des phénomènes naturels que ne le font les figures sur lesquelles on s'appuie pour les illustrer. Ces considérations amènent Pereira à établir une distinction claire entre la *certitude* et la *scientificité*, cette dernière caractéristique ne s'appliquant pas aux démonstrations mathématiques.

À la suite de Pereira, la problématique de la « démonstration par les causes » s'élargit rapidement à la question du pouvoir explicatif des mathématiques, en particulier à l'égard des phénomènes naturels. Soulignons que les savants de cette époque ne voyaient guère d'alternative à une notion de l'explication scientifique intrinsèquement liée à la recherche des causes. Ceci étant, un nombre croissant de savants souligneront l'incapacité des mathématiques à expliquer le *pourquoi* des choses, notamment Rivaltus, qui, dans son célèbre commentaire de l'œuvre d'Archimède, déclare :

> Les géomètres ne nous parlent pas de la cause d'une chose, mais de la cause de notre connaissance de la chose. En effet, ils croient qu'il est suffisant de montrer qu'une chose est ce qu'elle est, sans se demander par quoi elle l'est[25].

Une opinion à laquelle se ralliera également Pierre Gassendi (1592-1655) qui, reprenant la construction géométrique au sujet du triangle évoquée par Pereira, renchérit en affirmant que celle-ci n'explique absolument rien : elle se contente en effet de rendre apparent aux yeux de l'esprit ce qui ne l'était pas auparavant, ce qui revient, selon ses termes, « à ouvrir une boîte fermée »[26].

Face à ces virulentes attaques, les mathématiciens seront contraints de prendre au sérieux ces difficultés. Plusieurs d'entre eux tâcheront d'y remédier : on trouve notamment chez Giuseppe Biancani (1566-1624), un disciple de Clavius, une tentative de réponse aux critiques philosophiques évoquées. Admettant tout d'abord avec Barozzi qu'il est nécessaire de distinguer les preuves causales de celles qui ne le sont pas (telles que les démonstrations par l'absurde), il entreprend, dans un ouvrage intitulé *De mathemati-*

25. D. Rivaltus, *Archimedis opera quae extant novis demonstrationibus commentariisque illustrata*, « Quadrature de la parabole », *Scholium*, 1615.

26. *Cf.* B. Rochot, « Gassendi et les mathématiques », *Revue d'histoire des sciences*, vol. 10, 1957, p. 71.

carum natura dissertatio[27], de classer les théorèmes du premier livre des *Éléments* d'Euclide selon le caractère causal ou non-causal de leurs démonstrations. Or, Biancani reconnaît nombre d'entre elles comme étant causales : par exemple la proposition 1.1 des *Éléments*, qui démontre comment un segment donné permet de construire un triangle équilatéral. Qui plus est, les démonstrations causales ne sont nullement cantonnées aux mathématiques *pures*, elles s'avèrent bien souvent parfaitement capables de fournir aux sciences de la nature certaines des causes requises dans l'explication des phénomènes physiques : Biancani affirme à cet égard que l'optique géométrique permet de fournir à la physiologie de l'œil les causes nécessaires à l'explication des modifications de formes que subit cet organe au cours de la vision[28]. Soulignons toutefois que ce ne sont que les causes formelles et matérielles qui sont invitées à jouer un rôle dans les démonstrations mathématiques, mais en aucun cas les causes efficientes et finales.

À la suite de ces discussions concernant le statut des démonstrations mathématiques, de nombreux mathématiciens s'intéresseront au problème de la causalité des preuves, et tenteront d'y remédier à travers le développement d'approches méthodologiques nouvelles[29]. L'une des principales stratégies utilisées consistera à tenter de remplacer les preuves indirectes (en particulier les démonstrations par l'absurde) par des preuves mathématiques directes et causales, ayant la prétention d'être explicatives. Mentionnons à cet égard les importantes contributions de Cavalieri, Torricelli, Barrow et Guldin.

LES *MATHÉMATIQUES MIXTES* EN CONCURRENCE AVEC LA PHILOSOPHIE NATURELLE

S'il y avait, avant la Renaissance, une coexistence pacifique entre les philosophes de la nature, les mathématiciens, et les ingénieurs, chacune de ces communautés travaillant de manière essentiellement

27. G. Biancani, *De mathematicarum natura dissertatio*, Bologne, 1615.

28. *Ibid.*, p. 29-31.

29. *Cf.* E. Grosholz, Emily, et H. Breger, *The growth of mathematical knowledge*, Springer, 2000, p. 110.

autonome et indépendante des autres, la polémique que nous venons d'évoquer marque le début d'une profonde restructuration disciplinaire de ces domaines du savoir. Du rapprochement des mathématiciens et des ingénieurs naîtra une corporation de savants entendant étudier les phénomènes naturels à travers une démarche s'opposant fondamentalement à celle des philosophes de la nature. Cette concurrence amorce un conflit qui contribuera à orienter dans des directions divergentes deux méthodes opposées d'investigation des phénomènes naturels, dont l'une conduira aux sciences exactes que l'on connaît aujourd'hui, tandis que l'autre, tout en persistant durant encore près de trois siècles, sera progressivement désertée par les philosophes, même s'ils n'abandonneront jamais totalement la réflexion dans ce domaine.

Comme on l'imagine, la polémique de la *certitude mathématique* dont nous avons parlé plus haut contribue fortement à durcir les relations entre la communauté des philosophes de la nature et les praticiens des *mathématiques mixtes*, comme l'illustre par exemple ce passage de Clavius :

> Il serait bon que les professeurs de philosophie s'abstiennent de traiter de ces questions qui n'aident pas à la compréhension des choses naturelles et portent atteinte à l'autorité des disciplines mathématiques aux yeux des étudiants, en particulier lorsqu'ils enseignent que les sciences mathématiques ne sont pas des sciences, n'ont pas de démonstrations, *etc.* L'expérience nous montre que l'étude de ces questions constitue un sérieux obstacle aux étudiants et ne leur rend aucun service, surtout parce que les professeurs qui les enseignent ne peuvent s'empêcher de tourner ces sciences en ridicule[30].

Ce climat conflictuel incitera les partisans des *mathématiques mixtes*, qui s'efforcent initialement d'établir un contact avec les philosophes de la nature et de répondre à leurs arguments, à s'éloigner progressivement des débats métaphysiques. De sorte

30. C. Clavius, dans un mémorandum intitulé *Modus quo disciplinae mathematicae in scholis Societatis possent promoveri* (1580). *Cf.* A. C. Crombie, « Mathematics and Platonism in the Sixteenth-century Italian Universities and in Jesuit Educational Policy », *in* Y. Maeyama and W. G. Saltzer, (eds), *Prismata*, Wiesbaden, Franz Steiner Verlag, 1977, p. 66.

qu'une volonté d'autonomie vis-à-vis de la philosophie accompagnera le développement de cette communauté scientifique naissante, ainsi qu'on le remarque déjà chez les pionniers de la mathématisation de la physique : Galilée, par exemple, ne se positionne guère au sujet de la polémique que nous avons évoquée plus haut, dont on sait pourtant qu'il était informé[31], ayant probablement lu Pereira, et possédant même un exemplaire de l'*Opusculum* de Barozzi[32]. Une quête d'indépendance du même ordre conduira Newton à tenter d'éviter tout recours à des hypothèses métaphysiques dans ses théories.

Cette rivalité entre les praticiens des *mathématiques mixtes* et les philosophes de la nature persistera, de façon plus ou moins explicite, durant les premiers siècles qui suivront la Renaissance, même si de nombreux échanges, forts bénéfiques, auront lieu malgré tout entre ces communautés. En effet, si, jusqu'au XIXe siècle, de nombreux philosophes de la nature s'opposent à la mathématisation de leur domaine d'étude, il en est d'autres qui, au contraire, s'efforcent de s'inspirer de cette méthode qu'ils jugent fructueuse. Descartes en particulier, qui a bénéficié, durant ses années d'études au collège jésuite de la Flèche, d'une initiation aux *mathématiques mixtes*, tente d'introduire en philosophie la rigueur démonstrative des mathématiques. Pensons également à la présentation géométrique adoptée dans certains traités philosophiques, tels que l'*Éthique* de Spinoza, ou encore à la tentative de Wolff d'appliquer la méthode des mathématiques à toutes les branches du savoir. Toutefois, malgré les travaux de ces savants favorables à la mathématisation, cette démarche rencontre un fort mouvement d'opposition parmi les philosophes, qui persiste au moins jusqu'au milieu du XIXe siècle. Car en dépit des remarquables succès pratiques que connaîtront les *mathématiques mixtes*, elles mettront plusieurs siècles avant de supplanter institutionnellement la philosophie naturelle. En effet, il faudra attendre le milieu du XIXe siècle pour que les activités appartenant à

31. *Cf.* R. Feldhay, « The use and abuse of mathematical entities : Galileo and the Jesuits revisited », *in* P. K. Machamer, *The Cambridge Companion to Galileo*, Cambridge, Cambridge University Press, 1998, p. 127.

32. *Cf.* A. Favaro, « La libreria di Galileo Galilei descritta ed illustrata » (1886), in *Bulletino di Bibliographia e di Storia delle Scienze Mathematiche e Fisiche*, XIX, Maggio-Giugno, p. 219-293.

ce domaine du savoir finissent par se distribuer progressivement entre une physique qui intégrera enfin des branches comme la mécanique et l'optique, et les *mathématiques appliquées*, qui auront à se construire à partir des scories laissées par la physique dans cette intégration.

Auparavant, les *mathématiques mixtes* auront à coexister avec une physique qualitative qui, tout en acceptant volontiers la démarche expérimentale, entend néanmoins rester dépourvue de mathématiques. Et durant trois siècles, les praticiens d'une telle philosophie de la nature, des savants tels que Castel, Goussier, De Marivetz, ou encore Demonville, continueront à s'insurger contre ce mouvement de mathématisation de la physique, dont ils contestent la légitimité [33]. C'est ainsi que, critiquant la physique newtonienne [34], le savant jésuite Louis-Bertrand Castel (1688-1757) s'exclame :

> Y a-t-il donc-là aucune sorte de *Démonstration* ou d'*Explication* ? Pour moi, je veux croire jusqu'à un plus amplement informé, que c'est-là en effet une *Démonstration, Mathématique s'entend* : mais j'ai bien de la peine à y découvrir une *Démonstration physique*, & une sorte d'*Explication* [35].

Aussi tardivement qu'au milieu du XIXe siècle, d'importantes frictions opposeront encore les partisans d'une philosophie naturelle qualitative à ceux qui pratiquent une physique mathématisée, comme l'illustre notamment la virulente critique du savant français Antoine-Louis Guénard Demonville (1779-1850) à l'encontre des travaux de Poisson dans ce passage du *Vrai système du monde* :

> M. Poisson, cet illustre Savant, malheureusement ne sait pas douter : sa foi est entière, aveugle. Je respecte tout-à-fait sa crédulité pour Copernic, Newton, Laplace, et j'apprécie sa franchise comme celle de M. Bouvard. Ce sont les seuls dans l'académie qui jugent ma théorie insoutenable : M. Bouvard, par habitude et par affection à des idées qu'il a caressées près d'un siècle ; M. Poisson, par monomanie mathématique, et n'étant pas homme à admettre aucune

33. *Cf.* Yves Gingras, « What did mathematics do to physics ? », *History of Science*, vol. 39, 2001, p. 383-416.

34. *Cf.* Donald S. Schier, *Louis-Bertrand Castel, anti-Newtonian scientist*, Iowa, 1941.

35. Louis-Bertrand Castel, *Le vrai système de physique générale de Newton*, Paris, 1753, p. 97.

> vérité nouvelle, s'il n'en peut dénicher l'esquisse dans un de ses axiomes d'algèbre. C'est un parti pris, arrêté pour toujours, ceci le regarde ; mais sous combien d'erreurs ne s'efforcera-t-il pas de nous étouffer en vidant son magasin de formules ! Je m'en rapporte à ceux qui connaissent sa Théorie mathématique de la chaleur. M. Poisson est un grand mathématicien. Celui qui ne sait pas douter ne sera jamais qu'un pauvre physicien[36].

Tout au long de la période qui sépare la Renaissance du XIXe siècle, de vives tensions diviseront ainsi deux communautés de savants prétendant étudier la nature d'une manière fondamentalement différente, en opposition sur le terrain de la mathématisation. Ce n'est qu'au cours du XIXe siècle que la philosophie naturelle qualitative s'essoufflera, pour disparaître progressivement vers la fin du siècle, cédant enfin pleinement la place aux sciences mathématisées que nous connaissons à présent.

3. LA SCIENCE A-T-ELLE COMPLÈTEMENT REMPLACÉ LA PHILOSOPHIE NATURELLE ?

Au terme de ces considérations historiques, nous pouvons nous demander à présent si la science mathématisée que nous connaissons aujourd'hui a totalement remplacé la philosophie naturelle d'antan. Le différend ayant orienté jadis la science et la philosophie dans des directions différentes n'aurait-il pas laissé dans son sillage un domaine de réflexion resté en jachère, que l'épistémologue contemporain pourrait tenter de reconquérir, au moins partiellement ? En particulier, la progressive désertion du terrain de l'étude de la nature par les philosophes n'aurait-elle pas laissé orphelins certains des objectifs que poursuivaient les savants d'autrefois ?

Comme nous l'avons montré, les philosophes de la nature du XVIIe siècle n'ont pas, de façon soudaine, modifié radicalement leurs pratiques pour y inclure des mathématiques ; bien au contraire, ils se sont montrés en général réticents au changement, en restant très attachés à la tradition aristotélicienne. La « révolution scientifique »

36. Antoine-Louis Guénard Demonville, *Vrai système du Monde* (1837), Deuxième partie, « Avis de l'auteur ».

ne provient donc pas tant d'un brusque revirement méthodologique de ceux-ci que d'une conquête du terrain de l'étude de la nature par des savants provenant de communautés y étant auparavant étrangères, celles des mathématiciens et des ingénieurs, qui y importeront de nouvelles façons de travailler. Or, ce changement de propriétaire a-t-il vraiment pu se faire sans introduire la moindre rupture téléologique, comme le prétendaient les partisans des *mathématiques mixtes* ? Il est permis d'en douter, car c'est là justement ce qu'ont contesté les opposants à la mathématisation durant plus de trois siècles ; le cœur de leur critique ne visant pas tant l'efficacité des *mathématiques mixtes* à résoudre des problèmes concrets que leur adéquation à un objectif auquel elles ne leur semblaient pas destinées : celui d'*expliquer* les phénomènes naturels.

On peut donc se demander dans quelle mesure cette critique pourrait rester pertinente aujourd'hui. Car même si l'efficacité pratique de la physique mathématisée est à présent incontestable, cela n'implique pas pour autant que les objectifs qu'elle s'efforce d'atteindre sont vraiment les mêmes que ceux que poursuivait autrefois la philosophie naturelle. En particulier, la question de savoir si les mathématiques sont en mesure d'*expliquer* les phénomènes naturels reste controversée à l'heure actuelle[37] ; tous les philosophes des sciences ne leur accordent pas un tel pouvoir, certains d'entre eux affirmant qu'elles ne jouent en physique qu'un rôle descriptif, voire même purement instrumental. Par ailleurs, si la méthodologie de la philosophie naturelle d'autrefois est sans aucun doute largement dépassée, rien n'indique en revanche que les objectifs qui étaient les siens ne puissent pas conserver aujourd'hui l'intérêt qu'ils avaient jadis. Certains arguments de ceux qui se sont autrefois opposés à la mathématisation de l'étude de la nature pourraient donc rester pertinents ; il convient dès lors de ne pas les reléguer trop rapidement aux oubliettes de l'histoire des sciences.

Ces considérations invitent le philosophe contemporain à repenser sa relation aux sciences exactes. En particulier, il convient

37. *Cf.* A. Baker, « Are there genuine mathematical explanations of physical phenomena ? », *Mind*, 114, 2005, p. 223-238, ainsi que O. Bueno & S. French, « Can mathematics explain physical phenomena ? », *British Journal for the Philosophy of Science* 63 (1), 2012, p. 85-113.

d'analyser le glissement *téléologique* qui a pu se produire lorsque la philosophie naturelle a passé le témoin aux *mathématiques mixtes* afin de mettre en évidence les questions relatives à l'étude de la nature qui reviennent en droit, encore aujourd'hui, à la philosophie plutôt qu'à la science. En inscrivant sa réflexion au sujet de la nature dans une relation de complémentarité, et non de subordination, à celle de la science, le philosophe d'aujourd'hui évitera la tentation d'essayer d'imiter la démarche de mathématisation des sciences exactes, pour se concentrer au contraire sur les questions qui échappent à cette méthode d'investigation des phénomènes naturels.

Recherches sur la philosophie et le langage 29 (2013)
192 p., ISBN : 978-2-7116-8410-6, p. 157-175, Vrin.

Philosophie, mathématiques et faits scientifiques chez Wittgenstein

Pierre FASULA*

RÉSUMÉ

Le but de cet article est de montrer qu'on ne peut se contenter de poser la question des rapports entre philosophie et science sous le seul angle de leur distinction ou de la réduction de l'une à l'autre. La philosophie de Wittgenstein est, de ce point de vue, particulièrement intéressante : quand bien même elle repose sur une distinction nette entre philosophie et science, on y trouve aussi et surtout l'affimation d'une analogie entre le raisonnement philosophique et celui des mathématiques, ainsi que la description d'un usage possible des faits établis par la science dans la clarification des concepts.

ABSTRACT

The aim of this article is to show that one cannot content oneself with understanding the problem of the relation between philosophy and science as a problem of distinction or reduction. From this

* Pierre Fasula, ATER à Paris 1 (2011-2013), a soutenu une thèse sous la direction de Ch. Chauviré, intitulée « Musil, Wittgenstein : l'homme du possible » (le 13 avril 2013).

point de view, Wittgenstein's philosophy specially is interesting: even if it rests upon a very clear distinction between philosophy and science, one can find in it the idea of an analogy between the philosophical reasoning and the mathematical reasoning, as well as the description of a possible use of scientific facts in the clarification of the concepts.

INTRODUCTION

Le but de cet article est de montrer qu'on ne peut se contenter de poser la question des rapports entre philosophie et science sous le seul angle de leur distinction ou de la réduction de l'une à l'autre. La philosophie de Wittgenstein est, de ce point de vue, particulièrement intéressante, quand bien même elle repose sur une distinction nette entre philosophie et science. Elle pose en effet deux questions essentielles : tout d'abord, à supposer que les mathématiques ne soient pas une science (au sens d'une description du réel) mais une méthode logique, n'y a-t-il pas une parenté entre la philosophie et les mathématiques ? Ensuite, à supposer que la philosophie ne soit pas une théorie mais une activité, quel usage peut-elle faire des faits établis par la science ?

1. LA DISTINCTION ENTRE PHILOSOPHIE ET SCIENCE. LE STATUT DES PROPOSITIONS LOGIQUES ET DES JEUX DE LANGAGE.

Il est vrai que la distinction entre philosophie et science est particulièrement nette chez Wittgenstein, et ce, quelle que soit la période considérée. Prenons l'un de ses premiers textes sur la question, les propositions 4. 11 *sq* du *Tractatus*. D'emblée, la distinction est affirmée :

> 4. 111 – La philosophie n'est pas une science de la nature.
> (Le mot « philosophie » doit signifier quelque chose qui est au-dessus ou au-dessous des sciences de la nature, mais pas à leur côté) [1].

La science de la nature est en effet définie ici comme la totalité des propositions vraies et se caractérise par le fait qu'elle propose des théories, alors que « la philosophie se compose essentiellement d'éclaircissements »[2]. Mais, pourrait-on objecter, pourquoi ces éclaircissements ne pourraient-ils pas être scientifiques ? Ce serait

1. L. Wittgenstein, *Tractatus logico-philosophicus*, Paris, Gallimard, 1993, trad. fr. G.-G. Granger, p. 57.

2. *Ibid.*

croire que Wittgenstein soutient l'idée suivante : les éclaircissements philosophiques sont des propositions qui ne sont pas et ne peuvent pas être scientifiques – ce que l'on chercherait alors à discuter. En réalité, sa position est bien plus radicale : le terme d'« éclaircissement » ne désigne pas tant un type de propositions, vraies ou fausses, établies ou non par la science, qu'un type d'action. C'est en ce sens qu'il faut comprendre son affirmation selon laquelle « la philosophie n'est pas une théorie mais une activité »[3], ce qu'il explique ainsi : « Le résultat de la philosophie n'est pas de produire des "propositions philosophiques", mais de rendre claires les propositions. »[4] Mais là encore, ne pourrait-on pas objecter que l'activité philosophique de clarification utilise des propositions pour en clarifier d'autres ? Dans la perspective du *Tractatus*, ce serait le rôle des propositions logiques, dans celle des *Recherches philosophiques*, le rôle de ces descriptions que sont les jeux de langage. On pourrait alors se demander quel est le rapport de ces propositions ou de ces descriptions à celles de la science, ou encore si ces propositions et ces descriptions ne peuvent pas être scientifiques.

Commençons par le cas des propositions logiques. Selon Wittgenstein, « l'explication correcte des propositions logiques doit leur conférer une position unique parmi toutes les propositions »[5], ce qui implique notamment qu'on ne les confonde pas avec les propositions des sciences de la nature :

> 6. 111 – Les théories qui font apparaître une proposition de la logique comme ayant un contenu sont toujours fausses. On pourrait croire, par exemple, que les mots « vrai » et « faux » désignent deux propriétés parmi d'autres, et que par conséquent ce soit un fait remarquable que chaque proposition possède l'une ou l'autre. Ce qui semble alors rien moins qu'aller de soi, pas plus que ne sonnerait comme allant de soi, par exemple, la proposition : « toutes les roses sont ou jaunes ou rouges », même si elle était vraie. Cette proposition acquiert alors tous les caractères d'une proposition des

3. *Ibid.*
4. *Ibid.*
5. *Ibid.*, p. 96.

> sciences de la nature, et c'est l'indice sûr qu'elle aura été conçue faussement[6].

Les propositions des sciences de la nature ont un contenu qui est vrai ou faux, elles disent quelque chose de vrai ou de faux du monde, alors que celles de la logique ne disent rien du monde ou des propositions qu'elles clarifient, mais en montrent la structure. Pour utiliser une image, on pourrait dire que les propositions des sciences de la nature sont des tableaux que l'on peut comparer à la réalité, alors que les propositions logiques sont le miroir dans lequel se montre la structure logique de ces tableaux, c'est-à-dire la structure des propositions douées de sens.

En même temps, comme le montre le passage suivant, on pourrait tout aussi bien dire qu'en un sens, il n'y a pas, d'un côté, les propositions scientifiques et ordinaires et, de l'autre, les propositions de la logique :

> 6. 121 – Les propositions de la logique démontrent les propriétés logiques des propositions, en formant par leur connexion des propositions qui ne disent rien.
> On pourrait appeler encore cette méthode : méthode de réduction à zéro. Dans la proposition logique, les propositions sont mises entre elles en équilibre, et cet état d'équilibre montre alors comment ces propositions doivent être logiquement agencées[7].

Cela ne revient pas à dire qu'en réalité, il n'y a pas de distinction à faire entre les deux types de propositions, mais que les premières sont connectées les unes aux autres et mises en équilibre dans les secondes, pour former des tautologies. Il est donc tout à fait possible de dire que la philosophie, ou en tout cas la logique, produit des propositions à partir de propositions scientifiques ou ordinaires, sans revenir sur la distinction entre science et philosophie, puisque les propositions produites sont des tautologies.

Qu'en est-il alors du rapport entre l'activité philosophique et ces propositions tout à fait particulières ? Ces propositions logiques « fournissent des schémas d'inférence universellement applicables »[8] qui démontrent les propriétés logiques des propositions douées de

6. *Ibid.*.
7. *Ibid.*, p. 99.
8. D. Vernant, *Introduction à la logique standard*, Paris, Flammarion, 2001, p. 56.

sens et comment elles doivent être agencées, notamment quand ces propriétés et ces relations sont masquées par le langage. Autrement dit, ces propositions ne sont pas les propositions fondamentales d'une science première, la philosophie, mais elles fournissent des schémas qui permettent l'activité philosophique : la clarification logique des propositions douées de sens.

Venons-en maintenant aux jeux de langage, dont Wittgenstein nous donne une série d'exemples au début des *Recherches philosophiques* : donner des ordres et agir d'après des ordres, décrire un objet en fonction de ce qu'on en voit ou à partir des mesures que l'on en prend, produire un objet d'après une description ou un dessin, etc. Le paragraphe 130 est essentiel pour comprendre leur usage :

> 130. Nos jeux de langage clairs et simples ne sont pas des études préparatoires pour une réglementation future du langage – ce ne sont pas de premières approximations, qui ne tiendraient compte ni du frottement ni de la résistance de l'air. Les jeux de langage se présentent plutôt comme des *objets de comparaison*, qui doivent éclairer, au moyen de ressemblances ou de dissemblances, les conditions qui sont celles de notre langage[9].

La description de jeux de langage n'est donc pas une ébauche de règles destinées à réformer le langage, mais elle n'est pas non plus une description plus ou moins approximative de son fonctionnement, que certaines sciences, dans un deuxième temps, viendraient préciser. Ces descriptions sont des points de comparaison qui permettent d'éclairer, par ressemblances et dissemblances, le fonctionnement réel de notre langage, qui, quand il est mal perçu, est à l'origine des confusions conceptuelles.

On peut alors faire deux remarques. D'une part, ce type de clarification conceptuelle se situe dans la lignée de la clarification logique du *Tractatus*. En effet, si, dans le *Tractatus* comme dans les

9. L. Wittgenstein, *Recherches philosophiques*, trad. fr. F. Dastur *et alii*, Paris, Gallimard, 2004, p. 88.

Recherches, le langage lui-même est en ordre[10], ce n'est pas le cas de la connaissance que nous en avons[11]. Dans cette perspective, ce qui est recherché, ce n'est donc pas une réforme, une fondation ou encore une explication du langage, mais la mise en évidence de son ordre. Or, cela passe, dans la clarification logique, par un certain type de mise en ordre des propositions en tautologies, c'est-à-dire par la constitution de schémas d'inférence universellement applicables, et, dans la clarification conceptuelle, par l'usage de descriptions comme de points de comparaison, c'est-à-dire par la construction de modèles permettant d'éclairer le fonctionnement du langage. D'autre part, cet usage des jeux de langage accentue ce qui était déjà présent dans le *Tractatus* : la démarcation de la philosophie par rapport à la science et son rapprochement avec l'esthétique, plus précisément avec l'appréciation esthétique (et non pas l'esthétique au sens précis d'une théorie du beau). En effet, la clarification, qu'elle soit logique ou conceptuelle, se fonde sur une pratique qui doit rendre visibles certains aspects de nos propositions et de notre pratique du langage au moyen non pas d'explications ou d'hypothèses, comme c'est le cas dans les sciences, mais de comparaisons.

2. LES DEUX PROBLÈMES DU STATUT DES MATHÉMATIQUES ET DE L'USAGE DES FAITS.

Si maintenant nous voulons revenir sur cette distinction entre philosophie et science, ce n'est pas pour la remettre en cause, mais pour montrer que cette manière de la présenter est insuffisante et manque certains aspects essentiels de la question et de la solution proposée par Wittgenstein. Pour le mettre en évidence, il faut revenir à certaines distinctions que l'on trouve aux propositions 4. 11 *sq* du *Tractatus* :

> 4. 11 – La philosophie n'est pas une science de la nature. [...]

10. L. Wittgenstein, *Tractatus logico-philosophicus*, *op. cit.*, p. 92 : « 5. 5563 – Toutes les propositions de notre langue usuelle sont en fait, telles qu'elles sont, ordonnées de façon logiquement parfaite. »

11. *Ibid.*, p. 89.

> 4. 1121 – La psychologie n'est pas plus apparentée à la philosophie que n'importe laquelle des sciences de la nature. [...]
> 4.1122 – La théorie de Darwin n'a pas plus à voir avec la philosophie que n'importe quelle autre hypothèse des sciences de la nature.
> 4.113 – La philosophie délimite le territoire contesté de la science de la nature[12].

Ces distinctions permettent de poser un certain nombre de problèmes généraux. Un premier groupe de problèmes a trait aux sciences mentionnées dans ce texte : les sciences de la nature, la psychologie, la théorie de Darwin. Une première question serait : peut-on parler de « la » science ou bien doit-on toujours insister sur la pluralité des sciences ? Mais Wittgenstein ne semble pas très sensible à cette question puisque « toute la science de la nature » et « la totalité des sciences de la nature » sont posées comme équivalentes : « la totalité des propositions vraies est toute la science de la nature (ou la totalité des sciences de la nature) »[13]. Une deuxième question serait : qu'en est-il des sciences humaines ? Là encore, il n'en fait pas mention dans le *Tractatus*, seulement par la suite et de manière plus ou moins approfondie. On trouve ainsi quelques remarques sur l'histoire dans *De la certitude* et surtout des notes assez importantes sur l'anthropologie dans les *Remarques sur le Rameau d'Or de Frazer*. Mais il y a une troisième question qui est nettement plus centrale, et ce, dès le *Tractatus* : qu'en est-il des mathématiques ? Comme pour les sciences humaines, on pourrait s'étonner de leur absence dans ces propositions. Mais ce dont il faut s'étonner, en réalité, ce n'est pas de cela mais du statut qu'il leur accorde dans d'autres propositions : « la mathématique est une méthode logique »[14] qui opère sur des propositions au moyen d'équations, là où la logique opère sur des propositions avec des tautologies. Comme la logique, les mathématiques ne sont pas une science, c'est-à-dire une description vraie ou fausse de la réalité. Donc, le premier problème qui nous intéressera est le suivant : s'il y a une distinction nette entre science et philosophie, mais que les mathématiques ne

12. L. Wittgenstein, *Tractatus logico-philosophicus*, *op. cit.*, p. 57-58.
13. *Ibid.*, p. 57.
14. *Ibid.*, p. 102.

peuvent être considérées comme une science, qu'en est-il du rapport entre mathématiques et philosophie ? Le problème se pose d'autant plus que Wittgenstein définit la philosophie comme une clarification logique et les mathématiques comme une méthode logique : y a-t-il alors une parenté entre elles ? De quelle nature pourrait être cette parenté ?

Un deuxième groupe de problèmes est lié à la distinction entre deux types de conceptions de la philosophie et aux conclusions qu'on doit en tirer concernant l'usage des faits établis par la ou les sciences, qu'il s'agisse des sciences dites « dures » ou des sciences humaines. Repartons de la distinction entre la philosophie comme théorie et la philosophie comme activité. Dans le premier cas, la question de l'usage des faits se pose assez simplement : la philosophie a-t-elle des faits qui lui sont propres, ou bien se base-t-elle sur des faits établis par d'autres sciences ? Et quoi qu'il en soit de la réponse à cette question, comment doit-elle se rapporter aux faits établis dans les sciences pour construire sa propre théorie ? Mais dans le deuxième cas, celui de la philosophie comme activité, et notamment comme activité de clarification des concepts, y a-t-il un usage possible des faits ? On pourrait croire que non. Après tout, Wittgenstein déclare lui-même que la clarification logique se passe de l'observation des faits :

> 5. 551 – Notre principe est que toute question susceptible d'être en général décidée par la logique, doit pouvoir être décidée sans autre apport.
> (Et si nous nous trouvons en situation de devoir résoudre un tel problème en observant le monde, cela montre que nous nous sommes engagés dans une voie fondamentalement erronée.) [15]

On posera donc le deuxième problème de la manière suivante : n'y a-t-il vraiment aucune place dans la clarification philosophique pour un usage des faits ? Qu'une clarification logique comme celle proposée par le *Tractatus* n'en requiert pas, on l'accorde, mais qu'en est-il de la clarification conceptuelle mise en œuvre par la suite ?

15. *Ibid.*, p. 91.

Pour répondre à ces deux problèmes, celui de la parenté de la philosophie avec les mathématiques et celui de la place de l'usage des faits dans la clarification philosophique, on partira d'un groupe de textes tirés des *Remarques sur la philosophie de la psychologie*, dans lesquels Wittgenstein essaie explicitement de montrer la nature de son raisonnement ainsi que la place des faits dans ce raisonnement :

> 47. Ce qui nous intéresse est par exemple d'établir que dans notre environnement des formes déterminées ne sont pas liées à des couleurs déterminées (que nous ne voyons pas toujours le vert en liaison avec la forme circulaire ni le rouge en liaison avec la forme carrée). Si l'on se représente un monde dans lequel formes et couleurs seraient attachées entre elles de cette manière, on trouverait alors compréhensible un système conceptuel dans lequel la distinction fondamentale - forme et couleur – n'existerait pas.
> Encore quelques exemples.
> Il est important, par exemple, que nous soyons habitués à dessiner avec des crayons, des plumes, *etc.*, et que par conséquent les éléments de notre façon de représenter soient des traits et des points (au sens de « petits points »). Si les hommes n'avaient pas dessiné, mais s'ils avaient toujours peint (et que par conséquent le concept de *contour* des formes n'eût pas joué un grand rôle), il y aurait un mot usuel, disons le mot « ligne », par lequel personne ne penserait à un *trait*, je veux dire à quelque chose de très mince, mais toujours simplement à la frontière de deux couleurs, et par « point » on ne penserait pas à quelque chose de minuscule, mais à l'intersection de deux frontières de couleurs, et dans ce cas-là peut-être tout un développement de la géométrie n'aurait-il pas eu lieu.
> Si nous ne voyions l'une de nos couleurs primaires, disons le rouge, que de façon extrêmement rare et dans des dimensions extrêmement réduites, et si nous ne pouvions fabriquer des couleurs pour peindre, le rouge n'apparaîtrait que dans certaines relations avec d'autres couleurs, par exemple la pointe des feuilles de certains arbres, qui peu à peu en automne passent du vert au rouge, et dans ce cas rien ne serait plus naturel que d'appeler le rouge « un vert dégénéré »[16].

16. L. Wittgenstein, *Remarques sur la philosophie de la psychologie*, tome I, Mauvezin, TER, 1989, trad. fr. G. Granel, p. 21-22.

3. HYPOTHÈSES, EXPÉRIENCES DE PENSÉE ET CALCUL

On se penchera tout d'abord sur la nature du raisonnement effectué dans ces exemples : « si l'on se représente un monde dans lequel […], on trouverait […] », « si les hommes n'avaient pas […], il y aurait […] », « si nous ne voyions […], le rouge apparaîtrait […] ». De quel type de raisonnement s'agit-il ?

Une première erreur serait de croire qu'on a affaire à la formulation d'hypothèses sur l'origine ou les causes de nos concepts, sur ce qui fait que nous possédons tels concepts et non pas tels autres. Cela ne veut pas dire qu'on ne peut pas formuler de telles hypothèses ou que ces formules ne sont pas, la plupart du temps, des hypothèses, mais que Wittgenstein dit ne pas les utiliser comme des hypothèses. Dans le paragraphe qui précède ces exemples, il insiste justement sur le fait qu'il n'utilise pas ces formules comme des prédictions : « Nous ne développons pas une science de la nature : notre but n'est pas de prédire quelque chose »[17]. Dans le paragraphe qui suit ces exemples, il en vient même à dire qu'il ne les utilise même pas comme des affirmations : « Mais *je ne dis pas* que si les faits étaient autres, nous aurions d'autres concepts. C'est là une hypothèse dont je n'ai que faire et qui ne m'intéresse pas »[18]. Mais s'il ne le dit pas, que fait-il ? Quelle est la nature de ces raisonnements, s'ils ne sont pas des prédictions ou des hypothèses ?

Une deuxième possibilité consisterait à en faire non pas des prédictions ou des hypothèses, mais des expériences de pensée. Le problème est que cela se heurterait aux objections que Wittgenstein adresse à celui qui les a popularisées, Ernst Mach : « Ce que Mach appelle une expérimentation de pensée n'est naturellement pas une expérimentation du tout »[19]. Le problème n'est pas épistémologique, mais conceptuel : « expérience » et « expérimentation » ne sont pas les bons concepts pour décrire ce que nous faisons quand nous disons faire des « expérimentations mentales » ou des « expériences

17. *Ibid.*, p. 21.

18. *Ibid.*, p. 22. Nous soulignons.

19. L. Wittgenstein, *Remarques philosophiques*, Paris, Gallimard, 1975, trad. fr. J. Fauve, p. 52.

de pensée ». La raison, c'est que, dans une supposée « expérimentation mentale », justement, aucune expérience n'est faite et aucun résultat n'est obtenu. L'expérience est imaginée, au lieu d'être effectuée, et le résultat lui aussi est imaginé, au lieu d'être obtenu, ce qui ne veut certainement pas dire que l'expérience est effectuée et les résultats obtenus d'une manière particulière : en imagination[20]. Le problème, ce n'est donc pas que l'on imagine des expériences que l'on chercherait ensuite à réaliser (cette pratique courante n'a rien de problématique), ce n'est pas non plus qu'on fasse de tels raisonnements (là encore, c'est très courant et n'a rien de problématique). Le problème, c'est qu'on utilise improprement le concept d'expérience pour qualifier la nature de ce raisonnement.

La question se pose donc à nouveau : dans ces raisonnements, que fait-on qui n'est ni la formulation d'hypothèses ou de prédictions, ni des expérimentations mentales ? Wittgenstein nous indique la solution dans une remarque des *Derniers écrits sur la philosophie de la psychologie* : « Apparemment je fais des "expériences de pensée". A ceci près que ce ne sont justement pas des expériences. Bien plutôt des calculs »[21]. On comprendra cette idée en se rapportant à un passage essentiel des *Dictées de Wittgenstein à Waismann et pour Schlick*, passage qui porte sur la notion de supposition :

> Si étrange que cela paraisse, cette invitation : « Suppose qu'il pleuvra demain » a ainsi une grande similitude avec l'invitation à écrire cette proposition comme le début d'un calcul. « Suppose la proposition » signifie : « Prends-la en considération ! », c'est-à-dire : « Réfléchis à ce qui s'ensuit ; par exemple, à ce que tu ferais si elle était vraie. Bref, fais-en le point de départ d'une série de raisonnements et de déductions »[22].

Ce que fait Wittgenstein et que l'on pourrait prendre pour des hypothèses ou des expériences de pensée, ce sont en réalité des

20. Voir L. Wittgenstein, *Grammaire philosophique*, Paris, Gallimard, 1980, trad. fr. M.-A. Lescourret, p. 205 : « Une expérience que l'on pense, revient au même qu'une expérience que l'on dessine, peint ou décrit au lieu de l'effectuer. Et le résultat de l'expérience pensée est le résultat fictif de l'expérience fictive. »

21. L. Wittgenstein, *Derniers écrits sur la philosophie de la psychologie*, tome I, Mauvezin, TER, 1985, trad. fr. G. Granel p. 182.

22. L. Wittgenstein, *Dictées de Wittgenstein à Waismann et pour Schlick*, trad. fr. C. Chauviré *et alii*, Paris, PUF, 1997, p. 194.

raisonnements qui sont analogues à un calcul, c'est-à-dire des raisonnements qui développent les conséquences d'une supposition initiale.

Pour comprendre l'importance de cette analogie avec le calcul, il faut faire intervenir un certain nombre de distinctions et de remarques. Premièrement, parler de calcul, c'est ici parler du développement des conséquences d'une supposition, par contraste avec l'observation des conséquences d'une modification dans le cadre d'une expérience. L'usage de ce concept par démarcation avec celui d'expérience met donc en évidence la distinction entre le développement d'une représentation et l'observation empirique, et range les raisonnements wittgensteiniens dans la première catégorie. Deuxièmement, l'usage du concept de calcul permet de souligner la logique interne de ce type de raisonnement, indépendamment d'un de ses usages possibles : la prédiction. Autrement dit, il est vrai que ce type de raisonnement peut avoir un intérêt pour produire des prédictions, mais cela ne doit pas masquer la nature du raisonnement qui est effectué ici et qui peut servir d'autres finalités.

Troisièmement, si l'on fait une distinction entre calcul logique et calcul mathématique, on peut se demander à quel type de calcul Wittgenstein fait référence concernant ses propres raisonnements. Il nous semble qu'il s'agit du calcul mathématique, et ce, tout d'abord, pour une raison textuelle. Quand Wittgenstein revient au § 624 sur le concept de « vert rougeâtre », il compare explicitement la proposition « il n'y a pas de vert rougeâtre » à un certain type de propositions mathématiques : « 624. “Il n'y a pas de vert rougeâtre” est une proposition de même famille que celles dont nous usons comme d'axiomes en mathématiques »[23]. Il y a ensuite une raison plus conceptuelle. Comme l'analyse J. Bouveresse dans *Le pays des possibles*, « Wittgenstein décrit le mathématicien comme inventant sans arrêt de nouvelles formes de représentation »[24], ce qui n'est pas le cas de la logique mais des exemples de raisonnements cités plus haut, qui sont des constructions de concepts nouveaux. Si ces

23. L. Wittgenstein, *Remarques sur la philosophie de la psychologie*, *op. cit.*, p. 139.

24. J. Bouveresse, *Le pays des possibles. Wittgenstein, les mathématiques et le monde réel*, Paris, Minuit, 1988, p. 63.

raisonnements ont une parenté avec les mathématiques, c'est au sens où, dans les deux cas, il s'agit de construire des concepts.

Enfin, ce concept de calcul est à distinguer de celui de preuve. En effet, le propre des preuves mathématiques, selon Wittgenstein, c'est la nécessité de ce qu'elles énoncent, leur dimension normative, que l'on doit distinguer des prédictions des sciences de la nature : « 31. Il doit en être ainsi ne signifie pas qu'il en sera ainsi. Au contraire : "Il en sera ainsi" sélectionne une possibilité parmi d'autres. "Il doit en être ainsi" ne voit qu'*une* seule possibilité. »[25] Dans cette perspective, une supposition n'est ni une norme, ni une prédiction, mais le développement d'une possibilité : elle est un calcul possible là où la preuve dit ce qui doit être et la prédiction dit ce qu'il en sera. La conséquence, c'est que les raisonnements cités plus haut non seulement ne prédisent rien, mais en plus ne prouvent rien, ce qui, de manière plus générale, les différencie des raisonnements et déductions des autres disciplines, qui ont pour fonction de prouver ce à quoi ils aboutissent.

Quelle conclusion peut-on en tirer ? Ce passage sur la nature de la supposition éclaire ce que l'on disait des jeux de langage, ces points de comparaison qui rendent visible, par ressemblances et dissemblances, le fonctionnement de notre langage et donc nos concepts. Les jeux de langage ne sont ni des descriptions ou des observations empiriques, ni des hypothèses ou des prédictions, ni la formulation de normes, mais sont analogues à des calculs. C'est-à-dire qu'ils sont des constructions de concepts, dont la fonction, répétons-le, n'est pas de décrire nos concepts, de prédire ce qu'ils seront si l'on modifie telle ou telle chose dans notre vie, ou encore de dire ce qu'ils doivent être, mais d'être des points de comparaisons permettant de les comprendre. C'est donc en pensant aux constructions mathématiques que l'on doit comprendre le passage connu des *Remarques mêlées* : « Rien n'est pourtant plus important que l'élaboration de concepts fictifs, qui seuls nous apprennent à comprendre les nôtres. »[26]

25. L. Wittgenstein, *Remarques sur les fondements des mathématiques*, Paris, Gallimard, 1983, trad. fr. M.-A. Lescourret, p. 207.

26. L. Wittgenstein, *Remarques mêlées*, Paris, GF, 2002, trad. fr. G. Granel, p. 146.

En même temps, on le voit, qu'il y ait une parenté des constructions philosophiques avec les constructions mathématiques, ne signifie pas qu'il faille mathématiser la philosophie ou même introduire plus de mathématiques en philosophie, mais seulement reconnaître l'analogie des raisonnements philosophiques avec les constructions mathématiques[27]. Une autre limite du rapprochement réside dans l'usage de ces constructions : les constructions de concepts des mathématiques sont destinés à servir, notamment dans les sciences, alors que les constructions de concepts de la philosophie sont vouées à disparaître, une fois les confusions conceptuelles dissipées et nos propres concepts reconnus. Mais quoi qu'il en soit de ces limites, reste une idée essentielle : qu'il y ait une distinction radicale entre philosophie et science n'empêche pas qu'on puisse rapprocher la philosophie des mathématiques. Bien au contraire, c'est l'analogie avec le calcul qui permet de distinguer au mieux la spécificité du raisonnement philosophique par rapport à celui des sciences empiriques.

4. LA MISE EN ÉVIDENCE DU RÔLE DES FAITS DANS L'USAGE DE NOS CONCEPTS.

Passons à la question de la place des faits dans ces raisonnements, avec deux remarques préliminaires pour commencer. Tout d'abord, on notera que ces exemples de raisonnements illustrent une des recommandations principales de Wittgenstein concernant la clarification des concepts : aller voir du côté de leur usage. Autrement dit, nos concepts se montrent le plus clairement dans l'usage que nous en faisons. Ensuite, l'accent est mis sur les faits dont cet usage est solidaire : le rapport des formes et des couleurs dans la réalité, la présence d'objets techniques (le crayon, les

27. Cette idée est à comparer à celle de Kant dans la *Critique de la raison pure* : « Or, toute connaissance de la raison est une connaissance par concepts ou par la construction de concepts ; la première s'appelle philosophique, et la seconde mathématique. ». *Cf.* Kant, *Critique de la raison pure*, trad. fr. A. Delamarre, Paris, Gallimard, 1980, p. 694. Pour Wittgenstein, la philosophique n'est pas une connaissance par concepts, ni même une connaissance, mais une construction de concepts dont la fonction est de clarifier nos propres concepts.

pinceaux) ou encore la régularité de certains phénomènes. Les concepts sont à chercher dans leur usage, mais des usages qui sont mêlés à des faits.

La question est alors : comment les faits sont-ils mêlés à notre usage des concepts ? Voici comment Wittgenstein répond :

> Je ne dis pas que si les faits naturels étaient autres, nous aurions d'autres concepts. Je dis simplement ceci : Si tu crois que nos concepts sont les bons, sont ceux qui conviennent à des hommes intelligents, et que quelqu'un qui en aurait d'autres ne comprendrait par conséquent pas ce que nous comprenons, imagine alors certains faits généraux de la nature autres qu'ils ne sont, et d'autres formations conceptuelles que les nôtres te paraîtront *naturelles*[28].

Et Wittgenstein de préciser : « Naturelles, non pas nécessaires »[29] La fonction immédiate de ces raisonnements n'est donc pas d'expliquer, au sens d'indiquer les causes, la formation des concepts, mais de montrer à la fois la contingence, l'absence de nécessité de nos concepts, qui auraient pu être différents étant donnés d'autres faits généraux, et le caractère naturel des concepts imaginés, justement en raison de la possibilité d'imaginer des faits naturels dont ils dépendraient.

À partir de là, on peut comprendre le rôle des faits dans ce type de raisonnement. Quand Wittgenstein imagine d'autres faits généraux, il adopte un point de vue non scientifique. La démarche scientifique consisterait à montrer comment certains faits (physiques mais aussi physiologiques) ont causé les concepts que nous possédons et déterminent l'usage que nous en faisons. Or, la démarche philosophique se démarque de cela en s'intéressant à un autre type de relations entre les faits et les concepts, une relation non-causale. Autrement dit, elle ne considère pas les faits comme des causes, mais autrement : comme ce qui rend naturels telle formation, tel usage ou encore telle modification de concept. Comment alors qualifier ce rapport des faits aux concepts et à leur usage ? On avancera que cette relation est pratique ou pragmatique, au sens où ce qui est en jeu ici, c'est le rôle des faits dans un certain type d'activité humaine : l'usage, la modification ou encore

28. L. Wittgenstein, *Remarques sur la philosophie de la psychologie*, *op. cit.*, p. 22.
29. *Ibid.*

l'invention de concepts. Il faudrait insister notamment sur la diversité des rôles de ces faits : ils peuvent rendre possible ou se prêter à la création et à l'usage de tel ou tel système de concepts (c'est l'exemple des plumes et des crayons dans l'apparition de la géométrie), ils peuvent être les raisons plus ou moins explicites de l'adoption d'un système de concepts (ce pourrait être l'exemple du rôle de certains faits dans le choix d'une unité de mesure), ou encore ils peuvent être parfois des contraintes dans l'usage des concepts (ce serait l'exemple des données de la perception dans l'usage des concepts de couleurs).

Ceci étant dit, pour notre propos, l'essentiel se trouve ailleurs : dans l'idée qu'on trouve bien un usage des faits dans les raisonnements philosophiques, mais un usage de faits qui sont particuliers. Tout d'abord, le point de départ des exemples de raisonnement cités plus haut, c'est la représentation, l'imagination de faits généraux possibles qui sont différents de ceux que l'on trouve dans la réalité : la liaison systématique des formes et des couleurs, l'usage de la peinture et non du dessin, une autre fréquence du rouge et l'impossibilité d'en produire. Ensuite, ce sont des faits d'une grande évidence, qui ne requièrent pas leur établissement par la science pour devenir visibles. Enfin, comme on l'a déjà souligné, ces faits n'y sont pas considérés comme les causes de nos concepts[30]. Bref, cette démarche, pourtant attentive aux faits, ne semble en rien liée aux sciences, ne semble pas faire appel aux faits scientifiques.

En ce sens, la perspective wittgensteinienne met en évidence un problème essentiel. En effet, la question du rapport entre philosophie et science est bien souvent liée à celle des faits sur lesquels la philosophie devrait reposer. Mais, à supposer que la philosophie doive reposer ou même simplement s'appuyer sur des faits, les faits « scientifiques » sont-ils ce dont elle a besoin ? La science a-t-elle le monopole des faits dont la philosophie a besoin ? A-t-elle même le monopole des faits tout court ? Dans une perspective wittgensteinienne, la réponse est non : les faits intéressants sont les faits

30. « [...] la correspondance entre notre grammaire et les faits naturels universels (rarement exprimés) nous intéresse aussi, mais notre intérêt ne remonte pas jusqu'à ces causes possibles. », *ibid.*, p. 21.

généraux possibles qui nous font imaginer d'autres concepts à partir desquels il est possible de revenir aux nôtres. Pourtant, même si l'on accepte que l'essentiel se joue dans cette manière d'imaginer d'autres faits généraux, n'y a-t-il donc aucune place, dans l'examen de l'usage des concepts, pour les faits scientifiques ? Surtout, peut-on vraiment séparer les faits scientifiques et les faits généraux dont parle Wittgenstein ?

L'idée que l'on soutiendra est la suivante : de même que la philosophie ne s'intéresse pas à tous les faits généraux de la nature mais seulement à ceux dont l'usage des concepts est solidaire, de même, elle ne s'intéresse pas non plus à tous les faits établis par la science, mais seulement à ceux dont dépend l'usage de nos concepts. La science a un intérêt philosophique seulement quand elle met en évidence des faits généraux dont l'usage des concepts est solidaire. La conséquence immédiate est qu'il ne faut pas attendre des faits scientifiques qu'ils nous disent d'eux-mêmes ce qu'ils peuvent nous apporter, ou de la science qu'elle nous dise quels faits sont intéressants d'un point de vue philosophique. En philosophie, nous savons ce que nous cherchons, à savoir tout ce qui peut contribuer à la clarification de nos concepts, et c'est ce critère qui doit nous permettre de faire le tri dans la masse des faits découverts par la science. En même temps, dire cela, ce n'est pas sous-estimer la nécessité de la science. Les faits qu'elle met en évidence et qui intéressent la philosophie sont caractérisés par un défaut d'évidence auquel elle seule peut remédier. Dans les exemples de Wittgenstein, au contraire, les faits généraux qui sont intéressants philosophiquement sont caractérisés par leur si grande évidence qu'on ne les voit plus, mais ils ne requièrent alors qu'une autre direction de l'attention pour être saisis, et non une démarche scientifique. Prenons un exemple : Wittgenstein met en évidence l'importance, pour nos concepts de formes et de couleurs, du fait que les formes et les couleurs ne sont pas liées en permanence dans notre expérience perceptive. Mais on pourrait tout aussi bien en appeler à un fait établi par la psychologie cognitive expérimentale : jusqu'à un certain âge, formes et couleurs font l'objet d'un traitement neuronal différent, ce dont nous n'aurions pas pu nous douter et nous rendre compte à l'aide de notre seule attention aux faits de la nature[31].

La conclusion est alors que, si la démarche scientifique est nécessaire pour établir certains faits philosophiquement intéressants, ce n'est pas elle qui permet de faire le tri dans les faits qu'elle a établis, de montrer l'intérêt philosophique de tel ou tel fait. Inversement, même si l'on doit souligner qu'il revient à la philosophie de sélectionner les faits qui lui importent, il ne faut pas oublier qu'il revient à la science de les mettre en évidence. Elle ajoute aux faits généraux dont parle Wittgenstein, ceux qui sont trop évidents pour être remarqués, d'autres faits généraux qui le sont moins. Mais, ce faisant, elle peut aussi renouveller notre représentation des faits généraux. Or, cela a une double conséquence. D'un côté, elle contribue à quelque chose d'essentiel dans la clarification des concepts, l'imagination d'autres faits possibles : « Le progrès de la science est-il utile à la philosophie ? Certainement. Les réalités découvertes facilitent pour le philosophe la tâche d'imaginer les possibilités »[32]. En même temps, d'un autre côté :

> c'est un fait d'expérience que les hommes modifient leurs concepts et leur en substituent d'autres lorsqu'ils prennent connaissance de nouveaux faits ; lorsque, par exemple, ce qui leur semblait important auparavant cesse d'avoir de l'importance et *vice versa*. (Quand on s'aperçoit, par exemple, que ce qui passait d'abord pour une différence de nature *n'*était *qu'*une différence de degré)[33].

Et si ces périodes de modification et de substitution de concepts sont propices aux confusions conceptuelles, on peut alors se demander si la science, par ses découvertes, ne contribue pas aussi à ces confusions qui sont l'objet même de la philosophie.

31. Je remercie Jérôme Dokic pour cette information donnée lors du colloque dont est tiré cet article.

32. L. Wittgenstein, *Derniers écrits sur la philosophie de la psychologie*, *op. cit.*, p. 270.

33. L. Wittgenstein, *Fiches*, Paris, Gallimard, 2008, trad. fr. J.-P. Cometti et É. Rigal, p. 89.

Table des matières

Numéros déjà publiés

Cahier n° 1

Septembre 1981 – 148 pages (épuisé)

Présentation du Groupe de Recherches, par Janine Chêne. *Lecture, lecteurs, lettrés, littérature*, par Pierre Bourdieu. *Les origines frégéennes de la distinction entre ce qui « se dit » et ce qui « se voit » dans le* Tractatus Logico-Philosophicus *de Wittgenstein*, par Jacques Bouveresse. *Valéry, Wittgenstein et la philosophie*, par Régine Piétra. *Essai sur la rationalité et la pensée mythique grecques*, par Henri Joly. *Le « Récit scientifique » à l'âge baroque : l'exemple du récit de la découverte de la circulation du sang*, par Jacques Lambert.

Cahier n° 2

Juin 1982 – 180 pages

Entre temps et récit : Concorde/Discorde, par Paul Ricœur. *Le temps du conte et le non-temps de l'inconscient*, par Monique Schneider. *Le rôle du récit dans l'avance en âge*, par M. Philibert. *La notion du sujet parlant*, par Oswald Ducrot. *La peinture tirée du tombeau*, par C. Stanislas. *L'Être (et le Néant) dans sa lettre*, par François Heidsieck. *Le corps-langage – Inscription, parole, phantasme dans l'hystérie de conversion*, par Janine Chêne. *Le corps-langage – le corps anagrammatique*, par Monique Broc-Lapeyre.

Cahier n° 3 – La Philosophie dans sa langue

Juin 1983 – 177 pages

Vices et vertus des cercles (pour introduire aux problèmes de l'auto-référence), par Daniel Bougnoux. *La langue et le discours de la méthode*, par Jacques Derrida. *Rêver de ses plaisirs. Sur l'onirocritique d'Artémidore*, par Michel Foucault. *La philosophie entre le clair et l'obscur ou Kant et Hegel devant l'« Aufklarung »*, par Henri Joly. *L'archipel et le signe (sur la pensée kantienne de l'historico-politique)*, par Jean-François Lyotard. *Secret, dissimulation et art de persuader chez Pascal*, par Louis Marin. *L'*Aufklarung *et la problématique de la langue : enjeux culturels et université scientifique*, par Marianne Schaub.

Cahier n° 4 – Langage et philosophie des sciences

Juillet 1985 – 219 pages (épuisé)

Les formes fondamentales de la prédication : un essai de classification, par Jules Vuillemin. *Connaissance des mots, connaissance des choses : théorie du signe et *épistémologie à l'âge classique*, par Ukich Ricken. *Le synthétique* a priori *et la science moderne*, par G. Granger. *Platon, Aristote, Descartes, sur l'espace*, par Jean Largeault. *Logique médicale*, par Anne Fagot. *Lecture et identification dans l'histoire naturelle; Cuvier et le déchiffrement des organismes*, par Jacques Lambert. *La recherche contemporaine sur le mythe : une révolution pas encore conçue*, par Kurt Hubner. *Wittgenstein critique de Frazer*, par Jacques Bouveresse. *Identité, désignation et matérialisme*, par Pascal Engel.

Cahier n° 5 – Pratique de langage dans l'antiquité

2 e trimestre 1985 – 175 pages (épuisé)

La sophistique dans l'Antiquité : Grèce, Inde, Chine, par Régine Piétra. *L'égalité du droit à la parole dans la démocratie grecque – la notion d'*isegoria, par Janine Chêne. *Pourquoi Baubô a-t-elle fait rire Déméter?*, par Monique Broc-Lapeure. *Épicure : un langage pour la sagesse*, par François Heidsieck. *Remarques sur la logique du changement*, par Frédéric Nef. *Le mot, la phrase, le roman et l'existence chez Flaubert*, par Claude Boyard. *Le langage des droits de l'homme*, par Jean-François de Raymond

Cahiers n° 6 et 7 – Philosophie du langage et grammaire dans l'Antiquité

Avril 1987 – 464 pages – Actes du Colloque du 3 au 6 septembre 1985

Avant-Propos, par Henri Joly. *Les mots et les choses : la philosophie du langage chez Démocrite*, par Aldo Brancacci. *Dire et savoir* (legein – eidenai) *chez Xénophane et Parménide*, par Anna Kelessidou. *Observations concernant* legein *et* logos *chez Héraclite*, par François Heidsieck. *Théorie et langage. Le langage comme* logos théorètikos, par Georges Antonopoulos. *Comment faire des choses avec des mots grecs. Les actes de langage dans la langue grecque*, par Françoise Letoublon. *Les mots et les formes dans le* Cratyle *de Platon*, par Charles Kain. *Platon entre le maître d'École et le fabriquant de mots. Remarques sur les* grammata, par Henri Joly. *Discours des vieillards et discours sur la vieillesse chez Platon et aujourd'hui*, par Michel Philibert. *Isocrate et le langage de la culture*, par Jean-François de Raymond. Logos-*phrase et* logos-*texte chez Platon et Aristote*, par Anna Maria Thornton. *Structure sémantique et forme logique d'après l'analyse aristotélicienne des phrases d'action*, par Pascal Engel. *Symbole et signe dans le* De Interpretatione, par Curzio Chiesa. Legomenon *et* Kategoroumenon *chez Aristote*, par Lambros Couloubaritsis. *Paradoxes linguistiques. À propos de* lexis *chez Aristote*, par Denis Zaslawsky. *Pour une réinterprétation des catégories stoïciennes*, par Claude Imbert. *Remarques sur la classification des propositions simples dans les logiques hellénistiques*, par Jacques Brunschwig. *Le problème de l'expression et de la communication dans le scepticisme grec*, par Françoise Caujolle-Zaslawsky. *Critique de la théorie du signe et langage chez Sextus Empiricus*, par Venant Cauchy. Elementa. *Remarques sur le rôle de l'écriture dans la linguistique antique*, par Francoise Desbordes. Pecuslpecunia, *un acte de parole*, par Claire

Feuvrier-Prévotat. *La sémantique de St Augustin est-elle vraiment mentaliste ?*, par Frédéric Nef. *L'électisme et le développement de la grammaire hellénistique et romaine : les unités du discours*, par François Charpin. *L'ordre de la langue. Observations sur la théorie grammaticale d'Apollonius Dyscole*, par Jean Lallot. *The Treatment of the Greek Middle Voice by the Ancient Grammarians*, par A. Rijksbaron. *Donat ou Priscien : syntaxe et figure de construction dans la grammaire latine au XVIe siècle*, par Bernard Colombat.

Cahier n° 8 – Le Langage et le mental
Année 1987 – 145 pages

Épistémologie du sommeil paradoxal, par Claude Debru. *Pierce, lecteur de Berkeley : l'esprit et les signes*, par Claudine Engel-Tiercelin. *L'individuation des états psychologiques et le statut de la psychologie populaire*, par Daniel Laurier. *La linguistique aux frontières de l'anthropologie et de la phénoménologie*, par Françoise Letoublon. *La notion de système en philosophie*, par Daniel Parrochia. *Retour aux Grecs : Réflexions sur les « pratiques de soi », dans l'usage des plaisirs*, par Henri Joly.

Cahier n° 9 – La Métaphore
Année 1989 – 338 pages

Henri Joly (1927-1988). La philosophie comme métaphore, par Henri Joly. *Métaphores sporadiques et linéarité du signifiant chez Gorgias de Léontinoi*, par Alonso Tordesillas. Métaphora : *le fonctionnement sémiotique de la métaphore selon Aristote*, par Jean Lallot. *Métaphore et* methesis *dans la* Rhétorique *d'Aristote*, par Alain Petit. *L'euphorie de la langue*, par Pierre Rodrigo. *La question du sens figuré dans l'interprétation de l'écriture*, par François Heidsieck. *Métaphore et théorie des classes de noms chez Hobbes*, par Martine Pecharman. *Le problème de la métaphore et la controverse sur l'imagination à l'âge classique*, par Ulrich Richken. *La métaphore chez Nietzsche*, par Monique Broc-Lapeyre. *Nietzsche et le métaphorique : des métaphores, des concepts et des catégories*, par Monique Dixsaut. *La métaphore et les philosophes : quelques réflexions sur l'invention philosophique de la métaphore*, par Silvana Borutti. *Symbole et métaphore*, par Lambros Couloubaritsis. *La métaphore vive dans les langues mortes*, par Françoise Letoublon. *Le sens littéral des métaphores*, par Pascal Engel. *Les conditions d'acquisition de la métaphore chez l'enfant*, par Joëlle Gardes-Tamine. *Images et métaphores poétiques*, par Régine Pietra. *Dialogue de la musique et de la métaphore chez Michel Butor*, par Jean Sgard. *Comique et jeu métaphorique*, par Michel Gilot. *Le transfert à l'idiolecte : sur Paul Celan et l'antagonisme des langages*, par Jean Bollack.

Cahier n° 10 – Sémantique formelle et philosophie du langage
Année 1989 – 332 pages

Introduction : la sémantique formelle a-t-elle un intérêt philosophique ?, par Pascal Engel. *La sémantique kripkéenne et les doctrines logiques de Leibniz*, par Maurice

Boudot. *Peirce ou la version sémantique-sémiotique de la logique formelle*, par Claudine Engel-Tiercelin. *Comparabilité et incomparabilité des théories physiques*, par Jules Vuillemin. *Can there be a Substantive Account of Truth ?*, par Thomas Baldwin. *The Sorites Paradox and its Significance for the Interpretation of Semantic Theory*, par Crispin Wright. *Adverbial modification and perception reports*, par Martin Davies. *States of affairs, Bedeutung and the Contingent* a priori, par Graeme Forbes. *Sémantique et psychologie : la sémantique des attributions de croyance*, par Pierre Jacob. *The Onogenesis of Conceptual Roles*, par Andrew Woodfield. *Représentation du sens ou représentation des connaissances*, par Daniel Kayser. *Quelques propriétés formelles élémentaires des fantômes*, par J. Jayez. *Événements et propositions : quelques aspects de la référence anaphorique en allemand*, par R. Bauerle. *Conclusion sur la table ronde*, par Frédéric Nef.

Cahier n° 11 – Valéry : la philosophie, les arts, le langage

Année 1989 – 281 pages

In Memoriam Henri Joly, par Régine Piétra. *Avant-propos*, par Régine Piétra. *Paul Valéry devant les paradoxes de la philosophie*, par Simon Lantiéri. *« Penser ce qui n'existe pas »*, par Ned Bastet. *Un système éclaté*, par Florence de Lussy. *Croisée de perspectives : Paul Valéry et Ortega y Gasset*, par Monique Allain-Castrillo. *Le chef d'orchestre dénubien furibond et Monsir Follerie*, par Monique Broc-Lapeyre. *Alain et Valéry*, par Judith Robinson-Valéry. *Valéry, William James et le problème de « l'Expérience Mystique »*, par Paul Gifford. *Suivre Léonard ou la Question du récit*, par Jeannine Jallat. *Teste et l'Impossible réel*, par Jean Levaillant. *« Plus je pense, plus je pense » ou concerto pour cerveau seul*, par Nicole Celeyrette-Piétri. *Valéry et le Socrate de son* Eupalinos *: écrire ou ne pas écrire*, par Silvio Yeschua. *Valéry et le cratylisme*, par Robert Pickering. *Langage et inspiration poétique : le témoignage valéryen*, par E. A. Moutsopoulos. *Le fonctionnement théâtral du dialogue philosophique chez Valéry :* L'Idée fixe, par Huguette Laurenti. *L'autre, l'obscur, du discours*, par Shushi Kao. *Le Modèle valéryen de l'esprit à la lumière des sciences naturelles de nos jours*, par Ulrike Heetfel. *L'art de l'ingénieur et la pensée valéryenne*, par A. Kaufmann. *Construire, connaître, douter*, par Vittorio Ugo. *Le fort et le ban : Valéry ou la récusation de l'art moderne*, par Jean-Charles Gateau. *Valéry et l'esthétique du cinéma*, par K. A. Bluher. *Langage musical/ langage poétique : Valéry à la recherche de son chinois poétique*, par Brian Stimpson. *« Océan sonore » : la genèse du* Cimetière marin, par M. T. Giaveri.

Cahier n° 12 – Hommage à Henri JOLY

Année 1990 – 470 pages

Avant-propos, par J. C. Pariente, F. Letoublon, R. Piétra. *Bibliographie d'Henri Joly. La construction sociale du sexe*, par Pierre Bourdieu. *De la vertu « rapetissante » d'une grande biographie. Mais comment les plus petits détails de la vie originaire font extraordinaire le destin de Nietzsche*, par Monique Broc-Lapeyre.

Le titre des Indalmoi *de Timon ; d'Ulysse à Pyrrhon*, par Jacques Brunschwig. *La grande illusion : pour servir à une mise en scène de l'*Hélène *d'Euripide*, par Barbara Cassin. *La forme éponyme. Participation et éponymie chez Platon*, par Curzio Chiesa. *Prolégomènes à la cosmologie de Pléthon*, par L. Couloubaritsis. *L'enfant, le cru et le philosophe. Orthopédie et sauvagerie dans les dialogues de Platon*, par Éric Debardieux. *La voix de l'ami*, par Jacques Derrida. *Thalès ou Socrate, qui commence ? ou : De l'ironie*, par Monique Dixsaut. *La philosophie du langage entre le clair et l'obscur*, par Pascal Engel. *L'argent dans les* Topiques *de Cicéron*, par Claire Feuvrier-Prévotat. *L'idée de forme logique dans les Six* Essais d'un art des signes *de J. H. Lambert*, par Gilles-Gaston Granger. *Le naturel et l'institué. Réflexion sur deux héros-types*, par Stéphan Imhoof. *Plato as a Socratis*, par Charles Kahn. *Le renversement platonicien :* logos, épistémé, polis, par Anna Kelessidou. *Poésie, Philosophie, Politique*, par Philippe Lacoue-Labarthe. *Quelques remarques à propos des notions de l'espace*, par Jean Largeault. *Le Temps s'en va*, par Françoise Letoublon. *« C'est moi que je peins... ». De la figuration du langage à la figuration du moi chez Montaigne*, par Louis Marin. *Les états généraux de la philosophie : l'École d'Athènes de Raphaël*, par Régine Piétra. *Prélude à une brève rencontre : la correspondance de Descartes avec la reine Christine de Suède*, par Jean-François de Raymond. *Du sens, de la méthode*, par Dominique Sainte-Rose. *Autour de l'*Aufklärung, par Marianne Schaub. *Lieux de parole, temps du discours dans « Sur* les sophistes *d'Alcidamas »*, par Alfonso Tordesillas. *Le comique comme idée. De la toquade à l'extravagance et au rire déchaîné : comparaison entre Racine et Aristophane*, par Jules Vuillemin. *Henri Joly, professeur*, par J. P. Carlet, D. Falcy, J. P. Falcy, A. Ribaud, A. Rubino, E. Buissière, V. Blanchard, I. Poulain, V. Coussedière.

Cahier n° 13 – Simone Weil et les langues
Année 1991 – 305 pages

Simone Weil et le refus de la langue de bois, par Monique Broc-Lapeyre. *Langage et réflexion politique chez Simone Weil : les années de formation (1926-1931)*, par Domenico Canciani. *« Ma solution, si j'avais pu... : L'analogie », ou l'analectique entrevue*, par Robert Chenavier. *Les rapports entre la science et la politique chez Simone Weil. Le problème de la forme*, par Francis Chiappone. *La langue des* Upanisad *chez Simone Weil. Une herméneutique retrouvée selon l'expérience intérieure*, par Alyette Degraces-Fahd. *Simone Weil : le langage d'une écriture*, par Gabriella Fiori. *Quelques oppositions de termes obéissance/révolte, malheur/bonheur chez Simone Weil. Une démarche linguistique à rapprocher de certains principes de méthode weiliens*, par Patricia Fogarty. *Simone Weil, traductrice de l'*Iliade, par Simone Fraisse. *Sur quelques problèmes de traduction et d'interprétation du* Timée, par François Heidsieck. *La critique de l'algèbre à la lumière des idées de Simone Weil*, par Pierre Kaplan. *Grandeur et misère du langage chez Simone Weil*, par Patricia Little. *Le problème du « nous » entre l'individu et le collectif*, par Florence de Lussy. *Pensée poétisante, poésie méditante*, par Adriano Marchetti. *Simone Weil* *et la cité platonicienne*, par Michel Narcy. *Langage de la place publique – langage de la chambre nuptiale. Quelques remarques sur le sens théologique d'une distinction philosophique chez Simone Weil*, par Heinz Robert Schlette. *Le langage des mathématiques chez Simone Weil*, par Michel Sourisse. *Des paroles à la parole. Ressources weiliennes pour un nouvel humanisme chrétien*, par Eric O. Springsted. *La recherche de l'homme par Dieu. Le sens mystique du folklore dans les écrits des derniers jours chez Simone Weil*, par Mayumi Tomihara.

Cahier n° 14 – Du Dialogue
Novembre 1992 – 352 pages

Prologue, par Denis Vernant. *La fonction des prologues dans les* Dialogues *de Platon. Faire l'histoire de Socrate*, par Marie-Laurence Desclos. *Idéal du dialogue ou idéal de la science ? Un débat entre Ugo Spirito et Guido Calogero*, par Évelyne Buissière. *Heidegger, philosophe du dialogue*, par Alain Boutot. *Le dialogue et l'apprentissage du langage*, par Sandra Laugier. *Signification et fonctions du dialogue chez Galilée*, par Jacques Lambert. *Le « dialogue » homme-nature*, par Marie-Dominique Popelard. *Dialogicité et subjectivité*, par Pierre Million. *Peut-on et doit-on définir un* a priori *communicationnel ?*, par Francis Jacques. *La volonté de s'entendre : dialogue et intentionnalité*, par Éric Grillo. *La violence dans le débat philosophique. La controverse Derrida/Searle*, par Mathieu Potte-Bonneville. *La logique dialogique par Gerhardt Heinzmann. Le sens dans l'interaction*, par Daniel Luzzati. *Modèle projectif et structure actionnelle du dialogue informatif*, par Denis Vernant. *Attitudes cognitives et actes de langage en situation de communication homme-machine*, par Jean Caelen et Anne-Lise Fréchet.

Cahier n° 15 – Merleau-Ponty, le philosophe et son langage
Année 1993 – 464 pages

Avant-propos, par François Heidsieck. *Ouverture du Colloque*, par Jacques Merleau-Ponty. *Le langage entre chair* [Leib] *et corps* [Korper], par Bernard Andrieu. *De la parole à l'être : le problème de l'expression comme voie d'accès à l'ontologie*, par Renaud Barbaras. *La dicibilité du monde, la période intermédiaire de la pensée de Merleau-Ponty à partir de Saussure*, par Mauro Carbone. *Faire parler les événements*, par Janine Chêne. *Le processus dialectique ouvert de la chair et le problème du chiasme comme accession à l'intro-ontologie*, par Roger Decriem. *Culture et mémoire dans* Le visible et l'invisible, par Jean Deprun. *L'institution de l'œuvre chez Merleau-Ponty*, par Koji Hirose. *Merleau-Ponty et Machiavel*, par Giovanni Invitto. *Merleau-Ponty, entre Husserl et Heidegger, de la phénoménologie à la « topologie de l'être »*, par Arion Kelkel. *Langage et signification*, par Jésus Martinez-Velasco. *La dette symbolique de la phénoménologie de la perception*, par Kasuo Masuda. *L'ambiguité de la liberté, « La liberté, en particulier chez Leibniz » de Merleau-Ponty*, par Shoishi Matsuba. *Topologie phénoménale : sur l'actualité scientifique de la phusis phénoménologique de Merleau-Ponty*, par Jean Petitot. *L'histoire de la philosophie dans la philosophie de Merleau-Ponty*, par André

Robinet. *La possibilité de la réflexion philosophique*, par Urs Schällibaum. *La genèse de la peinture et/ou la constitution du monde esthétique*, par Makato Shimizu. *La démarche ontologique de Merleau-Ponty*, par Xavier Tilliette. *La fibre poétique de la pensée de Merleau-Ponty*, par Anne-Marie Vidal. *Le soi incarné, Merleau-Ponty et la question du sujet*, par Maria Villela-Petit.

Cahier n° 16 – Stanislaw Lesniewski aujourd'hui

Année 1995 – 336 pages

Prologue, par Denis Miéville et Denis Vernant. *Remembering Stanislaw Lesniewski*, par Czeslaw Lejewski. *Lesniewski and Ontological Commitment*, par Peter Simons. *Les démonstrations de la non-existence des objets généraux chez Lesniewski*, par Georges Kalinowski. *Sémantique et ontologie : réflexions sur la théorie des objets et les propriétés*, par Frédéric Nef. *Stanislas Lesniewski et l'importance d'une logique développementale*, par Denis Miéville. *Logique et pragmatique : la genèse du concept d'assertion*, par Denis Vernant. *Une descendance des systèmes de Lesniewski. Le calcul de Lambek (de la grammaire logique aux grammaires de logiques des types)*, par Alain Lecomte. *Représentations centrées objets, formalisation en linguistique et systèmes de Lesniewski*, par Jacques Rouault. *Implémentation des principes méréologiques*, par Mounia Fredj. *Anaphore associative et méréologie*, par Alain Berrendonner. *Le « langage méréologique » ajoute-t-il quelque chose aux descriptions psychologiques ?*, par Olivier Houdé.

Cahier n° 17 – Max Weber et le destin des sociétés modernes

Année 1995 – 292 pages

Prologue, par Pierre Million. *Regard sur les rationalités wébériennes*, par Pierre Million. *Max Weber d'après la tradition « formiste »*, par Michel Maffesoli. *Les ambiguïtés de la sociologie compréhensive et ses conséquences sur la pratique sociologique*, par Monique Hirschhorn. *Les valeurs de l'homme Weber*, par Henri Leroux. *Max Weber et les contradictions de la modernité*, par Carlo Mongardini. *Max Weber, le prophète de la modernité*, par Robert Motta. *La discipline de soi comme base de la personnalité moderne. Différenciation, processus de civilisation, religion : aspects d'une théorie de la modernité*, par Aloïx Hahn. *La conception wébérienne de la discipline et le thème de la* Lebensführung, par Pierangelo Schiera. *L'Image de l'Europe chez Husserl et Weber. Le processus de rationalité chez Weber et l'appel à la raison chez Husserl*, par Elisabeth Suzanne Kassab. *L'éthique de la responsabilité et le décisionisme*, par Philippe Raynaud. *L'Entreprise politique de la société de masse : l'approche wébérienne du mode occidental de différenciation du politique*, par Patrick Lecomte. *Max Weber et les problèmes actuels du religieux*, par Jean-Pierre Sironneau.

Cahier n° 18 – Réflexions contemporaines sur l'Antiquité classique

Année 1996 – 288 pages – Journées Henri Joly

La Stasis *dans la démocratie par Lucio Bertelli. La notion de* fqÒnoj *chez Platon*, par Luc Brisson. *La déconstruction du « Connais-toi toi-même » dans* *l'*Alcibiade Majeur, par Jacques Brunschwig. *Le mythe, une catégorie hellène?*, par Claude Calame. *Écrire dans l'âme* (Philèbe, *38b-39c*), par Curzio Chiésa. *Socrate, poète et rhapsode. Quelques remarques sur l'*Ion, par Marie-Laurence Desclos. *Hérodote, les fleuves et l'histoire*, par Gian Franco Gianotti. *Philosophie ou science? La question des mondes multiples chez Anaximandre*, par Ada Neschke. *Le « cornu » : notes sur un problème de logique éristico-stoïcienne*, par Daniel Schulthess. *Le* logos *dans le* Phèdre *de Platon (265d, 266a et 270c)*, par Michel Fattal. *L'entrelacs et la bigarrure dans la pensée grecque antique*, par Anne Gabrielle Wersinger.

Cahier n° 19 – Religiosité, religions et identités religieuses
Année 1998 – 376 pages

Religion et politique en Europe, par Pierre Brechon. *L'Identité catholique dans les conflits actuels d'appartenance en France*, par Mrg Gérard Defoix. *La catégorisation religieuse*, par Francis Jacques. *Le noyau identitaire du religieux face à l'analyse compariste*, par Yves Lambert. *De l'identité de Dieu*, par Pierre Magnard. *L'Influence des auto-compréhensions religieuses sur le droit étatique*, par Francis Messner. *Peut-on penser un Dieu? Réflexions sur quelques stratifications du langage religieux*, par Pierre Million. Homo religiosus *et expérience du sacré*, par Julien Ries. *L'Héritage d'Héra. Réflexions sur l'identité de la cité grecque et sur les syncrétismes antiques*, par Pierre Sauzeau. *Identité et religions séculières*, par Jean-Pierre Sironneau. *La mise en cause de la validité intellectuelle de la religion dans la France de Louis XIV (1661-1685)*, par Jacques Solé. *L'oscillation de l'intention dans les métaphores religieuses : déisme ou foi chrétienne*, par Antoine Vergote. *Quel est le sujet de la religion?*, par Jean-Louis Vieillard-Baron. *Traditions, traditionalité, traditionalisme. Diversité confessionnelle des représentations et des modes de gestion de « la » tradition*, par Gilbert Vincent.

Cahier n° 20 – Esthétique : des goûts et des couleurs
Décembre 1998 – 293 pages

Présentation, par Régine Piétra. *Pourquoi « des couleurs »*, par Dominique Chateau. *De la possibilité d'une révolution copernicienne en esthétique*, par Alain Roger. *Pour une Critique impure de l'esthétique*, par Régine Piétra. *Fin et renaissance de l'esthétique*, par Bernard Lafargue. *Le goût à rien*, par Monique Broc-Lapeyre. *Esthétique épidermique, critique viscérale*, par Michel Philippon. *Art, plaisir, esthétique*, par Jacques Morizot. *Propriétés esthétiques, force évaluative, et différences de sensibilité*, par Jerrold Levinson. *Réalisme et anti-esthétique dans l'attribution des propriétés esthétiques*, par Roger Pouivet. *Description ou évaluation. Sur les définitions de l'art*, par Jean-Pierre Cometti. *Hume, De la norme du goût : la voie moyenne de l'expertise*, par Carole Talon-Hugon. *Adorno, un certain goût pour la rumeur*, par Jean-Louis Déotte. *La guerre des nomades. Controverse esthétique et rivalité des œuvres selon Adorno*, par Daniel Payot. *Au théâtre (juger selon le goût?)*, par Maryvonne Saison. *La poésie relève-t-elle de l'esthétique?*, par

Françoise Armengaud. *Le cas de l'émotion esthétique en architecture*, par Jean-Maurice Monnoyer. *Pourquoi j'aime Lipatti*, par Christian Doumet.

Cahier n° 21 – Biographie des hommes, biographie des dieux
Année 2000 – 274 pages

Avant-propos, par Marie-Laurence Desclos. *La forge d'Héphaïstos ou le malheur d'être dieu*, par Silvia Milanezi. *Une blessure d'Athéna*, par Renée Piettre. *« Biographie divine » et aspirations de l'aède. Une lecture de l'*Hymne homérique IV *à Hermès*, par Maria Vamvouri. *Sappho sans sa vie*, par Martin Steinrueck. *Vie et portrait d'Ésope*, par François Lissarague. *Raconter la vie du héros ou la biographie entre mythe et histoire*, par Colette Annequin. *Biographie historique ou roman héroïque : la* Vie de Pyrrhos *de Plutarque*, par Claude Mossé. *Sur la notion de « vies parallèle » dans Plutarque*, par Catherine Darbo-Peschanski. *Biographie et stèle funéraire attique*, par Geneviève Hoffmann. *Écrire la vie de Socrate : analyse de quelques biographèmes*, par Marie-Laurence Desclos. *Un processus de mythisation à partir de la Vie d'Apollonios de Tyane*, par Philippe Hanus.

Cahier n° 22 – Fichte : Idéalisme, Politique et Histoire
Année 2003 – 190 pages

Avant-propos, par Jean-Marie Lardic. *Fichte et la querelle des interprétations*, par Jean-Marie Lardic. *La grammaire de l'effectuation*, par Isabelle Thomas-Fogiel. *Fichte, lecteur de Kant*, par Jean-Michel Buée. *L'unité originairement synthétique de l'aperception chez Kant, Reinhold, Maïmon, Schulze et Fichte*, par Martin Bondeli. *L'éthique fichtéenne : autonomie ou autodétermination*, par Myriam Bienenstock. *Fichte et la liberté de penser*, par Jean-François Goubet. *Droit et nature : le droit naturel chez Fichte*, par Ives Radrizzani. *Le droit pénal chez Fichte*, par Jean-Christophe Merle. *Peuples, État, Histoire universelle*, par Claudio Cesa.

Cahier n° 23 – Hare et la philosophie morale
Année 2004 – 252 pages

Avant-propos, Hare en perspective, par Jean-Yves Goffi. *Hare et l'ontologie*, par Jean-Pierre Clero. *Les deux niveaux de la réflexion morale : J. S. Mill et R. Hare*, par Catherine Audard. *L'autre versant de la philosophie morale britannique : genèse et enseignements du sentimentalisme*, par Philippe Saltel. *Hare : principes, situations et éducation morale*, par Brenda Almond. *Le prescriptivisme universel, l'identité personnelle et les valeurs qui ne « peuvent dire leur nom »*, par Alan Montefiore. *Hare et la métaéthique contemporaine*, par Stélios Virvidakis. *Prescription, motivation et rationalité*, par François Clementz. *Survenance : le moral et le mental*, par Ruwen Ogien. *Trois remarques sur le langage et la morale ou l'apport de la pragmatique à la métaéthique*, par Denis Vernant. *Prescriptivisme et internalisme chez Hare*, par Christine Tappolet. *Du bon usage de la Règle d'Or : R. Hare et la question de l'avortement*, par Bernard Baertschi. *La philosophie *morale de Hare et les limites de son application : la question de l'esclavage*, par Helena Kalokairinou. *Le principe des actions à double effet*, par Jean-Yves Goffi. *R. Hare, Une bibliographie.*

Cahier n° 24 – Du nouveau dans les sciences

Année 2006 – 574 pages

Introduction, par Sarah Carvallo et Sophie Roux. *La Nouveauté comme valeur culturelle : lieux, formes et norms des revendications de nouveauté chez les érudits des sociétés islamiques*, par Sonja Brentjes. *Histoire du tonus : ruptures ou continuité ?*, par Sarah Carvallo. *Les Origines d'un nouvel élément chimique : l'affaire du chlore*, par Hugues Chabot. *Qu'y a-t-il de nouveau dans l'œuvre scientifique de D'Alembert ?*, par Pierre Crépel. *La Psychologie : une nouvelle science entre sens commun, physiologie et métaphysique ?*, par Michel Dufour. *Comment naît un instrument ? Étude de l'invention de l'actinomètre*, par Jérôme Fatet. *Découvertes multiples en chimie pharmaceutique et analytique*, par Philippe Jaussaud. *Les nouveautés de Stahl et Lavoisier vues par Kant*, par Mai Lequan. *Poincaré, précurseur du chaos ?*, par Loïc Petitgirard. *Découvrir le principe d'inertie*, par Sophie Roux. *Les contributions de Clausius et Boltzmann à l'élaboration de la signification physique de l'entropie à partie du travail de Carnot*, par Jérôme Viard.

Cahier n° 25 – La logique et les normes. Hommage à Jean-Louis Gardies

Année 2008 – 172 pages

In memoriam Jean-Louis Gardie, par Jean-Marie Lardic. *L'héritage frégéen dans l'œuvre de Gardies*, par François Schmitz. *Prolégomènes au principe d'identité. Gardies, critique de Leibniz et de Frege*, par Ion Vezeanu. *Le raisonnement par l'absurde*, par Denis Vernant. *La philosophie mathématique de Jean-Louis Gardies*, par Jean-Claude Dumoncel. *La « grammaire pure » : une grammaire des normes*, par Alain Lecomte. *Nature et fonction de l'intuition phénoménologique dans la philosophie du droit de Jean-Louis Gardies*, par Pol Boucher. *Bibliographie de Jean-Louis Gardies.*

Cahier n° 26 – L'invention philosophique humienne

Année 2009 – 300 pages

Avant-propos, par Philippe Saltel, *L'intérêt de lire Hume aujourd'hui* par Jean-Pierre Cléro, *Les naturalismes de Hume* par Cédric Brun, *Le problème de la substance corporelle dans le* Traité de la nature humaine *de David Hume* par Richard Glauser, *L'invention humienne du concept de* croyance naturelle par Claire Etchegaray, *Hume, Realism or Quasi-Realism ?* par P. J. E. Kail, *Scepticisme cartésien et scepticisme humien* par Pascal Engel, *Hume et la fiction de l'identité* par Ion Vezeanu, *Peut-on échapper de façon kantienne au problème humien de l'identité personnelle ?* par Wayne Waxman, *De la sympathie à l'interaction, la dette de la sociologie américaine à l'égard de David Hume* par Céline Bonicco, *Hume and the Concept of Convention* par John Latsis, *L'invention des conventions de justice chez Hume et sa* skepsis *envers la rétribution* par Ignace Haaz, Happiness and Dignity : *remarques sur la théorie de l'obligation chez Hume* par Philippe Saltel.

Cahier n° 27 – Figures de la rupture, figures de la continuité chez les anciens.

Année 2011 – 256 pages

Avant-propos, par Marie-Laurence Desclos. *Ruptures et continuités généalogiques dans l'Iliade : le parthénios entre temps des dieux et temps des hommes*, par David Bouvier. *Le discours d'en dessous. Rupture et continuité dans l'épopée*, par Catherine Darbo-Peschanski. *Un élan infini : Sappho, Tithon et Aurore. À propos de « Sapho and the Crack of Dawn » (1990) de John J. Winkler*, par Sandra Boehringer. *D'Hésiode à Eschyle : Prométhée, un mythe de souveraineté entre rupture et continuité*, par Marie-Laurence Desclos. *Ruptures et continuités dans l'image de Sparte d'Hérodote à Plutarque*, par Claude Mosse. *La figure de rupture dans les* Vies de philosophes et de rhéteurs *d'Eunape*, par Martin Steinrück. *Ethologie du couple « rupture/continuité » en stoïcisme : fondation d'un système d'estimation*, par Sandrine Alexandre. *La phantasia chez Aristote : un exemple de généalogie du concept*, par Marie-Laure Binzoni. *Rupture et continuité : les divisions du Sophiste de Platon*, par Annick Jaulin. *Polyphonie et dialogisme. Rupture par et pour la continuité et continuité de la rupture chez Platon*, par Isabelle Milliat-Pilot. *Penser, raconter et représenter la violence : encore une leçon des Grecs ?*, par Anna Beltrametti.

Cahier n° 28 – Histoires et définitions de la philosophie sociale

Année 2012 – 282 pages

Présentation. Histoires et définitions de la philosophie sociale, par Éric Dufour, Franck Fischbach et Emmanuel Renault. *Le déni du social. Deux exemples contemporains : Abensour et Rancière*, par Franck Fischbach. *Après Winch. La philosophie sociale et le tournant pragmatique*, par Robin Celikates. *Aux limites de la philosophie sociale : la question de la technique*, par Jean-Yves Goffi. *La tradition sociologique à son origine. Thèse, antithèse, synthèse, hypothèse. Sociologie et philosophie sociale*, par Jacques Guilhaumou. *Individu et société dans* L'Entraide *de Pierre Kropotkine*, par Jean-Christophe Angaut. *Politique et critique sociale. Sur la lecture kantienne de Rousseau par Cassirer*, par Géraldine Lepan. *La notion de philosophie sociale chez Natorp*, par Éric Dufour. *Économie et politique dans la pédagogie sociale de Paul Natorp*, par Julien Servois. *John Dewey (1859-1952) : philosophie sociale, droit et éducation*, par Lucie Chataigné-Pouteyo. *Raison et déraison du social chez Hegel et Marcuse*, par Mohamed Fayçal Touati. *Sartre, Marcuse, et la philosophie sociale au prisme du marxisme*, par Emmanuel Barot. *Adorno : de la philosophie sociale à la théorie sociale*, par Emmanuel Renault.

Hors-série – La structure du monde : Objets, Propriétés, États de choses

Année 2004 – 664 pages – sous la direction de Jean-Maurice Monnoyer

Combinatorialism, par David Arsmtrong. *« Sur ce qu'il y a » : la question et la réponse selon Boltzmann*, par Jacques Bouveresse. *Still Here : in Defense of Primitive Identities*, par John Bigelow. *The Place of Relations in a Trope Philosophy*, par Keuth Campbell. *Why There are no Tropes*, par Jerrold Levinson. *Worldmakking made hard*, par Michael Devitt. *Modal Problems for Australian Metaphysics*, par Chris Daly. *Le problème des universaux : aspects historiques et perspectives contemporaines*, par Claudine Tiercelin. *The State of the Laws*, par Stephen Mumford. *The Causal Efficacy of Mental States*, par Peter Menzies. *Rightness and Right-makers*, par Jonathan Dancy. *Fictionalism about Universals*, par Graham Oppy. *The Space of Perceptual Objects*, par Brian O'Shaughnessy. *Geography of the Reality*, par Barry Smith. *Individualiser les propriétés ?*, par Frédéric Nef. *Relations, dispositions et propriétés causales*, par François Clémentz. *Apologie du particulier*, par Roger Pouivet. *Why Nearly – but not Quite – Everything is an Object*, par Peter Simons. *Des premiers compas : l'origine de la théorie symplectique des groupes*, par Jean-Marie Souriau. *Reply to Michael Devit*, par Paul Boghossian. *Truth and Truth-makers*, par Paul Horwich. *Reply to Paul Horwich*, par David Armstrong. *Reply to Jonathan Dancy*, par Franck Jackson.

Hors-série – Lambertiana. Hommage à Jacques Lambert

Année 2010 – 470 pages – sous la direction de Pierre Édouard Bour et Sophie Roux

Hommage à Jacques Lambert, par Michel Meulders. *« Comment l'anatomie a trouvé le cœur… » : la métaphore anatomique chez les moralistes classiques*, par Bernard Roukhomovsky. *Les fausses évidences : dire et représenter la mort à l'âge classique*, par Sarah Carvallo. *Les pharmaciens français dans les grandes institutions scientifiques*, par Philipe Jaussaud. *Georges Canguilhem : la connaissance de la vie*, par Claude Debru. *L'Un et les figures de la rationalité chez Jérôme Cardan*, par Jean-Marie Lardic. *Un miroir des Princes Florentins : la lettre de Coluccio Salutati à Charles de Duras, roi de Naples*, par Jean-Yves Goffi. L'Essai de logique *de Mariotte : une naturalisation de la méthode ?*, par Sophie Roux. *Les tentations bibliothécaires du conseil, Montesquieu entre Machon et Lamy*, par Robert Damien. L'Encyclopédie *sans Lumières ? Perspectives sur la mémoire industrielle à la lumi.re de Jacques Lambert*, par Jean-Claude Beaune. *La philosophie du* comme si : *Hans Vaihinger et Henri Poincaré*, par Christophe Bouriau. *Vailati et Mach*, par Jacques Lambert. *La légende des faits objectifs*, par Christiane Chauviré. *Peirce, épistémologue de la vertu ?*, par Pierre Édouard Bour. *L'espace et le problème corps-esprit chez Riehl et Schlick*, par Michael Heidelberger. *Ce que peut nous apprendre le pragmatisme en philosophie de la perception : la réponse de Hilary Putnam*, par

Yannick Chin. La théorie de l'espace Poincaré, par Philippe Nabonnand. *L'idée d'une théorie générale des classifications*, par Daniel Parrochia. *Explication scientifique et explication non-scientifique*, par Michel Dufour. *Biologie moderne et science des matériaux : éléments pour une approche comparative*, par Yves Brechet et Franck Bruckert. *L'effet de serre : un dialogue exemplaire entre citoyens et spécialistes*, par Jacques Villain.

Imprimé sur les presses de Jouve - Mayenne
2131943M - dépôt légal : novembre 2013 - date d'impression : novembre 2013